Military Manpower Procurement

Military Manpower Procurement

A Policy Analysis

Steven L. Canby

Lexington Books
D.C. Heath and Company
Lexington, Massachusetts
Toronto   London

227254

Published simultaneously in Canada.

Printed in the United States of America.

International Standard Book Number: 0-669-81489-x

Library of Congress Catalog Card Number: 70-178917

Contents

List of Tables

List of Figures

Introduction

Since 1965, when large numbers of American troops began to arrive in Vietnam, the draft has become a major public policy issue that has generated considerable literature. Most of these publications are (1) analyses of the operation of the Selective Service System; (2) cost estimates of a proposed volunteer military force; or (3) polemics for a particular recruitment system.

This study attempts to take an impartial and comprehensive look at the entire military recruitment issue. It asks: What are the attributes desired in a military recruitment system for the United States? It lists 17 criteria for assessing the relative merits of alternative recruitment systems. They are:

Manpower Demands. How well does the procurement system respond to the military's requirements for its active and reserve forces?

Industrial Protection. Does the system adequately protect the industrial base and public welfare?

Economic Cost. What are the real resource costs of the procurement system?

Budget Cost. How much does the system cost DoD and the Treasury?

Efficiency. Does the manpower system induce efficiency in the military?

Ex-ante Equity. Does the system treat all individuals equally? Or are some given preferential treatment?

Ex-post Equity. Do those selected think the system is fair?

Rejectee Equity. Do those unable to meet military acceptance standards think the system is fair?

Pay Equity. Are those selected being paid wages comparable with their age cohort in the civilian sector?

Uncertainty. Is the system causing undue uncertainty to potential selectees?

Career Interruption. Does the system unnecessarily interrupt the careers of the selected?

Social Class Equity. Is the system fair to all social groups?

Social Instrument. How can the military upgrade human resources without degrading its primary mission?

Conscience, Tradition, and Law. Is the procurement system consistent with society's notions of conscience, tradition, and law?

Threat to Democracy. Does the system threaten democratic government?

Decision making Considerations. Can manpower procurement be designed to insure more optimal decision making?

Technical Workability. Is the system simple enough for the public to understand and workable under changing conditions?

The study then examines 6 ways of procuring manpower for the military. They are:

Selective Service. An alternative based on the principle of universal liability but not equal probability of service. It generally implies that certain valued or overburdened individuals should be deferred or exempted from military service. A more encompassing variation is Selective National Service, assigning young men (women) to a multitude of worthy social activities, including military service.

Voluntarism. An alternative based on individual choice, free of draft pressures. Its two variants are (1) a market military in which wages are set just high enough to clear demand and supply and (2) a queuing system in which wages are set above the market and the best qualified are selected from among those volunteering.

Lottery. An alternative based on random selection emphasizing equal probability of service.

Universal Service. An alternative based on universal service of all able-bodied young men (and occasionally women). Its two variants are (1) Universal Military Training (UMT) and (2) Universal National Service.

Sequential System. Any alternative joining together several single systems in a defined sequence of contingencies, in order to take advantage of each system's strengths.

Mixed Systems. Any alternative which has attributes of more than one "pure" system. Most of the mixed systems can be classified as draft systems which permit volunteering within the conscription framework. (A pure draft system would exclude all voluntarism.)

Each of these 6 alternatives is at some point in the discussion considered appropriate or inappropriate for three conditions, or contexts: peace, limited war, and full mobilization.

The important issues affecting the choice of alternatives in peacetime have traditionally been socio-political. Economic issues became dominant only after Korea, because of the apparent scarcity of critical skills and the high budgetary costs of the traditional voluntary system. Consequently, feasibility of a return to voluntarism was determined by economics. Its desirability, however, remains socio-political.

Among the policy-relevant findings of this study, five are salient. First, since the relative importance of the criteria change depending on whether there is peace or war, no single procurement system is appropriate in all contexts. A sequential system that suits the requirements of each context is preferable: voluntarism in peacetime; a lottery without exemptions for limited conflicts such as Vietnam; and selective service for possible nation-in-arms conflicts like those of the past. Second, military manpower policy remains geared to a mobilization strategy rather than to current strategies of nuclear deterrence and less-than-general war. Third, many of the military's manpower difficulties stem from its inefficient compensation system. Fourth, the additional budget cost of a peacetime volunteer force would be $2.1 to $2.5 billion,* much less than the $4 to $17 billion estimates formerly cited in the public debate. Fifth, except under special conditions, deferments are militarily unnecessary, economically undesirable, and can be unfair.

Chapter 1 develops an analytical framework for evaluating policy alternatives. Chapter 2 is the central chapter. Various arguments for and against specific alternatives are discussed; many arguments are shown to have only a slight effect on the choice of alternatives. Risk to life and service structure are related in an appendix to show the unappreciated implications of the high concentration of risk in the ground combat branches. Another appendix shows that voluntarism does not lead to a black military. Blacks and whites differ sharply on their Armed Forces Qualification Test scores. By changing acceptance standards, the proportion of blacks entering military service can be dramatically altered. The real problem is that present acceptance standards are set too high for most blacks to enlist; of those who do qualify, few score high enough to qualify for the technical specialties. A very important point—though not a topic of this study—is that many statistics used to allege military discrimination correlate with AFQT scores.

Chapter 3 discusses why deferment policies are contrary to the conceptual underpinnings and actual working of the American economic system. Deferment policy is premised on an outdated strategy of mobilization. Even if the strategy were still valid, peacetime deferments are generally unjustifiable and may be avoided by lowering the age of induction. No economic and military grounds exist for student deferment; its rationale is individual convenience. However, as long as student deferments are abolished in wartime and not pyramided into other deferments, public policy should consider permitting students a choice of induction date. Such choice also ensures wider social participation in wartime.

Part 2 contains the detailed analysis to support the budgetary arguments summarized in Chapter 2. Part 2 is highly specialized and designed for those directly concerned with cost. However, the layman who skims Part 2 will see why even experts err and derive erroneous policy conclusions. Chapter 4 is a short chapter which summarizes and references the intricate procedures of costing military manpower. Chapter 5 analyzes the military pay system. The structure of the pay system significantly affects the calculation of incremental costs. At present, large wage increases can be given to volunteers with less than two years' service without causing wage inversion and expensive, across-the-board wage increases to all personnel. Because of the military's substantial non-cash benefits, the relevant wage base for calculating wage increases is the individual's perceived valuation of these benefits, not their nominal value or cost to the

---

*[Editor's note: This is a long-run, steady-state estimate. Short-run transitional costs are considerably less if the full-range of techniques outlined in Chapter 6 are used. If these procedures are not followed, the costs of voluntarism can be quite high, as the Nixon Administration has discovered.]

government. Other conclusions of this chapter are: (1) DoD underestimates its retirement costs by over 50%; (2) present compensation practices are causing a disproportionate growth in retirement costs, which will be an increasing burden to defense managers; (3) the cost of the military's compensation package for its careerists considerably exceeds the compensation received by civilians of comparable age and education; and (4) military personnel costs could be considerably reduced if the military pay system were brought more in line with civilian practices.

Chapter 6 considers the complex institutional factors involved in properly costing military manpower due to the military pay structure, standards for acceptance, personnel flows, and interservice differentials. The chapter also shows the sensitivity of cost estimates to different force levels, enlistment attitudes among youth, elasticity estimates, unemployment rates, and reenlistment rates. The last appendix develops the argument that the incremental budget costs of voluntarism would actually be *negative* if structural changes were made in manpower policies to conform to the military's real manpower requirements (that is, without the constraints imposed by a draft system and adherence to the demands of a nation-in-arms military expansion).

Chapter 7 discusses the military-manpower debates after World War II and indicates the imperfect knowledge that was available to decision makers.

The debates and literature of military manpower are full of loaded words and connotations. By a choice of seemingly synonymous words, powerful prejudicial value judgments can be introduced. A neutral definition of terms is therefore in order. In this study the words *professional* and *careerist* will be used synonymously in the sense of "one who has voluntarily chosen to pursue a military career." This differs from Samuel Huntington's more rigorous definition of professionalism as expertise, responsibility, and corporateness which by definition can be located only in the officer corps; Huntington calls the career enlisted man a tradesman or craftman. *Mercenary* means a long-term volunteer who has no attachment of national loyalty. This usually suggests a foreign volunteer. The general notion is that the mercenary is unscrupulous and dangerous to the society which employs him; in fact, however, mercenary conduct has often been exemplary overseas and at home when supplemented by strong national forces. Though a mercenary by his nature is inherently less socially constrained than a native, too much emphasis on the monetary aspect obscures the fact the primary attraction of most modern vocations is monetary, although professional groups in particular tend to downplay this aspect. A *market military* is manned by participants who see the military vocation as the best among existing alternatives. Monetary reward is an important ingredient, as well as social prestige, cost of entry (prerequisite education and training), and the burdensome aspects of the specific job. A market military is part of the national civilian labor market and therefore no more like a mercenary force than any other occupational group.

Research was begun at Harvard University in the spring of 1967, when I was rapporteur for The Harvard Institute of Politics' faculty seminar on selective service, chaired by Thomas C. Schelling.* Many of the ideas developed here owe their origin to this seminar. As rapporteur, my responsibility was to develop and interrelate the many ideas brought forward on this relatively uncharted but important aspect of national policy. Parts of this study were completed at The Rand Corporation and were published as *The Budget Cost of a Volunteer Military*, RM-6184-PR, S. Canby and B. Klotz, August, 1970.

*Other members were John T. Dunlop, Henry Rosovsky, Jack Rawls, Charles Fried, Stephen Marglin, Lester Thurow, Gerald Rosenthal, Graham Allison, Jack Carlson, Robert Herzstein, and Robert Zupkis. Occasional participants were Samuel Huntington and Michael Walzer.

Part I:
The Policy Issues of
Manpower Procurement

1

An Evaluative Framework for Military Manpower Procurement

Prologue: Manpower Recruitment and Its Relationship to Foreign and Domestic Policy

Every society develops policies for achieving its foreign and domestic goals. Because implementing these separate policies requires economic and political resources, tradeoffs are inevitable. A major focus of these tradeoffs is military policy, which attempts to meet the demands made on its strategic component by *foreign* policy with material and political resources supplied its structural component by *domestic* policy.[1] American military policy has tended to be warped by overemphasis on one goal or the other. During periods of peace before World War II, the emphasis was internally oriented, with limited concern for the international arena. The cost was military unpreparedness and unnecessary prolongation of recurring conflicts. After 1940, the emphasis shifted to national security. Nowhere was this more apparent than in the allocation of young men coming of military age.

Selective Service since World War II has pursued a structural policy consistent with an outmoded strategy of mobilization but not with the existing strategy of deterrence. The two corollaries of the mobilization strategy were the nation-in-arms concept and a strong scientific and economic mobilization base. Manpower was the critical commodity, to satisfy immediate military requirements and to provide the technical base for sophisticated military hardware. Sacrificed for presumed necessity was the fundamental principle of equal treatment for individuals and for social classes; substituted for this democratic principle was the elitist principle of differential value to the State. Such a discriminatory policy can be legitimized in a democracy only by the doctrine of necessity and social survival.

Military forces-in-being for a deterrence strategy may have required conscription; but they did not require a selective scheme that neglected issues of equity and other socio-political considerations in order to minimize the draft's economic and potential military impact on the mobilization base.

That a false premise could underlie major national policy is a problem of considerable importance. Why were these inconsistencies not perceived?; and if they were perceived, why were no steps taken to remove them until after so much public discontent? The military's limited perspective should not be blamed. This is the realm of policy analysts—in particular, economists and political scientists. Economists did criticize military resource allocation pro-

3

cedures and the compensation system; but their criticisms tended to be based on marginal analysis that skirted deep-seated ills. Political scientists placed their emphasis on foreign policy and broad strategic issues; a few at the other end of the spectrum concerned themselves with civil-military relations. But few realized and none analyzed the disequilibria among the components of military policy:[2] that the design and tactical doctrine of our general-purpose forces were no longer appropriate for their intended use; that the manpower and personnel policies, of which manpower procurement was but one part, had become inappropriate by failing to evolve with the change from mobilization to a deterrent strategy; and that the system of procuring military manpower had become undesirable by its failure to reflect the new manpower requirements of the military services, the differing circumstances of peace and war, and the evolutionary changes in cultural mores. Thus, the critical meshings that form the framework of the American military system were left unanalyzed.

Evaluative Criteria

Military manpower procurement alternatives have to satisfy both military requirements and domestic goals. During wartime, when social survival is threatened, greater emphasis is placed on military requirements. In other periods the emphasis shifts to domestic goals, as before World War II, or to some balance among the various objectives. The analytic task is to determine a balance among the various military and domestic goals, considering their relative importance and the impact on them of military manpower procurement. Some posited goals are important for society as a whole; others are trivial or thought important by only a few. Others may be peripheral to military manpower. Still others may be closely related to military manpower, but relatively insensitive to the choice of procurement alternatives, particularly those in the politically feasible subset. Which goals are insensitive is not always obvious. Where such weak links exist, meaningful trade-offs among goals can be expensive in terms of other goals more closely related to manpower procurement. If such weakly affected goals are important, it is often possible to obtain them through specific instruments outside the procurement system. This satisfies the goal but not at the cost of trading off other goals. For example, voluntarism's alleged threat to democracy is only moderately sensitive to the choice of enlisted procurement; the real problem is the career officer corps. If voluntarism is preferable in other respects, the appropriate solution is not to choose an otherwise second-best procurement alternative, but to find nonprocurement means to neutralize the political influence of an officer corps.

The military goals that Selective Service focused on are straightforward and stated in the preambles of the various Universal Military Training and service acts and Selective Service acts, to wit:

Sec. 1(b) . . . an adequate armed strength must be achieved and maintained to ensure the security of this nation.

Sec. 1(c) . . . adequate provision for national security requires *maximum* effort in the fields of scientific research and development, and the *fullest possible* utilization of the nation's technological, scientific, and other critical manpower resources. (Emphasis added.)

The domestic goals are complex and elusive. Though generally neglected in the cold war era, they have become a source of dissension since Vietnam. In recent years several groups and authors have come forth with menus of domestic goals related to military manpower procurement. The most famous has been the Marshall Commission; the most comprehensive, the Harvard faculty seminar on selective service. The Marshall Commission cited these domestic criteria:[3]

(1) fairness to all citizens,
(2) minimal uncertainty and interference with individual careers and education,
(3) social, economic, and employment conditions and goals,
(4) budgetary and administrative considerations, and
(5) other factors deemed relevant.[4]

The Harvard group's criteria included the Commission's and touched upon most domestic impacts of military manpower procurement. Its criteria were:

(1) fairness with respect to who serves,
(2) fairness in respect to conditions of service,
(3) efficiency in the use of the nation's manpower,
(4) efficiency in the use of military manpower within the services,
(5) the satisfaction or resentment of those rejected and those selected,
(6) the impacts of alternative systems on politics and on policy making,
(7) the impact on race relations, education, and poverty,
(8) the technical workability of alternative systems,
(9) the uncertainty of disruption in the lives of young men,
(10) the career opportunities in the military service, and
(11) matters of conscience, tradition, and law.[5]

A more developed version of the Harvard criteria are broken out and briefly defined in Table 1-1.

Procurement Alternatives and Variations

The major generic procurement alternatives are displayed and explained in Table 1-2. The eight specific variations which have been discussed since World War II are shown in the vertical axis of Table 1-3. The variations under the heading "parity pay," which imply some form of wage comparability with civilians of

Table 1-1
Criteria

I. Military Requirements
   Manpower Demands. How well does the procurement system respond to the military's requirements for its active and reserve forces?
   Industrial Protection. Does the system adequately protect the industrial base and public welfare?

II. Economic Considerations
   Economic Cost. What are the real resource costs of the procurement system?
   Budget Cost. How much does the system cost DoD and the Treasury?
   Efficiency. Does the manpower system induce efficiency in the military?

III. Individual Considerations
   Ex-ante Equity. Does the system treat all individuals equally? Or are some given preferential treatment?
   Ex-post Equity. Do those selected think the system is fair?
   Rejectee Equity. Do those unable to meet military acceptance standards think the system is fair?
   Pay Equity. Are those selected being paid wages comparable with their age cohort in the civilian sector?
   Uncertainty. Is the system causing undue uncertainty to potential selectees?
   Career Interruption. Is the system unnecessarily interrupting the careers of the selected?

IV. Social Considerations
   Social Class Equity. Is the system fair to all social groups?
   Social Instrument. How can the military upgrade human resources without degrading its primary mission?
   Conscience, Tradition, and Law. Is the procurement system consistent with society's notions of conscience, tradition, and law?
   Threat to Democracy. Does the system threaten democratic government?
   Decision making Considerations. Can manpower procurement be designed to insure more optimal decision making?

V. Technical Workability
   Is the system simple enough for public understanding and workable under changing conditions?

---

similar attributes, have received only limited public attention. The two universal systems are listed in Tables 1-2 and 1-3 for completeness.[6]

Criteria, Alternatives, and Context

For evaluation, alternatives and criteria have to be related. Table 1-3 is an ordering device for this purpose. Each manpower alternative can be judged by a vector of attributes (criteria) whose relative importance varies according to the continuum of peace and war.

If dominating procurement alternatives could be found, the decision rule would be simply: choose that alternative at each point along the continuum that meets the conditions $A_j^i \geqslant A_j^k$, where the superscripts stand for alternatives and subscripts for attributes. Changing the procurement system at each possible point in the continuum is administratively and politically infeasible; but pegging for these three generic environments is feasible: a peacetime (P) context for a nonexpanded military of less than 3 million men, with no immediate prospect of conflict; a limited war (LW) context of an expanded military to fight a less than full-scale conflict, as in Vietnam; and, finally, a full mobilization (FM) context for nation-in-arms conflicts, as in World Wars I and II. These pegging points are shown in the diagonal of Table 1-3.

Some alternatives, especially variants, can be eliminated by dominance. However, for the three archtypes—selective service, the lottery, and voluntarism—dominance does not exist. Lack of dominance is a potentially serious limitation because of the reliance that must therefore be placed on subjective judgment concerning the relative importance of the criteria. Fortunately, the procedure of evaluating each alternative according to specific contexts intro-

Table 1-2
Alternative Procurement Schemes

Selective Service. An alternative based on the principle of universal liability but not equal probability of service. It generally implies that certain valued or over-burdened individuals should be deferred or exempted from military service. A more encompassing variation is Selective National Service, assigning young men (women) to a multitude of worthy social activities, including military service.

Voluntarism. An alternative based on individual choice, free of draft pressures. Its two variants are (1) a market military in which wages are set just high enough to clear demand and supply and (2) a queuing system in which wages are set above the market and the best qualified are selected from among those volunteering.

Lottery. An alternative based on random selection emphasizing equal probability of service. The two crucial caveats are: (1) a lottery with widespread disqualifications, deferments, and exemptions is substantially identical to a Selective Service System except for timing, and (2) the virtues of a lottery extend only *within* a given age cohort and become dissipated when several age cohorts are lotteried together.

Universal Service. An alternative based on universal service of all able-bodied young men (and occasionally women). Its two variants are (1) Universal Military Training (UMT) and (2) Universal National Service.

Sequential Systems. Any alternative joining together several single systems in a defined sequence of contingencies, in order to take advantage of each system's strengths. Gearing systems recognize that the various alternatives have strong points that can be matched with the context.

Mixed Systems. Any alternative which has attributes of more than one "pure" system. Most of the mixed systems can be classified as draft systems which permit volunteering within the conscription framework. (A pure draft system would exclude all voluntarism.)

Table 1-3
Three-Dimensional Military Manpower Matrix of Program Alternatives, Criteria, and Context

System alternatives	Context	I Military requirements	Manpower demands	Industrial production	II Economic considerations	Economic cost	Budget cost	Allocative efficiency	III Individual considerations	Ex-ante equity	Ex-post equity	Rejectee equity	Pay equity	Uncertainty	Career interruption	IV Social considerations	Social class equity	Social instrument	Conscience, tradition, and law	Threat to democracy	Decision making considerations	V Technical workability
Current mixed volunteer-SS without parity pay	P LW FM																					
Current mixed volunteer-SS with parity pay	P LW FM																					
Mixed volunteer-lottery without parity pay	P LW FM																					
Mixed volunteer-lottery with parity pay	P LW FM																					
Pure lottery with parity pay	P LW FM																					
Volunteer	P LW FM																					
Universal military training	P LW FM																					
Universal national service	P LW FM																					
Sequential systems	P LW FM																					

duces near-dominance. In one context, one alternative may appear much better than others. In another setting, this same alternative fares poorly. For instance, in the comparisons of procurement alternatives, voluntarism looks attractive in peacetime but objectionable elsewhere; the lottery has desirable attributes during limited wars, but not during full mobilization; and selective service appears attractive during full mobilization, but poor in the other two contexts. Such findings suggest a *gearing*, or sequential system that permits the overall procurement system to capture the strengths of each single alternative in its appropriate context without its major liabilities under other circumstances.

2

Criteria Analysis and Evaluation of Procurement Alternatives

This chapter fleshes out the evaluative framework. Each criterion is analyzed in turn and its implications developed for the three pegging contexts of peace, limited war, and full mobilization. The findings are then related to the feasible alternatives.

Criterion: Manpower Demands

Procurement alternatives must above all satisfy the military's quantitative and qualitative manpower requirements. An alternative that is not flexible enough to satisfy changing demands is not feasible and can be eliminated from further consideration. Draft systems can obviously satisfy the military's quantitative requirements in all contexts; volunteer systems may not. Arguments "proving" voluntarism's inadequacy often fail to note the low wages given enlisted entrants or that historically the supply curve of volunteers has often shifted sharply downward and to the right at the beginning of hostilities, when enthusiasm is high. In the case of Vietnam, it has been alleged that few men would volunteer for service; yet the available data up to early 1969 do not support this contention.[1] Voluntarism can and has supported large military establishments in this country. Even at low wages, voluntarism can on occasion support a large military, as in Britain in 1914-1916. Nevertheless, voluntarism, though more flexible than commonly thought, is a frail system to support national security during emergencies.

An important and often neglected point concerning procurement alternatives is their consistency with the strategic component of military policy. The special characteristic of a modern military is its two distinct capabilities: nuclear strategic and conventional/limited warfare. Nuclear capability requires forces-in-being to deter direct threats to national survival. General-purpose forces (GPF) represent the traditional military; they are no longer vital to protection against direct and immediate threats to national security. Their use can always be finessed by the threat of nuclear warfare; yet theirs is an important function. In Europe, conventional forces-in-being are necessary for a strategy of graduated response. Elsewhere, GPF do not serve an immediate vital function. Token forces are permissible; no materializing threat is so serious that it cannot be met initially by relatively small forces backed by a reinforcing capability. Immediate response with large forces may be desirable, but the benefits must be weighed against their cost and the possibility of success using more subtle approaches. Moreover, forewarning precedes most conventional attacks; whether the time gained is used advantageously is another matter.

The net result is that military necessity no longer calls for the maximization of military power; rather, something less than maximum power is now sufficient.[2] Military technology has shifted the demand and supply curves for military forces to a position resembling the situation in pre-revolutionary Europe. This is a kinked demand curve, reflecting high value down to the kink and a sharply decreasing marginal value thereafter. Concurrently, technical complexity has shifted the supply curve up by increasing physical and human capital investments in the military forces. Thus, the supply and demand curves suggest a smaller, more highly trained, military as in monarchical Europe.

For the strategic forces, the strategies of deterrence and assured destruction require forces-in-being that need little wartime expansion; indeed the likelihood of mutual destruction implies that little would be possible. Deterrence forces are analogous to fixed overhead. High equipment cost and sophisticated skills suggest a labor force similar to that of a well-managed corporation: personnel continuity reduces human investment costs and increases job effectiveness. The military, however, has traditionally preferred malleable and vigorous youths. Since this technical segment does not engage in ground combat, the corporate-managerial model is more appropriate for the nuclear forces than the traditional pattern.

GPF requirements are more complex. Most GPF strategies require forces-in-being and an expansionary mobilization, particularly for ground combat forces. Manpower needs for GPF are basically designed for close combat and to develop an expansionary wartime capability. Close combat requires a youthful, physically vigorous, force to undertake its risks and hardships. An expansionary capability requires generating rapid peacetime promotion to create sufficient personnel experience in the event of accelerated promotion during large military expansions. Both criteria thus imply high personnel turnover.

A situation has thus arisen whereby two militaries having different manning requirements coexist. One requires a long-term volunteer force; the other a high-turnover force, whether short-term volunteer or conscripted. However, because of structural interdependence, *only one procurement system is possible at any one point in time.* A volunteer system is structurally satisfactory for both, but cannot satisfy wartime quantitative demands. Conscription satisfies demands, but is structurally unsatisfactory in peacetime because coercion in one segment of the military affects the other. If coercion is continued to man the relatively unskilled expansionary forces, noncareerists will be induced to volunteer into the skilled segment (which formed 56.5 % of pre-Vietnam enlisted strength, while ground combat formed only 13.4%.[3]) Bulk numbers as well as training costs indicate that peacetime recruitment should focus on the skilled segment.

This leads to the important policy conclusion that while voluntarism is quantitatively unsuited for large conflicts, draft systems are inappropriate for a modern military's peacetime structure. This, of course, implies a sequential system using voluntarism in peacetime and a draft system during large conflicts. For intermediate conflicts there is little difference between the volunteer and draft systems in their ability to satisfy quantitative and structural requirements because the effect of high wartime wages is similar to the draft's coercion in inducing noncareerists into the skilled segment.

Criterion: Industrial Protection

The second major function of SS has been to shelter the economic production base by deferring those with skills held vital or in scarce supply. The intent of deferment is efficient production. Over time this intent has broadened to include deferments for the "national wealth, safety, and interest"—often as perceived by special interest groups.[4]

Deferments justified by "national wealth, safety, and interest" assume actual and potential shortages of skilled manpower. If the nation's resources are underutilized or will never be fully mobilized for national security, then resources can always be released from civilian to military purposes. This criterion, therefore, asserts that market forces cannot assure an adequate supply of skills for either full mobilization or prolonged periods of high military requirements. Ergo, men (i.e., students) must now be channeled into skills determined to be in the national interest. The weaknesses of the argument are in its *assumptions.* Channeling was devised for a full mobilization strategy under the special conditions that were perceived in 1950, namely: (1) a temporary shortage of skilled personnel caused by World War II's temporary curtailment of new scientific talent and rapidly shifting technological demands, and (2) large military manpower demands for the indefinite future. A second critical assumption was the alleged inadequacy of the market system to meet scientific manpower demands. Its fallacy is in extending a valid short-run argument into the long run, where market forces *do* adjust to shifting demands.

In short, the criterion of "national wealth, safety, and interest," which has been an underpinning of the American draft system, is analytically invalid except during full mobilization or under very special circumstances.

During wars requiring full mobilization, a case can be made for *occupational* deferments to permit greater military production. During less than full mobilization, when society's resources are not so constrained and when younger men with few critical skills are liable for military service, the case for deferments is not convincing. Thus, all the manpower alternatives satisfy the industrial protection criterion during peace and limited war. But only selective service satisfies the criterion during full mobilization. Voluntarism is undesirable during full mobilization because patriotic zeal often induces men into the armed forces who are more valuable on the production front.

Criterion: Efficiency

This section discusses the economic efficiency of the possible procurement alternatives, their budgetary impact, and the relative importance of economic efficiency in the three peace-war contexts. It focuses on the efficient allocation of resources *to* the military and the efficient utilization of these resources *within* the military. In particular, it will be shown that achieving efficiency within the military requires more than voluntarism's rationalizing impact via higher labor costs.

Economic and Budget Costs

In peacetime, the economically efficient solution to military manpower procurement problems is the market: paying wages just sufficient to attract the required quantity and quality of personnel.[5] This is distinct from voluntarism per se, which can also mean high pay to queue prospective volunteers in order to choose the best qualified of those meeting acceptance standards.[6] Using unnecessarily high-quality manpower is economically inefficient, whether by voluntarism or by draft. The difference is that conscription may hide the cost of using high-quality manpower, while voluntarism's cost is explicit and eliminates any subsidy. The paradoxical result is that, while the budgetary cost of voluntarism may be greater than that of the draft,[7] its real costs may be less because lower opportunity cost volunteers replace higher-opportunity-cost draftees.[8] In this process money wages are necessarily increased as volunteers replace nonvolunteers. Efficiency is increased until opportunity costs are equalized at the margin and substitution is no longer beneficial; at this point military wages will equal or exceed each enlistee's opportunity cost.[9]

Voluntarism's budgetary costs are estimated in Chapter 6 to be on the order of an additional $2.1 to $2.5 billion/year for a pre-Vietnam force level of 2.65 million men.* This estimate is similar to other published estimates in that it uses similar econometric assumptions and procedures and accepts the present, anachronistic manpower system as the basis for analysis. These estimates are considerably lower than other published estimates because of the attention given to the institutional meaning of statistical relationships.[10] The consequence of Chapter 6's estimate and the more recent Gates Commission estimate is that the incremental budgetary costs of voluntarism are low enough to include voluntarism in the politically feasible subset of alternatives.

Economic Advantages and Insufficiency of a Market System

The Allocation Process. From an economic (but not political) viewpoint, *budgetary* costs are an inappropriate criterion; it is the *economic* costs which

---

*[Editor's Note: This is a long-run, steady state estimate. Short-run transitional costs are considerably less if the full-range of techniques outlined in Chapter 6 are used. If these procedures are not followed, the costs of voluntarism can be quite high, as the Nixon Administration has discovered.]

measure the real burdens on society's labor and capital resources. Using budget costs in lieu of economic costs biases the decision process towards a larger military and induces economic inefficiency. The transformation and community indifference curves of Figure 2-1 indicate this misallocation; the curves can also be used to illustrate the insufficiency of a market system for defense decision making. The transformation curve represents the locus of efficient points. Of the procurement alternatives, only voluntarism lies on the curve.[11] The draft subsidy (or externality) places society at point 1 on the lowest shown Scitovsky community indifference curve. If all the inefficiencies and externalities could be removed, society could reach the social optimum of mutual tangency at point 5 on the highest attainable Scitovsky curve. In practice these deficiencies cannot be fully removed and point 5 can only be approached. Most important is the fact that a price system strives for the static optimum at point 5 only by reallocations at the margin. Equally important are innovative activities which change existing production processes and cause an outward pivoting of the production possibilities curve to the new grand optimum at point 6. Consequently, a market system per se can at best approach a static optimum at point 5; it has little to do with the "creative destruction" movement from points 5 to 6.

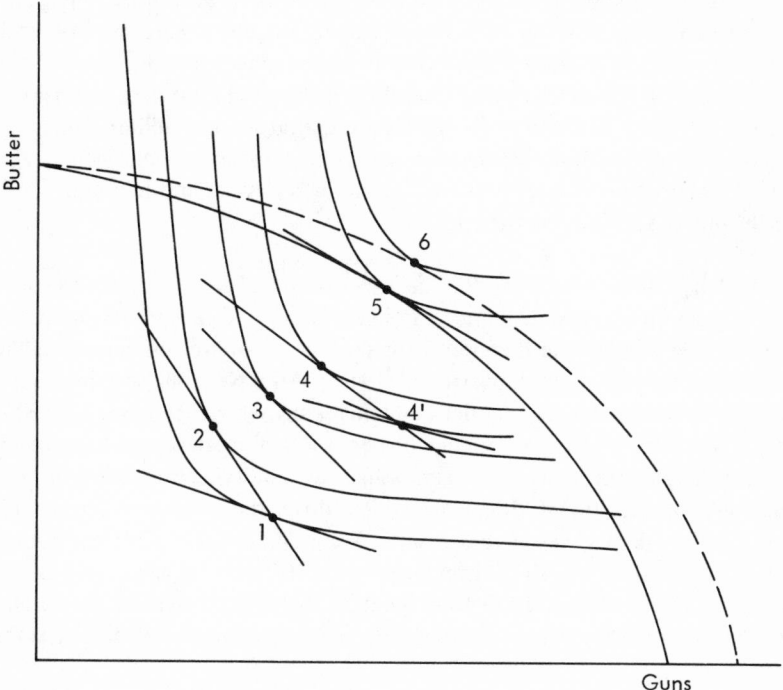

Figure 2-1. The allocating process.

Point 1 is not on the transformation curve of efficient points because of improper factor pricing. Low labor prices for noncareerists means a flatter price line for guns than the true cost, shown by the steeper price line through point 1. The externality of coercion is represented by the acute angle between the price lines. Replacing the externality of coercion by market wages causes guns to be priced at their true higher cost and a consequent reallocation on the margin between the two commodities (guns and butter) until the new tangency at point 2 is reached. Point 2 is on a higher welfare curve but remains off the contract locus. Point 2 simply pays these same noncareerists their opportunity-cost market wages (or a shadow wage). In other words, point 2 means a smaller military but no substitution of personnel and no change in underlying practices. Assuming that market wages permitted replacing higher-opportunity-cost draftees with lower-opportunity-cost volunteers, military labor prices would dip and a new tangency would occur at point 3, where greater efficiency provided more of both commodities.[12] Point 3 remains off the contract locus, since capital-labor decisions have not yet been affected by the new price ratios. At point 3 higher volunteer labor costs affect total costs but not internal allocative decisions.

The next step is the long-run movement to point 4. As equipment becomes obsolete and past decisions are reviewed, higher labor costs induce marginal capital-labor readjustments which lower or flatten the guns price line. This causes a further increase in efficiency, leading to more purchases of each commodity. However, contrary to the analogy from economic theory, the contract locus at point 5 is never reached because (1) static organizational efficiency is neither feasible nor dynamically desirable for a military organization because of wartime redundancy and expansionary requirements; and (2) some practices become customary, are never reviewed, and hence are both statically and dynamically inefficient.[13]

Behavior Adaptation. Removing the draft's subsidy and ease of labor accessibility will not automatically guarantee internal military efficiency. Service biases and preferences such as the preference for servicemen over civilians because the former can be ordered to work overtime,[14] will remain. Nevertheless, the impact of higher wages can only be beneficial and increasingly beneficial over time. But a strong argument can be made that higher wages alone will not have much effect. Significant impact requires reviewing and modifying fundamental conceptual and organizational principles which drive the military's production activities and its derived resource demands. Accordingly, voluntarism's impact is in (1) its potential in the shift from one system to another of permitting old assumptions to be challenged before bureaucratic rigidity again sets in, and (2) its change in relative factor prices strengthening an already existing case for change.

An argument against expecting too much impact upon long-run behavior patterns from the higher cost of voluntarism is that resources constraints have not been credible to the American military. In wartime the American military has traditionally received and come to expect an open checkbook. A good argument can be made that much of the difficulty concerning Vietnam was caused by the military's relying on more resources rather than better using its existing resources (i.e., constrained maximization).[15] This is consistent with Professor Richard Neustadt's observation that across-the-board reductions imposed by Congress in peacetime cut muscle, not fat. The apparent reason is that not only does fat entail psychic income benefits, but cutting muscle increases one's bargaining strength the following year. However, the fundamental cause is affluence. If resources were perceived to be in short supply and national survival were indeed at stake, as in Israel, the military would not cut muscle for the sake of future bargaining advantages. In short, the military does not fully consider or weigh resource costs; price signals can therefore not be viewed as a panacea for inefficiency.

An assertion often made, as in DoD's Project PRIME, is that a businesslike price system will solve the military's management and allocation problem. For those portions of the military with a measurable output, a pricing system can be a useful tool. The real problem, however, lies in the end-output operational units where benefits have defied quantification. For these units, there is no assurance that a pricing system would produce a rationalizing impact. Rather, the lack of quantifiable (or imperfectly stated) benefits to match against cost reductions could lead to undesirable competitive excesses among peers vying for the best efficiency report from commanders who are themselves in competition. The crucial point is that the two basic premises of a price system are missing: measurable profits (benefits minus costs) and the stabilizing pressures of competitors. Another fundamental difficulty is that a pricing system does not ensure that individual, organizational, and social welfare functions are identical. A commander's welfare function is not identical with his service's; and the services' are not identical with society's. In the U.S. military a successful command tour is the sine qua non for promotion; at the same time, command tours are short because there are many more staff positions than command positions. A commander, therefore, has a short time-horizon, which induces actions with short-run payoffs but which may have adverse long-run effects after his departure. This aberration, of course, is not unknown in business, where accounting profits are often manipulated by a variety of devices. Another flaw in the price system analogy is that even if the above deficiencies could be resolved, no military organization could function if the lowest organic commander were allowed to choose his own equipment, organization, etc. The logistic system would become inoperable, and non-standardized behavior patterns would complicate command and coordinating relationships among units.

Efficiency and Civilianization. Civilianization's primary significance for a volunteer military is that it reduces the number of men to be attracted by market wages.[16] Civilianization of some military functions is also cost-effective because military personnel often cost more on a total cost basis and are less motivated than civilians. The caveat is that the military's structure and the nature of its business must be properly considered. For instance, civilianizing KP may not be cost-effective due to non-peak loading of military units in peacetime; it may, however, accomplish other objectives such as upgrading service attractiveness and morale and providing more unskilled civilian jobs. The Navy in particular requires rotational billets, many of which could be more efficiently manned by civilians. Nonvesting of retirement benefits has also created a need for billets to place personnel who have outgrown their usefulness. Finally, and most important, static and dynamic efficiency are not coextensive. The military often builds in extra strength in peacetime to provide cadre for military expansion. The weak links in this "surging" and cadre argument are: (1) cadre requirements are often premised on a low-probability mobilization strategy rather than on more likely deterrence and limited war strategies, and (2) padded manning (i.e., supply) generates its own demand, thus undermining its reason for being by becoming a "requirement" over time.

While the focus of civilianization has been the substitution of civilians for military personnel, the greater potential lies in returning to the traditional military practice of before World War I of contracting for many logistical services.[17] Provided a medium of competition exists, civilian contracting has the advantage of outside management expertise, a more experienced labor force, and market pressures to maintain the contractor's vibrancy. The problem with contracting is that while civilian performance may be more efficient in peacetime than military performance, it has limited wartime deployment capability. Hence, the military may have to maintain a standby organization for wartime purposes. This means the relevant comparison is not total cost but the military's marginal cost versus the contractor's total cost. This puts contractors at a major disadvantage, for only if the military's incremental cost were greater than the contractor's total costs would it be efficient to permit contractor performance while the military unit trained only for the future. This leads to the important conclusion that if civilianization is to lead to major savings, ways have to be found whereby civilian organizations can substitute for military units in wartime.

Shadow Prices. If voluntarism is rejected, part of its economic advantages could be achieved by an accounting shadow price. Shadow prices would remove the externality and induce proper decision making (from points 1 to 2 in Figure 2-1). Shadow prices could also promote long-run efficiency changes. The main limitation of shadow prices is that they do not prevent the draft's economic costs of "mismatching" by drafting high opportunity cost individuals. Shadow prices therefore would not induce the move from point 2 to 3, but would induce the equivalent move as from point 3 to 4.

Another shadow price possibility is to let market forces determine wage levels but to add an accounting premium for decision making purposes in order to induce the substitution of capital for labor within the military. The justifications for an additive shadow premium are the relative scarcity of labor in wartime and the market's inability to value human life. Peacetime capital-labor ratios within military units are inappropriate for wartime. Yet the raison d'être of the non-strategic forces is combat. Unless some allowances are made for wartime scarcity prices and the probability of death, inappropriate labor-intensive peacetime organizations and tactics will be carried over into wartime. An internal shadow price would partially correct this error. Another minor justification for a shadow premium concerns the mechanics of present valuing. In the trade-off between discounted capital and labor in hardware development, labor's real costs increase relative to "front-loaded" capital as labor's productivity increases in the civilian sector. To the extent that hardware development responds to economic stimuli, neglect of dynamic increases in labor productivity induces a small labor-intensive bias in military hardware. Another factor leading to higher labor intensity has resulted from the systematic underestimation of true labor costs by estimates being based on annual wages rather than on a billet concept which includes all personnel and pro-rated accession, training, and terminal costs. However, given the imperfections of development procedures, an accounting wage premium to reduce one bias to labor intensity may not be beneficial because of the more general bias towards capital intensity from pushing the state-of-the-art in weapons procurement.

Effect on Military Strength. Figure 2-1 can be used to indicate the military's direct loss from voluntarism and the potential for at least partial recovery from greater efficiency. The immediate and most obvious impact of higher wages would be loss in strength occasioned by the movement from point 1 to 2. The extent of the recovery from greater efficiency depends on the military's adaptive behavior and the shape of the community indifference map. The general shape of these curves means that the military can benefit from both "income" and "substitution" effects. That is, the releasing of resources through improved efficiency provides a cheaper product and a higher national income to be divided between military and other programs, as in the movement from point 3 to 4. If reappraisals of existing production processes were extensive enough, efficiency could conceivably more than offset the initial loss incurred through higher wages. However, this depends critically on the Scitovsky map: the more the curves reflect income inelasticity and converge to the left, the greater the difficulty in overcoming the initial loss.

Three implications concerning military incentives follow from this diagramatic analysis. First, the military has, in principle, an incentive for greater efficiency through the substitution and income effects. Second, even if society and the very top military hierarchy found and preferred points 5 and 6, which provide more guns than point 1, the military institution as a whole may not. This would depend on the resource-saving techniques and innovations used to reach these points.[18] Military rank (and monetary and psychic income) structure is based primarily on supervisory authority and span of control. Labor-saving changes would reduce the military's strength and hence its rank and promotion potentials; greater capital intensity (particularly human capital) would be only partially offsetting. Innovations would often be both factor-saving and disruptive by changing established patterns. Extant careerists could therefore be expected to be biased against such changes because they reduce career potential and threaten existing expertise.

Finally, the military can always gain a short-run advantage from reintroducing coercion's subsidy and moving to a lower community position but a larger military, as at point 4. This causes a military expansion, which is always advantageous for existing careerists. Even if an expansion does not occur, careerists may still benefit by this divergence if any fixed wage fund increase is concentrated on themselves, rather than more evenly distributed across the board. As long as coercion forces high-caliber but low-career-propensity individuals into service, the plausible argument can always be made that high personnel turnover "proves" that career compensation needs to be increased to attract and retain personnel.

Curve-Shifting Versus Marginal Analysis Along a Curve. The difficulty with the theoretical approach taken in Figure 2-1 is lack of operational guidance. The basic limitation is the transformation curve itself: it assumes that efficient production processes are already known. In sheltered industries, such as the military, this assumption is not realistic. Statistical estimates, even if available, would identify existing production processes, not the efficient processes assumed in trade-off analysis.

Focusing on marginal analysis by accepting institutional givens runs the risk of optimizing or performing trade-offs on a low-lying curve. Often the biggest gains come from shifting the curve through an analysis of the concepts that drive the institution's behavior. The more rigorous analytical procedures of optimization are appropriate only after the curve has been shifted. Moreover, it cannot be assumed that superimposing a rationalistic incentive structure over an institution will induce efficient behavior: manipulation by individuals within the institution and institutional rigidity may block its effect—as has occurred in the weapons acquisition process.

Costs and Alternative Systems

If economic efficiency were the sole criterion for a desirable manpower procurement system, voluntarism would be the preferred system, because self-selection excludes those with opportunity costs greater than the going wage. The least efficient procurement alternative is a random or lottery process. A selective system of exempting the better educated has the attribute of skimming off those with the higher opportunity costs. But unless such discriminating techniques as income earned are used, selectivity can only approach voluntarism's efficiency.[19]

Voluntarism is efficient in its disposition of real resources, but it can be budgetarily expensive because of intramarginal economic rent, particularly during military expansion. In limited war, sufficient manpower flexibility could be gained by adjustable enlistment bonuses among and within the services to match supply with demand. The advantages of the bonus are its "time preference" cheapness and its flexibility in adjusting supply and demand without disturbing the regular pay structure.[20] Discriminating among the services is particularly important. Supply projections indicate that the Army is the only service in peacetime with a recruitment deficit; moreover, military expansions are largely in the Army and Marine Corps. Only these services require large wage increases during military expansion. Economic rent can be further reduced if the largest increases are reserved for those with the greatest burdens and risks—the infantry. Thus, if devices are developed to contain economic rent, the budget costs of voluntarism during limited wars need not be unduly high. Only during full mobilization does voluntarism become unduly expensive and undependable.

The advantages of a draft are just the opposite of those of voluntarism. Impressment guarantees manpower flexibility. Undesirable intramarginal economic rents are avoided by coercing rather than enticing intramarginal individuals. There are no speculative and pay inversion problems. (DoD defines pay inversion as paying juniors more than seniors.) Careerists are usually paid their opportunity costs while draftees are not. Finally, as manpower requirements approach full mobilization, selectivity approaches market efficiency without its deficiencies and short-run adjustment lags. Market voluntarism is thus economically attractive in peacetime; and selectivity, in full mobilization. Both systems are more efficient than a lottery during limited wars.

In terms of military budget cost, selectivity and lottery are approximately equal in all contexts since both substitute coercion for monetary inducements. The main difference is that retention rates for a lottery system would tend to be lower; this implies reduced wage costs from fewer careerists but higher turnover costs. During peacetime the advantages of a draft over voluntarism are at a minimum, since relatively few men need to be enticed; as manpower requirements increase, voluntarism's budget costs increase sharply as the supply curve is climbed, unless economic rents can be contained or shifts occur in the supply curve from patriotism, sense of excitement, etc.

Any discussion of budgetary and economic criteria for evaluating alternative procurement systems must include their relative importance. Many economists assert budgetary costs are irrelevant; yet they are politically important. Moreover, budget costs are relevant in at least one economic sense—their impact on aggregate demand. Only if a government possesses the fiscal and monetary tools and the will to contain inflation are budgetary cost considerations economically unimportant. The fact is, however, that during full mobilization, governments may have the political will but not the desire to reduce work incentives through stringent taxation and credit policies. On the other hand, in limited war, only minor policy adjustments may be necessary but government may not have the political will, as the Vietnam experience poignantly illustrates. Thus the claim that budgetary costs can be excluded as a consideration for evaluating alternative procurement schemes applies only to peacetime. In war, budgetary considerations are important and weigh against voluntarism. Economic efficiency is always a valid, but far from dominant, consideration. Economic considerations are most important during full mobilization, when national survival may hinge on resource availability. During such periods, the social value of resources exceeds their market accounting value; the consequence is that efficient resource allocation often becomes the dominant non-military criterion and virtually coextensive with the criterion of industrial protection. In other periods, when national survival is not threatened and military requirements can always be satisfied by reallocating resources between the civilian and military sectors, economic efficiency is desirable but not critical.

Issues of Equity

Equity connotes fairness; but even in this limited philosophical sense, equity has many facets. The Harvard criteria subdivided equity into (1) fairness with respect to who serves, (2) fairness in respect to conditions of service, and (5) the satisfaction or resentment of those rejected and those selected. "Fairness with respect to who serves" can in principle be separated into free choice and equal probability of selection (ex ante equity). "Fairness in respect to conditions of service" can be separated into fairness as perceived by those selected (ex-post equity), fair pay relative to similar civilians (pay equity), and fairness in assignment within the military. Overlapping with (2) is the "satisfaction or resentment of those selected" in (5); (5) also includes rejectee equity for those desiring military service but unable to meet the military's qualification standards. A final form of equity implicit in these criteria is the aggregate effect of procurement alternatives on socio-economic classes (group equity).

The Economic Case for Free Choice

Free choice is fundamental to the American liberal tradition and economic system. Since free choice permits the individual to maximize his utility, many observers presume that free choice ensures fairness. It is therefore argued that voluntarism is the preferred system, provided military requirements can be satisfied. Accordingly, these observers assert that voluntarism is by definition the fairest system because it undercuts further consideration of equity, save rejectee equity.

Yet underlying the optimality of free choice from the utility maximization viewpoint are a number of crucial assumptions: the absence of imperfect knowledge, uncertainty, externalities, and institutional restrictions; and, finally, an acceptable income distribution. In addition to these standard limitations, military manpower procurement impinges on such extra-market considerations as political decision making, morality, and the privileges and obligations of citizenship.[21] For instance, citizenship implies certain inalienable features, such as voting, which cannot be overtly bought and sold, though voters are often appealed to through programs implying income redistribution. These extramarket considerations qualitatively separate military service from otherwise comparable civilian jobs. But, as we shall see, these qualitative distinctions are significant only in wartime or when war is an immediate prospect. In peacetime, military manpower, for all practical purposes, can be considered a labor submarket.

The economic assumptions underlying individual choice are relatively unimportant for military manpower procurement. Such manipulation as enticing youths to volunteer through misleading advertisements and training promises, can be readily rectified. Uncertainty and imperfect knowledge are found in all labor markets. They are more serious for *entrants* into military service; military careerists suffer less than their civilian counterparts. If it were not for enlistment contracts and the fact that it is legally impossible to opt out, there would be less uncertainty and imperfect knowledge in entering military service than the civilian labor force. Both labor groups invest their time, but the civilian also invests his limited financial resources in occupational training which may not conform to expectations. The difference thus hinges on the presence of an enlistment contract. Military careerists, on the other hand, know military life and cannot claim imperfect knowledge of its implications. Furthermore, a military career offers economic security and an attractive retirement annuity. Careerists are also less restricted by enlistment contracts: officers, after their initial tour, can generally resign at any time; enlisted men are still contracted but often can have their contract cancelled by repaying their reenlistment bonuses and, of course, forfeiting a retirement annuity. Thus, the main uncertainty facing careerists is unforeseen "hardship" tours with family separation caused, for instance, by limited wars.[22]

Military enlistment contracts can be disparaged on ethical grounds for their implied similarity to contractual or indentured labor. The argument runs that imperfect knowledge or changing conditions may cause a young person, in particular, to regret having committed himself. Critics also point out that personal labor contracts in the civilian market cannot be legally enforced, although the employee can be sued for financial damage in a breach of contract suit. (Often hidden in this argument is the hoped-for side benefit of hobbling foreign expeditions, if volunteers are permitted to opt out at propitious moments.)

On the other side of the argument, the military could not function without enlistment contracts. Opting-out at critical moments could produce chaos in a military organization.[23] No militarily threatened society could accept such a situation. Without at least a first-term contract, the military would have no way of ensuring that it could use the people it had trained. Whereas civilian apprenticeships emphasize prolonged, on-the-job training programs, the military typically telescopes a large portion of its investment in formal training. As long as the military procured its manpower through the draft and draft-induced volunteers, training had to be accelerated in order to obtain a reasonable payoff period from such short-term personnel. On the other hand, because contractual labor is unenforceable in the courts, civilian firms cannot ensure that the benefits of their human capital investment will not be lost to other firms or even their competitors. Both the military and civilian firms are thus operating under constraints that probably lead to economically nonoptimal results.

Free Choice and Extra-Market Considerations

While the standard assumptions underlying the economic case for free choice are not restrictive, such assumptions as externalities and acceptable income distributions are restrictive when evaluated in extramarket terms and can be used to build a case against free choice.

Paternalism. Social paternalism to protect the individual is one argument against free choice. In many fields, such as child labor, mine safety, air traffic, narcotics, etc., society interferes with individual and corporate choices, often after major disasters have crystalized public opinion. Traditionally, the military has been categorized as a high-risk, burdensome, industry with particularly onerous discipline and Spartan living conditions. Because of these burdens, many people feel that the individual choosing service has either not been fully informed of the burdens and risks, is over-discounting them, or, worse, is placing a pricetag on the probability of death. This is held to be illegal, since an individual cannot legally sell or take his own life. Moreover, risk to life carries socio-political and ethical implications that are above monetary considerations. The market is also an imperfect mechanism for pricing life and is in any case a rigged system because of underlying income distributions. Finally, society has an interest in insuring widespread sharing of wartime physical burdens in order to prevent recriminations which could occur if some classes suffered disproportionate casualties. Society, so the argument runs, should therefore interfere and prohibit voluntary entry into the military.

The difficulties with the paternalistic arguments are factual error, philosophic confusion, and attribution of the value judgments of a few to the population as a whole. Intellectuals and rugged individualists regard military discipline and its authoritarian paternalism as individually onerous and restrictive. On the other hand, the military's authoritarian paternalism provides social and economic security and a hierarchy of respect both given and received (i.e., Hegelian and Burkian corporateness). Those already possessing economic security and respect or those who can readily compete in a market economy tend to reject this blatant military appeal. To the many, however, who find these goals distant, the military is an attractive alternative.

As has just been pointed out, the individualistic tradition of American society dislikes military life because of its overt, distasteful, and coercive forms of discipline. This orientation reflects the value judgments of classic liberalism, which assumed that the ideals of the French Revolution—liberty and equality—would banish coercion; whereas, in reality, as Marx said, the Revolution stripped away the corporate security of the ancien régime from the proletariat while permitting the bourgeoisie to introduce new forms of economic coercion. An industrial society means coercion. Some forms are less overt and more palatable than others; but coercion remains. Coercion is a matter of degree; it can only be mitigated by the presence of alternatives.

Finally, the burdens and risks to life are not nearly as great as commonly believed. The ground combat arms (including the infantry) now comprise only 13% of peacetime strength; their burdens are not shared by the whole military. The risk to life in peacetime is low for all branches of the military; in wartime, risk is heavily concentrated on the infantry and the officer pilots. In the infantry, it is mainly newcomers who risk their lives; careerists suffer disproportionately only during the initial campaigns, before large-scale expansion.[24]

The risks and burdens of *peacetime* military service, therefore, are not such as to warrant paternalistic protection. Only in wartime are the risks sufficient to justify paternalism. However, in such periods, society has generally encouraged patriotic motives and the spirit of voluntarism.

Shifting the Burden Onto the Poor. A major argument against free choice is that the enticements of a volunteer system would primarily attract the less privileged and shift the burdens of war onto them. One aspect of this shifting is its impact upon political decision making, discussed on pp. 48-51. The other is the ethical notion that military service should be widespread and that the military should represent the nation as a whole. A volunteer military implies that economic status is a major determinant in enlistment decisions. This conflicts with an ethical notion shared by almost all societies, that the privileges and obligations of citizenship shall be borne proportionately. It has been noted that a characteristic of decadent societies is the shift of the military burden from the rich to the less-privileged classes.[25]

Several points deflate the burden-shifting argument. First, while physical burdens of service may indeed be shifted, their resulting disutilities can be offset by monetary compensation. From a utility viewpoint, both the rich and the poor can reach higher welfare positions by this division and specialization of labor.[26] A theoretical objection is that while such specialization may be efficient, it remains undesirable because the choices of the poor are significantly affected by their economic status. Second, the empirical fact is that the peacetime burdens of military service differ only in degree from those of civilian life. Burden-shifting is a wartime argument; only in wartime are the serviceman's risks and burdens distinctly greater than the civilian's. Finally, voluntarism, as shown in Appendix 2-B, does not lead to a black military, as is so often alleged.

A universal draft or an equal probability lottery for all members of an age cohort would ensure widespread sharing of military service. In these systems burden-shifting cannot occur among those liable for service, though of course certain social groups may be disproportionately represented among older careerists. Burden-shifting can occur only through either a selective or a volunteer system. If a selective scheme allows the better educated and those with higher incomes to be deferred from service, then selectivity and voluntarism lead to essentially similar social representation within the class of military recruits. The difference is that voluntarism at least fully compensates the burdened and ensures that the rich—while opting out of physical service—at least bear the military's financial burden. Selectivity (as traditionally practiced here and abroad) not only shifts the burden onto the less privileged but also levies higher tax rates on them.[27] A purely random process, on the other hand, would equally distribute the physical burden on all social groups, levy equal tax rates, and tax the privileged proportionately more.[28]

Due to the mechanics of assignment within the military, the burden-shifting argument actually *strengthens* the case for peacetime voluntarism, provided that a widespread draft is used to *expand* the military should war occur. The very fact that the less privileged opted for a peacetime military means that during a quasi-war (e.g., a Vietnam military expansion), the more privileged social classes would be drafted disproportionately into the expansionable segments of the military, namely, the infantry. Peacetime voluntarism, by reducing labor turn-over within the skilled "overhead" nuclear segment, would offer fewer relatively safe spaces during wartime for the better-educated volunteers who would otherwise fill them. And finally, when war occurs, careerists, even in the combat arms, will be largely remote from the direct fighting, in higher-rank cadre and staff positions. Thus a strong case can be made that peacetime voluntarism and an equal-probability wartime draft in the modern dual nuclear-conventional military would disproportionately endanger the *more* privileged, and not excessively burden the poor.

Top of the Bottom. A corollary to the burden-shifting argument concerns the restrictions society imposes on some ethnic/religious groups and the interdependence of individual decisions. Such interdependence in labor markets is normally not a consideration, since the impact of individual A's career decision on B is minimal except to the extent that oversupply is created, driving down occupational wages. The specific charge against voluntarism is that higher wages could conceivably draw off natural leaders among the blacks into the career military, thus improving a few individual positions but retarding social progress for the black community as a whole.

In principle this is an important question; there may not, however, be a real problem. First, only special deferment for natural leaders fully satisfies this argument. Even a lottery would draft a few who might be tempted later by the military's high career wages.[29] A volunteer system would probably draw off fewer natural leaders than has selective service, even with its student and occupational deferments. For example, in FY 1965 the propensity for qualified AFQT Category I blacks (.4% of the black cohort versus 9.8% for whites) to volunteer was only slightly higher than for comparable whites; however, such blacks were 2 1/2 times more likely to be drafted than Category I whites.[30] AFQT Category II blacks (3.8% of the black cohort versus 29% for whites) were 1.3 times more likely to volunteer, but also 1.8 times more likely to be drafted than comparable whites. Of course, over time these vying forces will diminish as the stock of high-caliber blacks increases; the effect is that the top-of-the-bottom rationale dissipates.

Another empirical consideration is that the entry wages necessary to staff a volunteer military are actually slightly *lower* than the mean earnings for the whole population age cohort. Such a wage would not be sufficient to attract the best of the black community, especially given the current emphasis on scholarships and special consideration for blacks in many prestigious universities and corporations.

Finally, top-of-the-bottom is really a second-best argument; the real goal is removing the prejudicial restrictions in the society at large. So long as these restrictions exist, a military career permits some individuals to reach the best position they can. The question thus is, does the long-run communal goal merit sacrificing the opportunities of some individuals in the short run? The answer depends on subjective value judgments and the empirical evidence of how much more of the natural leadership is in fact drained off by voluntarism than by alternative procurement systems.

Manipulation of Incentives. Another argument against free choice is the possibility that the power structure may manipulate incentives to shift the burden onto the less privileged. Those who hold this viewpoint concede that with given opportunities free choice leads to the highest attainable welfare position. The technical case for free choice is precisely this static efficiency. But if free choice produces dysfunctional changes, or hinders changes which otherwise would have occurred in the social framework, free choice may be dynamically undesirable and lead in the long run to a lower welfare position. The underlying fear is that voluntarism may curtail existing social programs and prevent the setting-up of new ones. The argument is, that the less income is redistributed to the underprivileged through social programs, the more responsive will be the poor to volunteer enticements. Voluntarism is thus seen as a threat to social reform.

Draft systems are free from this liability. More men at any given cost level can always be drafted; little incentive therefore exists to curtail welfare programs so that military service appears more attractive.

The Right to Kill. Another argument concerns the ethical question of whether an individual should be permitted voluntary admission into a profession whose members have the right to kill. An individual can be compensated for the risk of injury but he does not possess the right to kill except as the explicit agent of his society. The legal right to kill is reserved almost entirely to the military; even the police are assigned a preventive rather than a killing role. But what are society's alternatives in choosing its military agents? All of the politically feasible systems, including most draft systems, permit some degree of volunteer participation. Then there is the question of careerists (men with more than 4 years' service), who compose about half the peacetime force and who have voluntarily chosen a military career. Should this criterion also apply to them? If so, is society prepared to draft men into long-term military careers in order to maintain a pool of military experience?

The questions of when does killing occur, who does it, and are there different types of killing, also erode the importance of the right-to-kill criterion. The military does not kill in peacetime; the relevant question is, therefore, Who does what type of killing in wartime? Society tends to condone indirect and impersonal killing, as by strategic bombing and artillery; only direct and personal killing, as by infantrymen, seems to be ethically objectionable. In more specific terms, massacres such as the one at My Lai are thoroughly condemned,[31] but the far more extensive damage caused by indiscriminate use of artillery and air-delivered weapons tends to be glossed over. Though both result in killing, a sharp qualitative difference in morality exists. If it did not, the distinctions between weapon-system users, maintainers, producers, and so on, would become blurred—as, of course, a few do maintain they are. This distinction is significant because most of the "objectionable" killing is done not by those who volunteer in peacetime, but by those who enter during military expansions. Peacetime volunteers are largely in the more skilled specialities and operate and maintain the more sophisticated equipment (which kills impersonally).

Therefore, since the expansionary portions of the military are mainly involved in "personal" killing, free choice is objectionable mainly for those portions in *wartime*. The right-to-kill criterion has little relevance to peacetime voluntarism, or even to wartime voluntarism in the noncombat arms. Draft systems generally satisfy the right-to-kill criterion. But so does a manpower system coupling peacetime voluntarism with a wartime draft.

Mercenaries and Praetorianism. A final argument against voluntary choice is its alleged appeal to base monetary motives and its evolution into a mercenary force unresponsive and dangerous to democratic institutions. The 1966 Presidential (Marshall) Commission termed a volunteer military "a mercenary force unrepresentative of the nation."[32] The Clark Report predicted that voluntarism would place

a monetary value on the lives of citizens, creating the concept of defense of the nation by mercenaries, and abandon the unifying influence of the nation placing its faith in its own citizenry to rally to its defense. . . .[33]

The choice of the value-laden word "mercenary" is unfortunate.[34] The Marshall objection seems to refer merely to "a military force sustained only by financial incentive." Since Webster defines a mercenary as "now only a soldier hired into foreign service," the connotation is similar to the Clark Report's direct reference to noncitizens. Whether the Clark and Marshall groups were themselves confused, or intentionally attempted to confuse the public, is debatable. Voluntarism and "mercenarism" are not synonymous. Mercenarism requires volunteers; but voluntarism need not imply mercenarism.

Two misconceptions have been partly responsible for the charge that voluntarism leads to a mercenary force. Some have implicitly assumed that a volunteer system means voluntarism in all peace-wartime contexts. A second misconception has been caused by a number of economists in and out of DoD overestimating the budgetary costs of a volunteer force. These estimates made volunteer wages appear high even in peacetime. However, when correctly calculated, the additional wage necessary to attract the required *entrants* for a pre-Vietnam sized force is only $.5 to 1 billion/annum.[35] These statistical estimates show that market wages will not be much higher than the federal minimum wage and will be slightly less than mean earnings for the 18- to 22-year-old cohorts. This is not a wage that supports the contention of mercenary greed. If it is, then extant wages for the career force should be reviewed, for they actually *exceed* the mean earnings of comparable high-school and college graduates.[36] Correcting these two misconceptions largely dissipates the charge that peacetime voluntarism leads to a mercenary force.

Criterion: Ex-Ante Equity

Ex-ante equity means equal individual probability of service. A widespread confusion resulting in policy inertia against rectifying the draft's inequities has been caused by the failure to distinguish between equal obligation and equal probability of military service. Almost all draft systems formally propose equal liability; to do otherwise would violate democratic ideals. Selective Service has always meant equal obligation of service. However, from 1951 to 1967 the very title of the Universal Military Training and Service Act gave the impression that all had equal chances of serving. The chairman of the House Armed Services Committee, Carl Vinson, reflected this impression when he stated that the strength of Selective Service was that it applied "to everybody equally and alike."[37] During full mobilization, when manpower demands are high, most draft systems imply equal probability of service for the physically and mentally qualified *younger* cohorts who possess few critical skills. It is during periods when manpower calls are not exhaustive for an age cohort that the distinction between obligation and probability is important.

The criterion of equal probability of service is met in the most rigorous sense only by a universal draft of all but the mentally and physically handicapped. A pure lottery also implies equal probability of service. The lotteries which have been publicly discussed, however, are really mixed lottery-volunteer systems. The practical meaning of the lottery is therefore limited to equal probability for the draft-liable *pool*. A selective system imposes obligation on an age cohort, but effectively exempts many from service through its deferment policies and its implicit encouragement of the military to raise its acceptance standards. Such deferment policies and acceptance standards affect the population's ethnic and economic subgroupings differently, so that while the entire cohort is liable to be drafted, some are more liable than others. This form of group inequity can be eliminated only by equal treatment of individuals and, hence, equal probability of service for *each* draft-liable individual. Finally, in a volunteer system ex-ante equity is by definition satisfied because the probability of service is zero for all nonvolunteers.

Criterion: Ex-Post Equity

Individual satisfaction of selectees depends on their compensation,[38] understanding of the need for military force, and their answer to the fairness question, "Why me?" Given justifiable need and compensation, the individual tends to compare himself with his acquaintances. The more they have volunteered or been drafted, the greater his passive acceptance. He may complain about the military and his plight, but he does not necessarily feel *unfairly* treated. He begins to feel discriminated against only when he suffers, while his friends and perhaps other groups obviously do not. This raises the interesting question as to whether an individual feels more discriminated against by a random or a selective draft. A lottery (without deferments) provides greater ex-ante fairness by equal treatment for all age cohort members. But since one's acquaintances are usually peers in intelligence and education, selective service may provide a feeling of greater ex-post fairness by its narrowing focus upon the similarly situated. Such an acceptance, of course, depends on imperfect knowledge; to the extent that those serving become acutely aware that other sizeable groups are deferred or exempted for questionable reasons, the feeling of ex-post fairness dissipates and questions of group equity arise. The interesting point, however, is the clash between ex-ante and ex-post equity. A change to random conscription increases ex-ante equity but will continuously decrease ex-post equity as the population grows relative to military demands. During large mobilizations this interesting distinction disappears as the draft approaches universality.

Universal and volunteer systems do not have an ex-post liability. Universal systems by definition draft everyone and no person is singled out for special burdens or privileges. Voluntarism automatically rules out the individual's feeling of unfairness, although the larger society may still possess a different ethical sense of fairness and question the initial income distribution.

Criterion: Pay Equity

Pay equity is an aspect of fairness which tends to be overlooked in public discussions. Its ethics are independent of manpower selection: fair wages are consistent with conscription as well as voluntarism. However, fair and market wages are not necessarily synonymous. Peacetime market wages, sufficient to attract the required manpower because of differences in economic status, may be considered inadequate when measured by the social yardstick of desirable income distribution. Wartime market wages could also reflect extortionist demands by prospective volunteers, as in the Civil War. Pay equity is thus a neutral concept with respect to the choice of a manpower procurement system; it simply means offering a decent wage regardless of the selection scheme. For a volunteer system, a fair wage can be below or above the market wage necessary for attracting sufficient volunteers.[39]

Defining pay equity for the military is difficult. Figure 2-2 shows the two standard measures which Professor Pigou calls "wage unfairness"[40] and "wage exploitation." Since the rational firm does not hire labor past Qc, Pigou defines "exploitation" as the difference between the worker's marginal physical product value (QmR) and his wage (QmP); "unfairness," as the difference between the competitive wage (QcC) and actual wage (QmP).[41] For the military, however, demand (D_L) is not meaningfully defined. The military's well-known preference for satisfying requirements could conceivably cause a demand of Q_u. As long as the institutionally set military wage (Wm) exceeds QuU, wage exploitation technically does not exist as Wm > VMPP. However, the spirit of Pigou's definition suggests a new exploitation measure of QuT minus Wm; unfairness would remain as defined, QuS minus Wm. Generally, Pigou agrees with Marshall that

wages are fair relatively to wages in industries in general, if, . . . they are about on a level with the payment made for tasks in other trades which are of equal

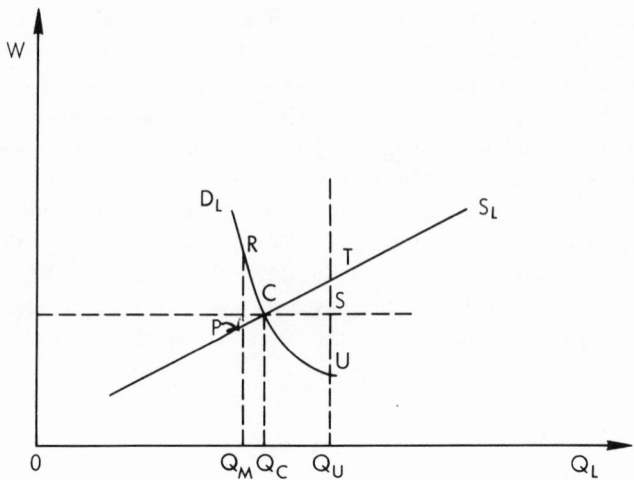

Figure 2-2. The Economic Meaning of Exploitation and Unfairness.

difficulty, and disagreeableness, which require equal natural abilities and an equally expensive training. As between persons . . . , fairness implies wages which . . . are proportioned to efficiency.[42]

The Marshall-Pigou definition of wage fairness seems the most logical criterion for pay equity. In theory a fair wage could be paid each entrant according to the natural abilities, human capital investment, and disagreeableness associated with each military occupational area. In practice, only a few broad categories are administratively feasible. The military has preferred in recent years a single wage and has opposed differential pay because of its sensitivity to discrimination against the less-skilled but more burdensome combat arms. Pressure of events from high losses among technical personnel has forced acceptance of limited differential pays for career personnel in the form of proficiency pay and variable reenlistment bonuses. Equity (and minimizing voluntarism's budgetary costs) requires similar discriminating differentials for entrants. The Marshall-Pigou criterion calls for wage premiums for both the more qualified and the more burdened. The wage premium for the more qualified, however, is tempered by their receiving, at government expense, valuable technical training that others do not receive.

The weakness of the Marshall-Pigou criterion is wage proportionment among entrants of *unequal* natural abilities assigned to similar tasks. The criterion assumes that individuals are given tasks which match their skills. Voluntarism roughly satisfies this assumption by the recruiting policy of permitting assignment choice by qualification. Conscription complicates this matching. Institutional arrangements prescribe that long-term volunteers receive training preference, relegating high-quality draftees to low-skill compartments. Moreover, except for very select drafts, the upper ability range of draftees is higher than the military's *enlisted* requirements. Consequently, while skill groupings may be paid wages comparable to civilian practices, mismatched individuals may not be.

The arguments against fair pay are: (1) that the cost would be astronomical; (2) that military service is an obligation of citizenship, rather than a marketplace transaction; and (3) that the military provides servicemen with the equivalent of free apprentice training.

(1.) Within the existing Selective Service framework, fair pay would mean increasing entrant compensation and higher budget costs. In peacetime, however, fair pay would necessarily reduce real economic costs as draft-induced accessions were replaced by volunteers. In 1967, first-year servicemen, using DoD's own nominal valuations, received only 63% of the federal minimum wage[43] (which represents a socially determined standard of sorts, even though it tends to lag behind current business practices). If the federal minimum wage is used as the criterion of fair pay, and adequate inter-rank differentials are maintained, the maximum budgetary increase for a Vietnam-sized force would have been $3.0 billion.[44] Based on pre-Vietnam strengths, the budgetary increase for a peace-time military paying the 1967 federal minimum wage would have been $1.8 billion. Costs to the Treasury in both cases is reduced by income taxes. In the long run, the increased budget costs of basing entry pay on the federal minimum wage somewhat exceeds voluntarism's $2.1 billion, because longer enlistments and higher reenlistment rates from substituting true volunteers for draft-induced accessions reduce accession and training costs but increase seniority and retirement costs even more.

(2.) Rationalizing low pay by reference to the obligation of citizenship is an emotive non sequitur. It assumes a universality which no longer exists. The Greek city-states and the Roman republic did initially rely on a low-paid citizen-militia with wage differentials according to family need. Low pay did not imply inequity. Equity is relative equality; if all able-bodied men are serving and receiving comparable low wages, no arithmetic inequity is involved. Neither is proportionate inequity involved; for the rich man's greater opportunity-cost of service is matched by his greater gain from the state's preservation. The Greeks and Romans also lacked the fiscal and monetary instruments to pay market wages without ruinous inflation. Thus, although historically correlated, low pay and obligations of citizenship need not be paired. Moreover, in American history, citizens undertaking these obligations by bearing arms have been amply compensated.[45]

(3.) A plausible argument for low entry pay is based on the apprentice analogy. The idea is that the apprentice receives low wages in return for the cost of his training. However, this assumes that the training will have general applicability, whereas in fact the military provides varying amounts of training for tasks pertinent only to military needs. When commercially useful general training is offered, the military can justifiably pay trainees their opportunity-marginal product, less the total cost of general training. The caveat is that market wages, based on acquired skills, would have to be paid during a subsequent enlistment period; this requirement would conflict with the existing pay structure's progression based on grade "responsibility" and longevity. Until draft-induced volunteering is terminated and wage policies rationalized, the military will continue to be what Professor Becker has termed

. . . a conspicuous example of an organization that both pays at least part of training costs and does not pay market wages to skilled personnel. It has had, in consequence, relatively easy access to "students" and heavy losses of "graduates" . . . . The military, of course, is not a commercial organization judged by profits and losses and has had no difficulty surviving and even thriving.[46]

To the extent that military training is useful only to the military (i.e., "training which has no effect on the productivity of trainees that would be useful in other firms"),[47] the costs of training ought to be borne by the military. Low pay for a conscripted foot soldier cannot logically be supported by reference to the training received in boot camp. The military is the sole beneficiary of this increased specific productivity and therefore ought to bear its costs.

In a 1966 *Reader's Digest* article, former President Eisenhower reiterated an old and respectable assertion, that military training is individually and socially beneficial.[48] To the extent that individual qualities of citizenship are thus improved, society benefits, and should therefore pay the bill through the military budget. To the extent that general training is offered, a case can be made for cost-sharing between the military and the trainee. (The respective proportions of such cost-sharing present a difficult question, however.)

The argument that military service provides opportunities to increase one's earnings is often supported by census statistics showing that the mean earnings of veterans are higher than those of nonveterans. But this is true only because simple averages obscure distinguishing characteristics. Harry Gilman argues that his studies show that veterans earn less than nonveterans.[49] Lester Thurow has also shown that, correcting for geographical and educational distribution, black veterans actually earn less than black nonveterans.[50] For blacks, correcting for distribution is particularly important because of their disproportionate concentration in the low-wage South and in the Armed Forces Qualification Test (AFQT) categories below peacetime acceptance standards. A skewed AFQT distribution also means that the relatively few qualified blacks receive predominantly specific training that had low commercial value.

A trivial but often-heard argument for low pay is: "I endured it; why should today's G.I.'s get a softer deal?" The advantage of repeating past errors is never explained. However, as Table 5-7 indicates, the argument is empirically incorrect. The draftees of 1946 actually had 11.7% more purchasing power than those of 1 January 1971, even though real civilian earnings increased 57.1%. In other words, even including the large military pay raises since 1964, the relative position of today's draftee has still deteriorated by 68.8%; the second lieutenant's, by 34%—while senior careerists have prospered with the economy.

Criterion: Rejectee Equity

Usually neglected—because most people do not want to serve in the military—is the need to consider the satisfaction of the rejected. Frequently, rejection is considered fortunate. But what of individuals who desire military service? A military career offers benefits often not found in the civilian sector. In an imperfect society, the military offers a haven against religious and racial discrimination. For the poor, the military offers training and a new start regardless of family background. The individual is judged solely by his ability to satisfy the military's peculiar criteria (though, of course, this is not independent of developed abilities and hence previous social background). The military also provides economic security and generous retirement benefits.

The rejectee's material dissatisfaction is caused by his exclusion from a desirable commodity—either the potential compensation or the training. The greater these perceived benefits, the stronger is the resentment at exclusion. This suggests an equity tradeoff: the higher the wage (for pay equity), the greater the feeling of inequity among the rejected.[51] High acceptance standards also increase the number excluded. Of course, higher acceptance standards and higher pay to support these standards would increase both the number of rejectees and their dissatisfaction.

Rejection for medical or mental reasons can be a positive stigma as well as an obstacle to maximizing individual welfare. In periods of patriotic fervor, rejection by the military has occasionally caused social rejection, particularly by women. In modern education-conscious America, inability to meet the military's minimum mental standards can adversely affect employment as well as self-respect. A wide gap exists between the public's image of acceptance standards and the military's pre-Vietnam standards. Whereas the public tends to think of low wartime standards, the Army has increased acceptance standards to exclude 31% of today's better-educated youth. If these standards are unreasonably high, then almost a third of the nation's youth and nearly 72% of its black youth have been unnecessarily stigmatized and excluded from a choice which might have been individually and socially desirable.

While such "mass" stigmatization is a function of high standards and imperfect knowledge about the rigor of these standards, any disqualification implies some stigmatization as well as rejectee inequity. This is an unpleasant fact which can only be minimized by ensuring that acceptance standards are no higher than necessary. This raises the question of how procurement alternatives affect acceptance standards. The importance of this question is seen in the fact that overall rejection rates increased steadily from 23% in the World War II-Korea periods to 35% in 1964.[52] Rather than being a manifestation of poor physical condition, as is often alleged, the increase was due to higher mental requirements, since medical rejections remained fairly constant and actually declined from World War II levels. Mental acceptance standards were raised by supplementing the Armed Forces Qualification Test (AFQT) with an additional battery of aptitude tests and continually increasing requirements. Equation (1) shows the effects of these procedures on Mental Category IV (10-30 percentile on the basic AFQT) pre-inductee acceptance rates.[53]

$$(1) \qquad R = -2.95 + .026P + .889U \qquad R^2 = .81$$
$$(3.28) \quad (2.40)$$

in which R = preinduction rejection rates (in percent), P = population of 18 year-olds (in thousands), and U = percent of 18-19 year-olds unemployed. The figures in parentheses are t-values. If P is redefined as excess supply (i.e., supply of 18-year-olds minus all enlisted accessories), 76% of the variation is accounted for by this variable alone.

Letting the military set acceptance standards for their convenience as supply changed was accompanied by a high social cost. By sharply curtailing its acceptance of non-high-school and low-test-scoring youths, the military in effect excluded those more prone to unemployment and hence inadvertently increased youth unemployment rates. In addition, the upward age creep of draftees (Figure 2-3) before the deferring of married men in 1963 meant that less-unem-ployment-prone older men were being drafted in lieu of more unemployment-prone younger men. No data exist to statistically measure their impact on unemployment rates; rough calculations, however, indicate a magnitude approxi-mating the unexplained residual in the debate, in the economic literature of the early 1960s, between the structuralists and the Keynesians. The importance of these phenomena can be seen in the rise in youth unemployment caused by constant manpower demand on the part of the nation's largest employer of these men—the U.S. military—during a period of rapid population growth, as shown in Equation (2).[54]

$$(2) \qquad Y = 1.446 + .070S + 1.900U \qquad R^2 = .96$$
$$(5.18) \quad (10.83)$$

in which Y = percent of 18- and 19-year-olds unemployed, S = supply of 18-year-olds minus all enlisted accessions divided by the number of 18- and 19-year-olds in the labor force (in percent), and U = percent of males 16 and over unemployed. The figures in parentheses are t-values.

In wartime the problem of artifically high acceptance standards is corrected by supply pressures generated by the overall scarcity of labor and the military's reduced *relative* demand for higher-quality manpower because of its reduced concern for stocking its career force and its disproportionate expansion in the quickly trained ground combat arms.

In peacetime, voluntarism seems to be the strongest corrective against overstated acceptance standards through the obvious mechanism of unnecessary cost. Draft systems have the disadvantage of allowing too-easy access to higher-quality personnel by simply raising standards. The corrective mechanism is the drafting of the more vocal and educated, who generally come from wealthier families. Thus, in universal and lottery systems, high acceptance standards would increase the probability of service for the better educated; the result would be pressure for a more reasonable standard. In selective systems, this pressuring mechanism can be perverse. Pressure for student and occupational deferments by the socially privileged lowers the qualitative manpower input to the services and reduces upper-class concern over acceptance standards. Consequently, the military, in an effort to maintain its mean quality when large percentages of the top of the quality distribution are exempted, is induced to raise its cutoff standards in order to increase its proportion of the middle group.

Criterion: Group Equity

The straightforward meaning of group equity is *like treatment of social groupings.* Group inequity can emerge if individual inequity can be associated with social groupings. Individual inequity produces only individual complaints and personal dissatisfaction. Group inequity, whether real or imagined, strains the social fabric.

Since the Civil War, society has been quite conscious of the group-inequity argument; yet Selective Service has again caused group inequity. The cause was a series of myopic innovations which led a system explicitly designed to avoid group inequity back into it by oversight. The World-War-I and 1940-41 drafts were explicitly designed to be a locally administered lottery to avoid the deficiencies of the Civil War draft. However, industrial deferments made the lottery cumbersome and actually more unfair and uncertain than the simpler, more systematic birthday selection scheme adopted in 1942 that produced nearly the same outcome during full mobilization. The next innovation was class-correlated student and occupational deferments, judged during the Korean period to be socially desirable. Finally, in the late 1950s, a burgeoning manpower pool, relative to military needs, induced a "rational" military to restrict entry and allocate entrants internally according to military convenience rather than social welfare.[55] In addition to narrowing the draft's social focus, the resulting "color-blind" system tended to exclude blacks from the skilled enlisted occupational areas, but disproportionately enlisted and drafted them to fill the low-skill, high-casualty occupational areas.

The cause of group inequity has been the selection and allocation of individuals according to criteria which produce nonrandom distributions. The solution is quite simple: either provide equal opportunities (e.g., education) or adopt a manpower system which distributes the burden satisfactorily. While the former is desirable, the latter may be more easily engineered by fiat. The pragmatic solution is therefore either a lottery or voluntarism (or some combination thereof). Within the military, allocation can also be partially revised by including social considerations, rather than only military ones. A socially correct criterion weighs both military and nonmilitary considerations. It need not downgrade national security, if it becomes the occasion for recognizing previously neglected or unrealized tradeoffs, such as allowing social groupings with higher reenlistment propensities lower cutoff scores into the more skilled specialties.

Group inequity is a particularly serious charge to avoid in wartime, even though it is technically inevitable during modern full-mobilization wars, because the important industrial and technical skills needed for deferment to support the military machine are concentrated among the better educated. The charge of unacceptable inequity, therefore, depends on how deferment policy is administered so that it is acceptable to all social groups in order to most effectively prosecute the war effort. Because group inequity often has attributes of economic exploitation, high home-front taxes and wage controls during full mobilization are ways to help avoid the charge by ensuring that deferees do not profit at the expense of those serving. During limited wars, group inequity is inexcusable. In this case, a war is not being fully prosecuted and society is not pressed for resources. Economic efficiency is therefore not critical for social survival, and the criterion of efficiency becomes secondary to noneconomic considerations.

Among alternative procurement schemes, selective service always causes group inequity. Universal and random selection schemes do not. For voluntarism, the relationship with group inequity is similar to the previously discussed issue of shifting the burdens of war onto the poor. Peacetime voluntarism, by definition, means no individual inequity, hence no summing process causing group inequity. A strict interpretation of this reasoning could also extend to wartime. However, the loss of life causes a qualitative distinction that undermines the acceptability of the underlying prior income distribution.

Criterion: Uncertainty and the Disruption in the Lives of Young Men

President Johnson referred to these criteria as "the objective of minimizing uncertainty and interference with individual careers and education."[56] The cost and degree of uncertainty and career interruption are a function of age, because employment and employer-sponsored training are often not available until after prospective military service.[57] Its two cost elements are: subjective disutility, which can be estimated by surveys indicating revealed preferences, and opportunity cost of temporarily reduced civilian earnings.

The upward creep of the median draft age caused by a growing manpower pool and the SSS's policy of "oldest first" is shown in Figure 2-3. This policy was administratively convenient and, according to the SSS, equitable, because it ensured equal treatment for those equally situated (those with similar SSS classifications). Population growth, however, caused the pool to grow to

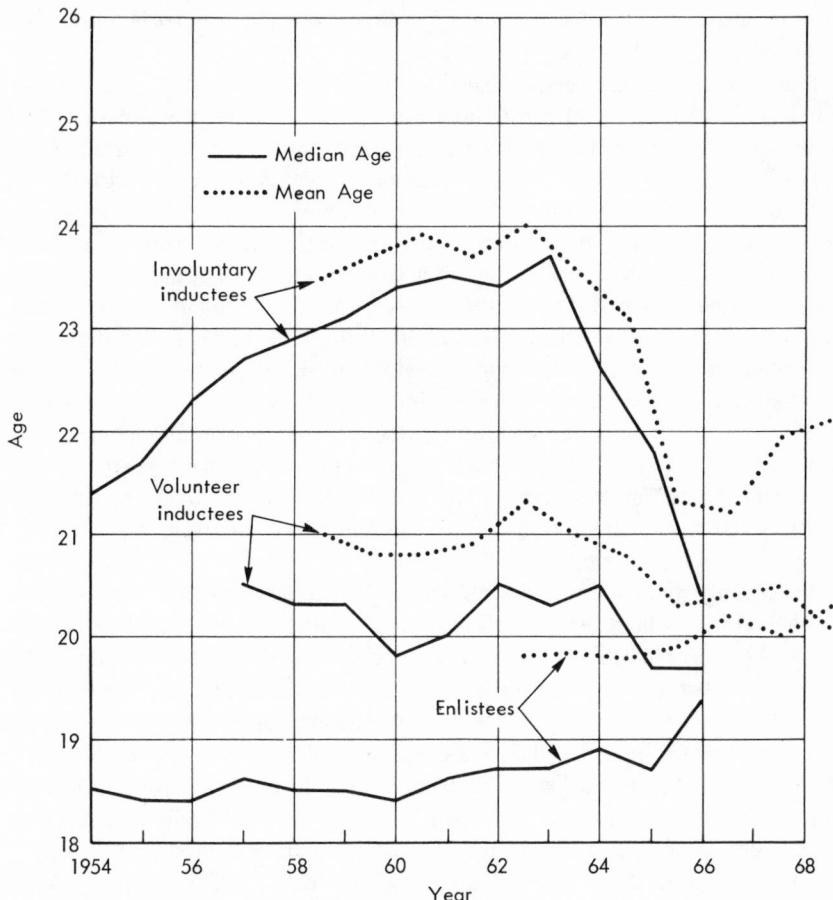

Figure 2-3. Age of Enlisted and Inductees, Median Age — Fiscal year 1954–1966; Mean Age - Calender Year 1958–1968. Source: *Health of the Army*, Office of the Surgeon General, 1962–1969; and RAOSSS, p. 10006.

unmanageable proportions which threatened the age-26 limitation and caused the Army to accept increasingly older draftees. Selective Service and DoD tried to solve the problem by having the military raise standards and Selective Service liberalize deferments. The problem is perhaps best illustrated by their inducing President Kennedy in 1963 to limit draft calls to single men, "which proved a highly effective method of lowering the draft age by reducing the size of the prime available group from which draft calls were filled."[58] Marriages thereupon accelerated, and the annual marriage rate increased by 10%.[59] Uncertainty for a politically favored group (married men) was reduced, but in a way that illustrates the haphazard manner in which the nation's youth has been manipulated to serve agency interests. Neither agency was guided by social criteria or subjected to detailed review procedures.

SSS and the military services have not desired to include the social costs of individual uncertainty and career interruption in their objective function. The military has favored such costs because they spur enlistments, though the Army has been somewhat unhappy that it alone among the services has had to pay the small price of accepting older, less malleable, draftees. The Selective Service System, on the other hand, viewed the removal of these costs as a major institutional threat. Significant reduction required either voluntarism or a lower draft age. Voluntarism at the very least means the elimination of SS's peacetime authority, though not necessarily the institution itself. A lower draft age undermines the system's classifying process and hence its decentralized local board structure. With a lower effective draft age, the system would have to shift to a lottery, because at age 18 or 19 few fatherhood exemptions exist and occupational deferments lack justification. This would have shattered the classifying process and the birthday technique of drafting by "oldest first." Once this step is taken, the rationale for a decentralized structure—the system's keystone—becomes questionable.[60]

Uncertainty and its resulting employment difficulties can be minimized either by voluntarism, which by definition implies no uncertainty except in case of war, or by a lowered induction age to reduce the period of liability. A lottery is preferable to selective service because of its lower induction age. The widely advocated age-19 lotteries produce a mean and median age of 20 (as against Figure 2-3's much higher median for selective service and 18.6 for voluntarism). Mechanical juggling could lower the mean age but lowering the age to below 19 would require an 18-year-old draft, which has not been politically acceptable in the absence of necessity. Except for full mobilization, an "oldest first" selective system is the least desirable procurement alternative to satisfy the uncertainty and career interruption criteria. Without heavy military demands selective service has a problem. An age creep is inherent with a constant-sized military and a growing population. Yet age creep cannot be reduced without increasingly arbitrary deferments leading to de facto exemptions. Even with increasing exemptions, selective service would only approach voluntarism's low median age by a change in the law to permit drafting 18-year-olds before older men.

Individual career interference, like uncertainty, is minimized by the same ordering of alternative procurement systems. Since free choice and interference are by definition mutually exclusive, voluntarism is again the preferred choice. Random selection's lower median age means less interference, because family and job responsibilities are age-correlated. Timing of educational interference depends on individual preferences; the presumption is that most young men would choose early rather than later disruption.[61] The lottery implies fewer college graduates' entering the military's enlisted-ranks, thus reducing misallocation of skills and ensuring wider social participation in the Army's more burdensome branches. A final point is that while the lottery's lower age means less individual interruption, SSS's de facto exemption of the best qualified may mean less aggregate interruption in terms of opportunity cost.

Criterion: Socializing Role—Impact on Race Relations, Education, and Poverty

Society may choose to cure its internal ills by a number of means. The military's massive contact with the country's various socioeconomic groups illustrates its potential as an integrative social force. The peacetime military absorbs 5% of the male labor force. During the 1950s as much as 63% of an age cohort flowed through the military establishment (exclusive of reserves), including 58% of the non-white male population.[62] Even a long-term peacetime volunteer force in the 1970s would require a 20% flow into the regular and reserve forces. Furthermore, the military operates a schooling system to impart appropriate civic virtues and important technical skills.

The military's socializing role has three strands. The classic strand emphasizes the civic value of a martial education and has been historically associated with universal conscription. Plato and Aristotle recognized its utility, as did Rousseau and innumerable other political theorists and military men. The harmonizing civic values usually emphasized are: submission to law, respect for authority, concern for the commonweal, and private sacrifice in public service. However, this indoctrination is purchased at the high opportunity cost of labor forgone by an age cohort and its cadre supervisors. There is also no assurance that a short period of military training will instill these civic benefits, which, of course, transcend quantification and are not registered in the national income accounts.

A second nonmarket strand is the military's social function of integrating diverse groups into the dominant social group. The military brings impressionable youth into contact with its authoritarian structure, which generally ensures compliance with official policy. During military service, the rough edges of social prejudice are generally rubbed off. As ex-servicemen flow back into the civilian sector, the social attitudes induced by the military are partially retained. Over time this should mitigate the harshness of white biases, though perhaps exacerbating black expectations and resentment.

The third strand is a market argument: military careers and military training can attract and uplift economically depressed groups. This is a new development which reflects the increasing technical complexity of modern militaries. But the military can help the poor only if two conditions are met. The first and more obvious is the admittance of those needing help; accepting too many, however, may place too much of a burden upon the military, considering its overriding mission of national security. A second condition is that those admitted be permitted either a military career or be trained in commercially valuable skills. Training in valuable skills implies higher personnel turnover and less extensive career opportunities for participants than careerism.

The civic value strand implies a universal system. Other drafts, while appealing to the collective civic values of a universal system, take only segments of the cohort population; the full cohort population is not exposed to the virtues of military life. Voluntarism, on the other hand, makes no pretense of calling on these values. A true lottery, being a proxy for a universal system, may capture portions of the civic virtues, but the reinforcing inclusiveness is lost. However, to justify a selective scheme by these values may be counterproductive. In fact, as many scholars have indicated, the civic values of military service may be completely vitiated by the cynicism and evasion which may be induced by a non-universal draft.[63] The smaller the number drafted and the greater the perceived inequity, the greater the tendency towards such adverse social attitudes.

The integrative function is also best satisfied by a universal system because it is inclusive and generally implies low acceptance standards to include those most in need. Of the nonuniversal systems, a lottery is preferable for its wider social representation and greater mutual exposure of various population groups. Voluntarism and a selective system with widespread deferments for the better educated lead to essentially the same narrow social representation. Of the two, selective service is preferable because its higher turnover increases the flow of personnel[64] and its deferments may not be so widespread as to converge with voluntarism's narrow representation.

The economic strand is best satisfied by voluntarism. Enlistments can be long enough to give both militarily and commercially valuable training. The military also benefits from the longer enlistments and consequent higher payoff periods (conscription implies relatively short periods of military service). Voluntarism's potential disadvantage is reduced turnover, which can be restrictive if demand for the military's training services exceeds supply. Among draft systems, universal systems are most handicapped because of the short training period available and the need to train such large numbers. Between random and selective systems, selectivity would be socially preferable because it includes larger numbers of the more underprivileged. The military would, of course, prefer the lottery because of the higher quality of the average draftee and the consequent reduced training requirement—an important military consideration in a short-tour, high-turnover, draftee force.

Criterion: Threat to Democracy

A much-discussed criterion for assessing the relative merits of alternative recruitment systems is their probable effect on domestic political institutions. Concern over how military recruitment affects civilian political life derives from a peculiar English bias against standing armies as an instrument for the abuse of power by the central authority.[65] The American Founding Fathers dealt with this problem not by altering the mode of military recruitment but by dividing power to avert tyranny and by interposing state militias and the states as recruitment agents between the federal government and the people. Until 1863, wartime debates concerning the "threat" associated with recruitment centered on the alleged dangers of permitting direct conscription by the central government. In peacetime, prior to World War II, with no serious external threat and little need for a standing army, distinctions among recruitment alternatives were not important.

The allegation that voluntarism is a threat to democratic institutions is a new twist to the old argument against standing armies, appearing only in the last decade. Voluntarism had always been preferred; it was conscription and its coercive effects that had previously been criticized as subversive. After World War II, for example, Universal Military Training (UMT) was defeated largely because many feared that mass conscription would undermine traditional American attitudes among impressionable youth and lead eventually to subservience to military interests. Only after voluntarism was tried in 1947-48 and it proved unable to meet the military's manpower requirements was a selective conscription system adopted in peacetime.

This section examines the pertinence of military recruitment to threats to the American political system. Since evidence suggests that the relationship is tenuous, the discussion turns to what in the military system does pose such threats and how to counteract it.

The Political Relevance of Alternative Recruitment Systems

The assertion that a high-turnover, socially representative military is less dangerous to democratic institutions than a volunteer force is not empirically supportable. Although the refusal of conscripts to obey their immediate superiors was a key factor in the collapse of the French Army coup against de Gaulle in 1960, other eclectic examples indicate that conscription is not a sufficient condition to insure against coups. Greece has universal conscription, and Brazil and Peru have selective conscription.[66]

Not only is conscription no insurance against coups, the conscription/voluntarism issue is only loosely related to political threats from the military as an institution. This is because the military threats to any existing political order generally come from the officer corps, which controls the military and is in the most direct position to influence political institutions. The operation of a viable military system requires a professional officer corps, and career officers and NCOs are perforce volunteers under all politically feasible recruitment systems. Even in a draft system, unless volunteering were expressly prohibited, those with the highest propensity for the military life would continue to enlist or be commissioned. The core group thus remains essentially the same regardless of the mode of recruitment. Some argue that high turnover is essential to a civilianized military. However, since young enlisted men (even junior officers) have relatively few contacts with senior officers, this consideration can be overstressed. Proponents of high turnover may forget that it is a double-edged sword: UMT was defeated because of fear of the military indoctrination of large numbers of youth.

The one condition under which voluntarism would be politically more dangerous than conscription is if there were such social dissension that military mutinies and social revolution occurred. A conscripted (hence more socially representative) enlisted force would in this case tend to neutralize the military politically. However, this situation is largely hypothetical. The conditions necessary for social revolution to occur are stringent and unlikely. Moreover, the difference in social representation between volunteer and conscription modes are a matter of degree. The percentage of minorities would not be significantly greater in a volunteer force and in any case could be readily controllable (see Appendix 2-B). Many young men would still enlist for a variety of non-monetary reasons, such as travel and training. A totally volunteer army would reduce the flow of young men through the system by an estimated 37% through longer enlistment contracts and higher first-term reenlistment rates (from 25% to an estimated 36%).

Often neglected in the consideration of how military recruitment affects political institutions is the coerciveness of the existing Selective Service System. Selectivity can be an instrument for the suppression of individual dissent. Universal and random conscription, which do not involve discretionary classifications, pose no such threat. The present selective service system, as described on pp. 56-57, has wielded a discretionary power unconstrained by the normal procedural safeguards. This potential abuse of power is checked only by the benevolence of individual boards, the willingness of the Justice Department to prosecute draft violators, and the strength of public opinion. The conformist and collectivist philosophy of Selective Service may be appropriate in major wars, but not necessarily at other times.

Selective Service's much-vaunted "adaptability to each individual registrant" is not individualism, as is often presumed, but a procedure to ensure the proper matching of each individual with the desires of the state.[67] In the words of the System's deputy director:

It is necessary to make a determination as to where these men will work, or where they will serve, or where they will study, and that is the determination that is made by the Selective Service. That is what the word "selective" means, to be able to select not only for the military service, but for the economy of this nation.[68]

Springing from this is channelization, which, according to John Lindsay (then a Congressman from New York), permits "the military to influence young men into jobs that relate to the Cold War, that enhance the position of the military in our society."[69] That Mr. Lindsay's concern was not idle speculation is exemplified by SSS's own publication:

Throughout his career as a student, the pressure—the threat of loss of defer-ment—continues. It continues with equal intensity after graduation. His local draft board requires periodic reports to find out what he is up to. He is impelled to pursue his skill rather than embark upon some less important enterprise and is encouraged to apply his skill in an essential activity in the national interest. The loss of deferred status is the consequence for the individual who acquired the skill and either does not use it or uses it in a nonessential activity. *The psychology of granting wide choice under pressure to take action is the American or indirect way of achieving what is done by direction in foreign countries where choice is not permitted.*[70] (Emphasis added.)

Factors in Military Threats to the Political System

Given the tenuous bearing of the voluntarism/conscription issue on threats to political institutions and values, what does pose a military threat? Theoretically, the mere existence of a standing army is the gravest threat. As mentioned above, the Founding Fathers sought to avert it by the division of power.[71] As for the danger of an army coup,[72] many factors make it less likely in this country than in other countries. Most important, besides the federal structure, is our tradition of economic liberalism, which reinforces the division of political power by making the economic reins more difficult to grasp. This contrasts with condi-tions in countries such as France, with its unitary government and with both political and commercial life concentrated in a single city. Also, the United States does not have an officer class or a tradition of military interference in political affairs.

The factor that currently receives the most public attention as a danger to democratic institutions is the isolation of the military from civilian life. Critics allege that the self-containment of the military engenders exclusivist military attitudes at variance with those of the bulk of the population. To put the military in greater touch with civilian life, many have advocated (some for their own narrow economic interests) the closing of on-post housing, military hospitals, post exchanges, etc. First of all, the isolation of military communities is improbable from civilian communities under normal conditions today. Mass communications, the automobile, and military personnel's exposure to public education insure abundant contact with civilian life and values. Proposals to force geographic integration of the military in civilian communities have marginal worth: geographic integration does not guarantee value integration, and, since military personnel would tend to live near military bases anyway, the closing of post facilities would not prevent near-post military concentrations. Isolation is further forestalled by the military's need to interact with civilian industry in the development of sophisticated weaponry.

Even if it were an actual condition, isolation of the military from civilian life would not be totally undesirable. It might prompt a productive self-analysis. In such a period of isolation after the Civil War, the American military achieved professional standing, becoming more militarily competent and adopting a code of ethics that proscribes military intervention in politics.[73] Furthermore, isolation does not of itself make a military politically dangerous. On the contrary, in modern times and in developed countries, the military can pose a threat only in alliance with some civilian group. However, should a military become isolated from civilian life and absorbed in its military efficiency, it may become less concerned about the ethics of its use as an instrument of the state. If the state in question is in the hands of anti-democratic forces, the military could then become a totalitarian tool. (Of course, this danger is possible also from an unisolated, politicized military that shares the same values as those in control of a totalitarian state.)

The most serious realistic threats to democracy, then, hinge not on the mode of military recruitment (although the recent system with its deferments was far from satisfactory in this regard), and not on the military's isolation from civilian interests and values, but on the politicization of the officer corps.

Ensuring a Politically Neutral Officer Corps

Prevention of a military threat to the political process should focus on politically neutralizing the officer corps[74] without undermining its legitimate role. Theoretically, there are at least four ways to neutralize the military hierarchy: (1) indoctrinating the officer corps, or, ensuring that its leaders share the perceptions of the controlling political group; (2) instituting formal political controls; (3) weakening the grip of senior personnel on their military juniors; and (4) splintering the officer corps into diverse socio-political groups. Initiating a policy of a large flow of young recruits and junior officers is but one means of accomplishing (3).

Which methods to use depends on the purpose. The communist totalitarian scheme is to neutralize the officer corps politically while ensuring full party control of the military institution. It therefore follows methods (1) and (2). Nazi totalitarianism attempted all four; the main effect was to create doubts in the minds of the generals whether junior officers could be depended on to obey orders to act against the Nazi regime.

In America, grip-weakening and maintaining a socially diverse officer corps are the approved modes. The intent of grip-weakening is to vitiate not legitimate military orders but those directed against the state itself or other blatantly illegal acts, such as those committed at My Lai. It is to create doubts in the minds of senior personnel that orders having an obvious political purpose will be obeyed. The real assumption behind the argument for civilianization through high personnel turnover is that men with low career commitments are less likely to obey blindly. The trouble is that these men are usually not high enough in the order transmission belt to see what is really happening. It is difficult for low-level enlisted personnel to discern at the crucial moment the intent of an order and to organize themselves against the chain of command. Neither are junior officers a bulwark because they can be short-circuited (because of the dual officer-NCO command structure at company level) by career NCOs, whose perceptions are generally similar to those of the career officers. The breakdown in the transmission belt must therefore occur in the command chain between the senior hierarchy and the executing troops. This means that the onus of blocking anti-state acts of senior officers is on career officers in the intermediate ranks. Given the vise-like control seniors have over their subordinates' careers, these imtermediate officers are in a difficult position. Any questioning of the legality of an order, correct or not, may well ruin their subsequent military careers unless institutional protection is provided by a grateful government.

This vise can be weakened in several ways, which as a side benefit should increase military efficacy. Raising mental standards for entry into the officer corps would provide higher-quality officers with, it is hoped, greater moral and economic independence due to higher intelligence, greater political sophistication, and better civilian opportunities. Another way to weaken control would be to make sure that the key communication and decision channels are staffed by the officers with the best educations and highest potentials. Implicit in this suggestion is, of course, the grooming of a true general staff. Most important, the rating system would have to be changed to reduce most officers' complete dependence on the goodwill of their immediate superiors.[75] A rating system balancing performance, which cannot be objectively evaluated, and intelligence, which can, would reduce this dependence. A rating system that gave increasing weight to intelligence at each higher rank would also do much to correct a fundamental weakness of the American military: an overemphasis on personal leadership qualities and deemphasis and even neglect of the cognitive aspects of generalship.

While grip-weakening is designed to eliminate the unthinking transmission and execution of subversive orders, officer diversification is designed to undercut the consensus leading to such orders. The two purposes of a diverse officer corps are to make political coalescence with any civilian faction more difficult and to confront the military with the prospect of fragmentation should it support any political faction.[76] High personnel turnover does not ensure diversity. Selective service does not make for officer diversity, because student and occupational deferments in effect permit many of the better-educated—hence upper-class and more liberal—members of the population to avoid military service. Diversity essentially requires making the military career more rewarding so as to attract and retain the desired college graduates.[77] Diversity is also promoted by recruiting college men through ROTC.[78] A third diversifying technique would be either to reduce the service academies in size or to broaden their curriculum. Broadening the curriculum might include replacing the military faculty (now largely academy graduates) with a rotating civilian faculty. It should be borne in mind, however, that a major reason for sending career officers to graduate school is to provide faculty for the service academies.

Criterion: Decision Making Considerations

An important and interesting criterion concerns alleged biases in the decision making process leading to foreign adventures. It is argued that the military is inherently predisposed to war and that decision makers too readily accede by not bearing their proportionate share of the ensuing burdens. The proposition is that more responsible decision making can be ensured by wide social representation because the rich would be unable to shift the burdens of war onto the poor. The questions to be asked are: What are these biases and are there controlling mechanisms other than manpower recruitment? The latter implies a broader term of reference to preclude second-best solutions from constrained analyses.

Military Influence

Military influence is often assumed to lead to a greater propensity for war, whereas in reality the military generally advocates caution and greater preparedness. In his classic study, Professor Huntington is at pains to point out that while characteristic military attitudes may be Hobbesian and authoritarian, professional military advice is usually "caution, sanity, and realism." While military advocacy of greater preparedness has been interpreted as warlike, it actually indicates a policy of risk minimization. On the other hand, Huntington's claim that "the stronger the military voice, the less likelihood of conflict"[79] is only true for a specific time, and does not allow for the interplay of events over time. In point of fact, by emphasizing objective capabilities (rather than subjective intentions) and neglecting oligopolistic interactions, the actions of the military are often destabilizing. Two other qualifications to the Huntington thesis also exist. Ex-ante, the military may caution against war; ex-post, the attraction of total military victory leads it inexorably into undesirable excesses.[80] Another qualification in Huntington's hypothesis is in its being based on European experience, in which opposing militaries tended to be balanced by coalitions.

Consistent with risk minimization is a large state's aggressive attitude towards, and domination of, small states without strong allies.

Many assert that the American military wields undue influence in American policy making. Many instances can be cited where military advice has been predominant. But the fault lies with civilians for not understanding military affairs and allowing to exist a vacuum for the military to fill. American public policy, as opposed to British, is plagued with civilian decision makers unable to understand or challenge the esoterics of the military profession. The American military has developed repertoires which often have little relevance to the strategy of civilian leadership.[81] The principal problem is that we do not have generalists with sufficient knowledge and prestige to synthesize and resist the pressures from the various input interests.[82] The result is often undue military influence during crises, as happened during World War II, Korea,[83] and even Vietnam, though this was obscured by civilian restrictions on bombing the North and invading the Cambodian sanctuaries.

Some would argue that the spectacle of a political leadership defaulting to its military advisers supports their advocacy of widespread service in order to expose future civilian leaders to military life and mores. However, since many past policy makers were exposed to military life as junior officers without apparent effect, the technique may be inappropriate in some respects: short-term soldiers are insufficiently exposed to the military system as a whole; usually too many years pass between the time of a public leader's military service and his assumption of public office; and military service by itself is not sufficient to convey an understanding of political-military strategy.

While the generalist approach strives to remove the primary reason for undue military influence, another approach is to co-opt the military leadership and to splinter the officer corps in general. Widening the base of the *career* officer corps by greater inclusion of graduates from the best-known universities accomplishes both. If these graduates eventually become the military's senior leadership, military recommendations would at least be somewhat more cognizant of, tolerant of, and adaptive to nonmilitary factors. The purpose of a diverse officer corps is to weaken the cohesion of political alliances within the military and with outside groups.

Wide Participation and Impact on Decision Making

The case for wide participation in the military is based on the notion that wars are not random events but conscious acts of state. Decision makers choose to fight wars according to their perceived benefits and costs. To make correct decisions, therefore, policymakers must perceive all the financial and human costs and be unable to shift them onto the lower classes. While appearing New Leftish, the argument that all should experience the pressures and burdens of government is Aristotleian and the basis of popular sovereignty. The idea is that if decision makers fully feel the "pinch" of their decisions through their families, friends, and associates, no war decision will be lightly made. This is not a "hobbling" argument which attempts to restrain decision makers by impairing military capabilities. Rather, it is an attempt at optimal decision making by removing any divergence between the objective functions of the rulers and the ruled. If military service is randomly distributed, no social class can shift the burden onto another; in fact it can be argued that a positive incentive is created for the rich to help the poor in order to reduce the poor's rejection rate. The case for wide participation in service is that it ensures identity of interests between decision makers and the body politic. Its practical importance in the American context, where class distinctions have generally been muted, is an unanswered question.

The wide-participation argument also has analytic deficiencies. It presumes that personal costs affect decision makers more than budget costs. Often implicit is a belief that Vietnam would not have occurred if selective service had been more universal in scope. But advocates for voluntarism can make an identical argument: voluntarism's higher costs would have made real costs more explicit. To the extent that decision makers are above personal considerations and motivated by national considerations, wide participation would have had little effect. But the no-effect argument cannot be made against voluntarism. Higher budget costs would have had an impact, as evidenced by the Johnson Administration's reluctance to disclose the war's budget costs or to raise taxes for its prosecution. A way out of this dilemma is a lottery for widespread representation while paying the going market wage for similarly aged men to ensure higher budgetary costs more accurately reflecting economic costs.[84]

A second deficiency of the wide-participation argument is its similarity to the rationale of deterrence. Ex-ante, wide participation, it is hoped, deters war decisions; ex-post, wide participation helps unleash emotions which intensify the conflict and complicate diplomatic efforts toward settlement.[85] Third, as an all-encompassing procurement system (in war, quasi-war, and peace), continuous conscription invites muddling or easing into war without a full-scale review of the situation. As the situation gradually worsens, draft calls are too easily increased, whereas a discontinuous system would focus attention on the issues before major decisions were undertaken. Fourth, if the object is to ensure that decision makers feel the personal costs of war, a lottery for both peace and war is less effective than peacetime voluntarism geared with a wartime lottery. This is because peacetime volunteers will be primarily assigned to the overhead portions of the military, whereas most of the disproportionately upperclass wartime draftees will enter the expanding ground combat arms. Fifth, pursuing wider participation for the perceived moralistic purpose of reducing the incidence of foreign adventures by curtailing the individual income-maximizing opportunities of peacetime voluntarism exposes advocates of wide participation to the charge of using the lower classes for their own moralistic purposes. This is contrary to Kant's categorical imperative, that the essence of morality is the treating of individuals as ends rather than means.

A System for Impact

A procurement system that captures the hoped-for advantages of wide participation on the decision making process is the Harvard group's gearshift, or sequential, system.[86] Peacetime voluntarism assures higher and more explicit budget costs; the wartime lottery ensures wide participation in wartime. The two systems in sequence increasingly place the burden on the upper class as the conflict expands. Moreover, sequential shifting is a discontinuous act which focuses public attention on decision makers. Decision makers would know that any action requiring a military expansion would precipitate a public debate. This would have no effect upon nuclear-war decisions, but it would dampen most uses of the general-purposes forces, especially in the internal affairs of others. Its psychological effect is therefore consistent with the Nixon Doctrine. The beauty of shifting is in its one-way reinforcing effect: if anticipation is insufficient to deter a decision for a military expansion, a shift into second gear at least assures wide participation, and nothing has been lost.

A possible weakness of gearshifting is that its anticipatory impact may be too strong. This would retard shifting and place the burden of war on the peacetime establishment recruited from among the less privileged. This would reinforce the allegation that peacetime voluntarism would be an instrument amenable to foreign adventures.[87] However, if an administration were not permitted military expansions except by widespread conscription, a reluctance to shift gears brings a number of offsetting benefits. First, if gearshifting is so potentially embarrassing to the party in power, that party will make its decisions with an eye to the next elections. Since there is no assurance that wars can turn out as anticipated or be prevented from escalating out of control, any administration will be even more deliberative in its foreign-policy decisions because of potentially higher domestic political costs. Thus, in effect, a discontinuous manpower system would act as an institutional damper on the decision making process. A pure lottery, or any other nongear and continuous system, lacks these built-in brakes.

Second, the military leadership would recognize the institutional damper as a potential resource restraint making manpower resources to support foreign adventures more difficult to obtain. In the long run this restraint can be translated into an incentive for the military to seek more efficient resource utilization and, most important, to reappraise existing techniques—a task that few militaries undertake willingly, barring necessity. Of course, the military would dislike the immediate implication of its not being permitted to out-escalate its opponents with massive force.

Third, given that escalation can be a two-sided interactive game which does not benefit either side, limiting a conflict to the regular military and slowing the rate of military expansion may be more desirable than uncontrolled massive responses, as occurred in Vietnam. Massive responses may be appropriate for conventional nation-in-arms conflicts where national survival is threatened, but are questionable in limited wars for limited objectives in which both sides can ante up and where the specter of nuclear war lingers in the background, as in Europe. When these two conditions exist, to slow successive responses seems desirable; but each step should also be large enough to cause the opponent to reconsider.[88]

Fourth, advocates of wide participation assume that socially representative armies bring pressures for peaceful settlements. A brief survey of history shows that they do not. Wide-participation conflicts tend to be ideological wars which are emotionally unrestrained; this leads to unrestrained destruction, which in turn leads to still greater emotionalism and destructiveness. Wide participation is an ex-ante deterrent to warlike intentions; but after a war has begun, the resulting emotions hamper diplomatic negotiations. In limited conflicts mass participation may cause personal costs to be perceived as too great for nonobvious benefits and hence bring political pressures to terminate the conflict. If decision processes for both opponents were symmetrical, both sides would gain. But if pressures are put on only one government, that side is placed at such an obvious disadvantage in the bargaining process that the other side may benefit from intransigence.[89]

Finally, to the extent that massive but relatively poorly trained armies are replaced with more efficient professionals, skill may replace reliance on mass-destruction artillery, mortars, and air weapons that cause so much collateral damage among the civil populace. For example, although the dynastic wars of Europe were all too frequent and often pointless, their sum total of pain and destruction was far less than that of the wars both before and after.

Other factors working against foreign adventures are the publicity of the mass media and casualty rates. Since the press is drawn to any news item, procurement alternatives have little differential impact. Vietnam was extensively reported even when it was primarily a career officers' war in 1961-64. It is difficult to say under which system casualties have greater effect on decisions. While the public may be more concerned about draftee casualties, the military would be more concerned about casualties among hard-to-replace professionals. If the military is as influential in the policy process as is alleged, then it will be less likely to fight with professionals than with a conscriptee force. Likewise, since the military is inherently cautious, if reinforcements and replacement of losses are uncertain or allocated reluctantly, the military will be less disposed towards foreign commitments and adventures.

Criterion: Matters of Conscience, Tradition, and Law

Conscience, tradition, and law are interrelated. Past ethical beliefs have shaped society's traditions and legal structure, just as these affect current ethical stances. The belief that a society has the right to impress its citizens for national defense is a long-accepted principle. Western political thought also presumes respect for the individual. Narrowly defined, collectivism and unfettered individualism are incompatible. The perennial dilemma in military manpower procurement is the balance between communal needs and individual rights. This balance is not immutable. When a society's survival is threatened, communal needs may dominate; in less dangerous periods, respect for liberal values may take precedence. In ambiguous situations, limited war for example, where a society is only indirectly threatened, still another balance may be sought.

Viewed collectively, conscription in itself is neither inequitable nor undemocratic. Universal conscription is the democratic and equitable manpower solution; it was the manpower solution of the egalitarian French revolutionaries and the libertarian American colonials. Nonuniversal conscription is less egalitarian and presents other difficulties, though random conscription approaches the universal solution through mathematical expectation. On the other hand, conscription conflicts with the fundamental American political value of individual liberty; the burden of proof is therefore on coercion to justify itself by a net gain in freedom when everybody's interests are counted. At the same time, voluntarism may be considered ethically undesirable and undemocratic if economic coercion exists or if voluntarism adversely affects the decision making process, even though it maximizes individual freedom of choice.

Changing the procurement system to reflect changes in external threats to the nation is a technique to obtain a more desirable balance between communal and liberal values. During large wars society normally coalesces and moves foward collectively. Hence, the appropriate solution is universalism, which selective service approaches during full mobilization. In peacetime the American preference for pluralistic and decentralized decision centers suggests voluntarism and freedom of choice.

The appropriate solution during quasi-war is ambiguous, though selective service is unambiguously ruled out. Society is often not unified; the nation is not striving for a single collective goal, such as national survival. Coercing some to satisfy a collective goal, while others are allowed to pursue individual objectives, introduces severe problems of equity, especially if there is risk to life. Yet voluntarism may create its own problems of possible social manipulation and narrow class participation. The pragmatic solution to this ethical dilemma is the pairing of the better parts of both systems. Fair pay would remove the sharp edges from individual inequity, while random conscription would spread the burden of achieving the collective goal among all social groups.

Tradition

Tradition provides legitimacy generated by customary practice. In the past, procurement practices were designed to support a small standing army in a situation where time was not critical.[90] Until the emergence of the U.S. as a world power, customary practice—as inherited from the English—was to maintain a small standing army recruited from volunteers supported (and neutralized) by a universal militia that relied on voluntarism to fill its quotas when military duty of extensive length or outside the locality was required.

The poorly designed and administered Civil War draft was of this tradition. Its primary and accomplished purpose was to spur volunteering. The practice of nonuniversal, selective conscription for military service dates back only to 1917; its conception and justification were based on universalism, constrained only by industrial requirements.[91] However, to the extent that it had been popularly accepted—at least before its glaring inconsistencies of the Vietnam period—it was becoming legitimized through customary practice. Both voluntarism and selective service can thus cite custom with some justification.

For peacetime recruitment, the traditional view still favors voluntarism. Peacetime conscription for national service began in 1940, lapsed in 1947, and reemerged in 1948 because of a temporary lack of volunteers. However, the existence of a standby draft assured 100% voluntarism from January 1949 to June 1950. After Korea, military manpower demands increased while the number of men coming of military age declined slightly. Thus peacetime national conscription has only a short history of "customary practice" and exists only because of shortages of volunteers.

Law

The rule of law is a general condition of good government. Without Platonic philosopher-kings and in the absence of military necessity, any action as important as the involuntary diversion of the nation's youth for an extensive period ought to be thoroughly consistent, substantively and adjectively, with legal custom. A youth facing two years' career interruption and the risk of death ought to enjoy the same degree of impersonal rules and procedural safeguards or "due process" as a defendant facing involuntary confinement. We may call one criminal punishment and the other an obligation, but the end result is still involuntary restraint.

Many of the difficulties of Selective Service stem from what might be termed its philosopher-king "rule of wisdom" approach. General Hershey has advocated that:

So long as we recognize the *wisdom* of allocating our manpower resources to support to the greatest possible degree both our Armed Forces and our national economy, we should also recognize the *wisdom* of approaching this allocation problem with the *best judgments* we can muster, rather than by chance.[92] (Emphasis added.)

Unfortunately, Hershey's selection instrument is "little groups of neighbors on whom is placed the responsibility to determine who is to serve the nation in the Armed Forces . . . and in industry, agriculture, and other deferred classifications."[93] Hershey's position is theoretically deficient. First, even in the best of circumstances, "little groups of neighbors" are hardly paragons of wisdom. Consequently, their rulings, however well intentioned, are no substitute for impersonal rulings without potential capriciousness.[94] The very "adaptability of the system to each individual registrant,"[95] another of the Selective Service System's alleged strengths, involves a danger. The rule of law is designed, among other things, to obviate the need for such personal adaptability. By its emphasis on "wisdom" and "best judgment," Selective Service has inadvertently fallen into the Platonic trap of implying that the rule of law is inferior to the rule of wisdom. Yet without the paliatives of wisdom and knowledgeable neighbors, the System's obviously discriminatory practices in the name of national defense would be politically unacceptable.

Administration by local boards composed of civilian neighbors, mentioned briefly, above, is an anachronism drawn from a post-Civil-War analysis of the public's violent reaction to the draft.[96] The two major lessons of the Civil War draft were that: (1) the American people still distrusted central authority, and (2) when conscription is employed, any appearance of injustice to some classes in society must be studiously avoided.[97] These lessons have little to do with adaptability to the individual and administrative discretion, which came into vogue because of industrial demands during both World Wars. Classification criteria in the Civil War were simple and objective.[98] The Selective Service System itself has noted that the Civil War lotteries conducted by *local* federal enrollment boards were susceptible to some manipulation and tampering, and the large number of boards served to multiply the possibility of such incidents.[99] Therefore, the only logical rationalization for local autonomy was to allay political fears of federal encroachment—a rationalization now largely outdated.

A potential theoretical justification for Selective Service procedures is the Lockian doctrine of Prerogative, which is relevant because the American constitutional tradition is a Lockian derivative. In general, Locke was harshly critical of ruling systems without well-defined laws. His general position was the rule of law:

The ruling power ought to govern by declared and received laws, and not by extemporary dictates and undetermined resolutions. . ." and "they [the ruling power] are to govern by promulgated established laws, not to be varied in particular cases, but to have one rule for rich and poor, for the favourite at Court, and the countryman at plough."[100]

But Locke recognized two exceptions: Prerogative and "preservation of the rest." While Locke could justify absolute power in the name of preservation, this discretionary power expressly did not include power over "any part of the subject's property." This exclusion includes unfair wages, for one's labor is one's source of income, hence one's property. His doctrine of Prerogative stated:

This power to act according to discretion for the public good, without the prescription of the law and sometimes even against it, is that which is called prerogative; for since in some governments the law-making power is not always in being and is usually too numerous, and so too slow for the dispatch requisite to execution, and because, also, it is impossible to foresee and so by laws to provide for all accidents and necessities that may concern the public, or make such laws as will do no harm if they are executed with an inflexible rigour on all occasions, and upon all persons that may come in their way, therefore there is a latitude left to the executive power to do many things of choice which the laws do not prescribe.[101]

This paragraph aptly summarizes Selective Service's justifications for its procedures; it also contains the reasons why the System has fallen from public favor. The means to the elusive goal of "the public good" are not invariant, for the goal itself changes with the threat to social survival. Wartime goals are not peacetime goals; hence, the means for one are unlikely to be appropriate for the other.

Prerogative is also a two-edged sword. Just as Prerogative can justify selective service, it can also destroy its legitimacy. The other edge is in Locke's statement that

This power, whilst employed for the benefit of the community, and suitably to the trust and ends of the government, is undoubted prerogative, and never is questioned. For the people . . . are far from examining prerogative whilst it is in any tolerable degree employed for the use it was meant—that is, the good of the people . . . . But if there comes to be a question between the executive power and the people about a thing claimed as prerogative, the tendency of the exercise of such prerogative, to the good or hurt of the people, will easily decide that question.[102]

This is especially critical for the SSS, since it has long justified itself by claiming widespread public support. Yet since the early 1960s its public support has been eroded first by its discriminatingly liberal deferment policies and later by its insensitivity to dissent and its nonuniform selection procedures, during the Vietnam period.

The major legal deficiency of the existing system is its lack of procedural safeguards. Such safeguards would be unnecessary if the System or local boards lacked the discretionary power to classify. But when classification standards are subjective and a board can arbitrarily reclassify, the draft is a potential substitute for criminal punishment and an instrument for stifling constitutional rights. In several well-publicized cases, boards have attempted to use their classifying authority to penalize dissenters. Procedural safeguards could remove this objection by offering the reclassified individual as much protection as criminals receive in court proceedings. The cost would be an intolerable slowdown of the processing machinery; this is a major reason why SS regulations prohibit legal representation before local and appeal boards.[103] Another cost, due to conscription's zero sum nature (one's gain is another's loss), is reduced social equity. The wealthier classes are both better informed and able to afford counsel; the inevitable result would be still further shifting of the burden onto the poor.

Thus, to institute formalized procedural safeguards in a selective system would require a high tradeoff in equity and the operational efficiency of the draft. These criteria can only be satisfied simultaneously by a high order of benevolence and fair play. In wartime, society may well place its trust in benevolence and decide that the abandonment of discretionary authority without adequate safeguards is worth the benefits gained. In peacetime, the value of this fiducial relationship is less clear; not only are the benefits less, but patriotic altruism is difficult to maintain.

The beauty of the lottery and voluntarism is their relief from these philosophical and legal entanglements. An age-cohort lottery is essentially a per se arrangement. The simplicity of its ex ante equality removes the necessity for decisions of "wisdom." The removal of discretionary power eliminates the relevance of procedural safeguards. A fortiori, a volunteer system is not concerned with legal questions of involuntarism. Rather, its legal problems are in the field of labor contracts; the main issue is whether contract-breaking ought to be a criminal matter, as currently, or a civil proceeding, as in the civilian economy. Traditionally, military necessity has urged the first approach. However, a more discriminating society might decide to distinguish among the differing contexts of peace, war, and the imminent threat of war.

Criterion: Technical Workability of Alternative Systems

Workability can be defined as administrative feasibility. A system which does not satisfy this criterion can be eliminated from further consideration. Of the frequently discussed procurement alternatives, only compulsory National Service fails this test.

National Service

National Service falters on two critical points: administration; and equalized burden, which means differential time periods according to assignment. To take the second point first, UMT implies 6 to 12 months' service, while National Service implies a minimum of 18 months for military service and 36 months for less onerous service. Assuming an average service of 2 years, 2 million men per year would flow in and out of a National Service force of approximately 4 million men. If women were included, as some advocate, the figure would double. Sheer numbers would make the scheme impractical.

The second point is the problem of assignment to diverse tasks. How are assignments to be administered? By a centralized authority? Decentralization to many needy social agencies raises difficult practical questions regarding agency qualifications, individual and agency assignment criteria, and supervisory capacity. Finally, efficient resource allocation would be impossible. If money costs to agencies were below social costs, the system would induce waste. Even worse, the consequent subsidizing of needy but inefficient industries such as medicine and education would act against institutional reform. In short, while Universal National Service has many desirable communal features in an otherwise materialistic and affluent society, its mechanics are foreboding.[104]

Universal Military Training

While it also takes in large numbers of people, UMT is operationally simple because its service period is short and the same for all. UMT is costly in its low military and debatable social benefits; but its administration is straightforward. Experience exists for handling large numbers in relatively homogeneous military programs. Its problems are familiar and consequently can be foreseen and programmed.

Selective Service

Of the three major alternatives, selective service has been a very simple and effective mechanism for satisfying the requirements of full mobilization: meeting the military's demands and protecting the industrial base and the welfare of local communities. The weak link in the system's administrative procedures is its reliance on implicit public support of its classifying and induction decisions. Without this support, the system can be readily swamped, since appeals and the threat of appeal make each decision considerably more lengthy.

Administrative procedures affecting SS's public standing have been geographic quotas, enlistment credits, and stratification of I-As. Draft calls—as inherited from the colonial period—are based on quotas handed down to the states and localities. Selective Service began in 1917 by allocating its quotas on the basis of each local board's total population. Because of significant population differences in age and numbers of exempted immigrants, quotas were soon changed and based on the numbers of available I-As and I-A-Os (conscientious objectors) after classification. This gave the appearance of geographic equity for those available for service. The result has been wide percentage differences in military service among communities and states. Wealthy communities with widespread student and occupational deferments have relatively few I-As, hence low quotas. At the other extreme, poor states, e.g., South Carolina and Mississippi, with mental disqualification rates of 50-60%,[105] also have few I-As and low quotas in relation to either total young men or population. Consequently, the midwestern prairie states, which have relatively low college attendance rates and the lowest mental disqualification rates (5-10%), are disproportionately burdened.

Another problem with the I-A quota is that the more diligent boards who are prompter in their classification of new registrants increase their locality's absolute quota. The system of I-A quotas, *minus* enlistment credits, also affects individuals through proration. Since each locality's quota is reduced by its enlistments,[106] credits benefit poor areas with higher volunteer rates by reducing the draft's incidence upon the remainder. A locality's incidence of military service is thus determined by the size of its I-A pool; its draft rate, by its I-A pool and its enlistment credits.

While the above are somewhat subtle consequences, stratification has produced serious anomalies that have shaken the public's faith in the System. While quotas are based on classified I-As, the induction sequence has depended on a hierarchy of subcategories within I-A.[107] This complexity has led to false accusations of arbitrary and nonuniform procedures. In fact, though two different draft boards may consistently adhere to uniform procedures, one may do no inducting because of enlistment credits, while the second may induct married men over 26 or even 18-year-olds. These quirks are caused by "accounting boundaries" inherent in any stratified system—the greater the stratification, the greater its occurrences.

Lottery

A lottery among members of a single age cohort, such as a lottery at 19, can be administratively simple. All men are registered, and those whose numbers are selected are drafted. The complications of a lottery are caused by deferments and the practices of subjecting multiple age cohorts to the same lottery, and dividing the national pool into local pools. During both world wars, a lottery—though workable—proved cumbersome and less equitable than a more systematic "oldest first" selection process. This has been General Hershey's administrative complaint against the lottery.[108] Thus, while the Marshall Commission, DoD, and Senator Edward Kennedy advocated an annual universal lottery, General

Hershey visualized Selective Service's unpleasant experiences during full mobilization when older classes would participate and industrial and hardship exemptions would be necessary. A lottery in such periods, gives at best only an illusion of fairness while increasing administrative workloads.

At its extreme, a lottery prejudiced by widespread deferments and state quotas remains selective service in all but name. A lottery by itself only eliminates internal stratification of I-As. Local quotas allow disparities in deferments and disqualification rates to shift the burden of military service from one region to another. Within a board's quota, enlistment credits make it possible for boards to call widely separated lottery numbers.

Three other features of a lottery system are noteworthy. First, a lottery does not rule out early selection and individual choice of induction date. As long as this choice does not interfere with wartime calls, the additional administrative details can be resolved. Second, age-19 lotteries are a misnomer. All the popularly advocated lotteries have a mean induction age of 20 and an age range from the 19th to 21st birthdays. If induction does not begin until all members are 19, then the oldest members will be 20 by the first induction date and 21 by the last induction date. An equal-percentage biennial lottery would reduce the mean age to 19 1/2 with a range from 19 to 20.

The third administrative question is the timing of mental and physical examinations. To examine an entire cohort is expensive. The advantages are statistical data unbiased by self-selection, referrals for corrective action by public health and social agencies, and *increased political focus and dramatization*. This last provides an incentive for the richer states to aid the poorer in order to increase the poorer states' qualification rates and hence their share of the draft burden. The advantages of examination after lottery selection are lower cost and *increased pressure on the military to accept those selected*. By shifting the onus of nonacceptance onto the military, greater political pressure is put on the military to widen its narrow "firm" acceptance criteria to more inclusive social criteria. If the military were unsatisfied with the quality of random selectees, it could set up special training programs, just as private industry does during full employment when it can no longer skim the labor market. Thus a lottery with ex-post examinations could induce the military to lower its acceptance standards and to upgrade selectees, rather than cast aside the disqualified and demand better replacements.

Voluntarism

The recruiting apparatus for voluntarism already exists. The inducement distinction between a draft system designed to spur voluntarism and market voluntarism is wages. If wages are to be the primary adjusting variable, the important questions are: (1) the frequency of change and (2) wage form. If wages can be changed only annually, recruitment could be plagued by shifting nonwage variables affecting volunteer supply, such as unemployment rates. Major shifts would create either a queue, which could induce undesirable recruiting practices, or large recruiting deficits. Small temporary deficits would not be serious, since their percentage effect on the total stock of military manpower would be miniscule; such deficits, however, would upset training programs and therefore reduce training efficiency.[109] Periodic wage adjustments would ensure better use of training facilities as well as an early correction of longer-run trends. Frequent settings and hence smaller adjustments would also reduce speculative enlistment timing among prospective volunteers. The argument against frequent wage changes is their disturbing effect on the compensation structure. The solution would be to unhook part of entry wages from the overall compensation structure. This would permit upward and downward wage adjustments to entrants without affecting other personnel. The obvious technique is the enlistment bonus. Bonuses are also cost-effective (through time preference) and can be discriminating among (and within) the services to offset the special recruiting handicaps of the Army in general and its combat arms in particular. This is particularly important because otherwise the Army's recruiting deficit drives the cost of voluntarism for all of DoD.

Sequential System

Combining several systems in sequence may appear administratively complicated. However, the recruiting mechanism for peacetime voluntarism already exists for draft-induced volunteers. For the two wartime contexts of limited war and full mobilization, a registration and classifying apparatus is also already operating. If random selection during limited war were part of this sequence, a lottery could be held annually, though no individual would be called unless war occurred. Alternatively, lotteries could be prepared but not drawn. Nor would a sequential system preclude preinduction examinations, if only to maintain the visibility of the obligation of citizenship. Thus, a sequential system would not be administratively infeasible or more complicated than present procedures. Its main effect would be to relegate Selective Service to a standby peacetime status while its staff planned and prepared to implement either random or selective conscription according to developing circumstances. Maintaining a standby draft system is necessary in an uncertain world to reduce the lead time for reinstituting the draft in an emergency.

Summary

This chapter has been concerned with the details of each criterion and how each relates to the alternatives. The problem is now to place this detail in perspective. The reader will find a review of Chapter 1 useful at this point.

No scientific method exists for reducing the detail so that the alternatives can be readily compared. One simplifying method is to emphasize the more important criteria. If the choice made on this basis is then compatible with the secondary criteria, a satisfactory, if not optimal, solution has been found.

The five most important criteria are manpower demands, industrial production, budget cost, ex-ante equity, and ex-post equity. In emphasizing these five, one quickly notices that no single system is satisfactory. A volunteer system is incompatible with manpower demands, industrial protection, and budget cost during a major war. Only selective service satisfies industrial protection in such a context. But in peacetime, selective service is incompatible with the two equity criteria, while voluntarism ranks high without being overcostly. A peacetime lottery founders on ex-post equity. The conclusion can thus be reached that selective service during full mobilization and voluntarism in peacetime are preferred choices.

The proper choice during limited wars such as Vietnam is more difficult. Selective service is unsatisfactory on equity grounds. Even if voluntarism were able to meet manpower demands within satisfactory budgetary limits, it does not satisfy ex-ante equity because of an ethical presumption that the burdens of war should not be shifted onto the poor through the mechanism of an underlying income distribution. The lottery, on the other hand, satisfies all the criteria, though weak in ex-post equity. The major policy conclusion can thus be derived that a sequential system should be adopted so that the strengths of each procurement alternative can be obtained without its more serious limitations.

Another more complex procedure is to rank each alternative by the criteria and then to combine the rankings for an overall rating as in Appendix 2-D. This procedure is instructive and forces a better understanding of the issues. The procedure's limitation is in its reliance on subjective judgment in determining the relative importance of the criteria.

Appendix 2-A

Risk to Life and Service Structure

Most arguments based on the burdens of military service implicitly emphasize risk of death. A military career is presumed dangerous. This, while plausible, is not true because of the military's structure and the distinct nonrandomness of casualty and death rates among and within the services.

Death and casualty rates are concentrated in one narrow segment of the military: the wartime rifleman. The structural characteristics of the U.S. military are such that few peacetime professionals fall into this category in wartime unless hostilities begin *before* a peacetime military has time to expand. Up until Vietnam, only 13.4% of the U.S. military was in the combat branches (infantry, armor, and artillery).[110] When a military expansion occurs, few peacetime riflemen remain riflemen due to the rapid promotion and cadre requirements of an expanding branch. Table 2-1 shows Army and Army Air Corps relative casualties in World War II. Not only were they concentrated in the infantry and armored branches, but only men in infantry and armored *platoons* (and medical aid men) suffered casualties exceeding the Army mean.[111] All the high-casualty positions except squad leader, platoon sergeant, and section leader are positions

Table 2-1

Wounded per Thousand Strength Overseas per Year By Arm or Service, December 1941 Through March 1946 and Summary Index

Arm or Service	Officers	Officer Summary Index	Enlisted Men	EM Summary Index
All Arms and Services	56.4	100	71.8	100
Infantry	251.0	445	264.9	369
Armored	a		228.5	318
Cavalry	165.1	293	163.1	227
Field Artillery	88.1	156	50.7	71
Air Corps	35.9	64	9.9	14
Chemical Warfare	31.0	55	29.6	41
Medical Department	9.2	16	26.7	37
Engineers	28.0	50	21.8	30
Coast Artillery	10.6	19	9.7	14
Other	4.8	9	3.8	5

Source: G.W. Beebe and M.E. DeBakey, *Battle Casualties,* Charles C. Thomas, Springfield, Ill., 1952, p. 38.
aDuring World War II officers assigned to armored units were carried under such arms as Infantry and Cavalry, and the designation "Armored" was used only for enlisted personnel.

filled by relative newcomers to the military service in general and the infantry in particular. Professionals largely escape the risk of death, which generally falls on those volunteering or conscripted for the wartime infantry.

Peacetime risk of life is now probably lower in the military than civilian life. In contrast to earlier wars, when disease was the major claimant, Table 2-2 shows that the nonbattle rate (other deaths) is now almost the same as the civilian rate for comparable ages. Since a peacetime statistic is not available, "other deaths" in wartime is an effective proxy and serves as a high peacetime estimate, since the military is more accident-prone in wartime than in peacetime. It must be observed, of course, that the military is a medically select group, due to initial medical acceptance standards. Table 2-2 also indicates that battle-death rates have decreased with each succeeding conflict. This is probably due to better care of the wounded and the increasingly small ratios of combat-to-service troops in the technically advanced militaries. Part of the decrease may also be attributed to the lessened intensity of each battle, though this is offset by longer periods of contact between opponents.

The mechanics of assignment are also important for a person entering the military during war. The service and occupational specialty (i.e., branch) are major determinants of the subsequent risk of death, which also correlates with rank and location. Tables 2-3 and 2-4 show that the Navy and the Air Force are low-casualty services, particularly in limited war. During both the Korean and Vietnam periods, these services suffered only 5% of the battle deaths, although they formed roughly half of the total armed forces. Put another way, a man entering the Army/Marines during Korea and Vietnam, respectively, had an a priori probability of dying 14.7 and 18.6 times greater than another entering the Navy/Air Force. In 1967 a man entering the Marines ran a risk 63 times greater than one entering the Air Force; and if the breakdowns for Marine riflemen and

Table 2-2
Military Death Rates (per 1,000 Population)

	Civil War (Union only)	Spanish American	WWI	WWII	Korean Conflict	Vietnam[a]
Total Deaths	104.4	36.6	35.5	11.6	5.5	
Battle Deaths	40.1	[b]	17.1	8.6	3.4	2.1
Other Deaths	64.3	[b]	18.4	3.0	2.1	
Comparable male civilian, age 24	[b]	7.1	15.6[c]	2.9	2.0	2.0

Sources: *Historical Statistics,* Series Y715-762 and B143-154
        1968 Statistical Abstract, #67, p. 54, and #371, p. 256.

[a]1967 and 1st quarter 1968 only.

[b]Not available.

[c]This figure is triple the 1915 rate of 5.2 because of the worldwide influenza epidemic which began in the closing years of World War I.

Table 2-3
Relative Casualties in Korea

	Deaths	Worldwide Strength	Summary Index[a]
Marines	12.7	7.4	1.7
Army	82.4	49.5	1.7
Navy	1.4	20.6	.07
Air Force	3.6	22.5	.16
Total	100	100	1

Source: *1968 Statistical Abstract*, #371, p. 256.
[a]Deaths/worldwide strength.

Table 2-4
Relative Casualties in Vietnam[a]

	Deaths	Southeast Asia Strength	Worldwide Strength	Summary[b] Index
Marines	36.8	13.8	8.4	4.4
Army	58.0	59.3	41.6	1.4
Navy	3.3	12.2	22.7	.15
Air Force	1.8	14.6	27.3	.07
Total	100	100	100	1

Sources: *Fact Sheet, Negro Participation in the Armed Forces in Southeast Asia,* OASD (M & RA), 28 March 1968. *Selected Manpower Statistics,* OSD, 15 April 1968, p. 21.
[a]Based on 1967 data.
[b]Deaths/worldwide strength.

flight crews were available, the discrepancy would be multiplied by several fold for these groupings.

Therefore, an individual volunteering for a professional career in peacetime does not unduly increase his chances of dying, since (1) the peacetime incidence is no higher than the civilian average; (2) 87% are able to volunteer for the noncombat arms; and (3) his risk is mainly in being assigned a combat leadership position in wartime. Whether an individual opting for a military career is exposing himself to death more than other members of his age cohort thus depends on (1) the overall incidence of service for an age cohort, (2) the probability of war during a cohort's draft exposure period, (3) enlistment timing, and (4) the military's structure. If the overall incidence of service is low or if no war occurs during the period of a cohort's liability to military service, a military career is necessarily more risky than a civilian's due to the probability of war *later*, even if the careerist is occupying a relatively safe position. However, if war occurs and the incidence of service is not low, a careerist volunteering at age 19 has a *lower* risk of death during his military career than his twin brother who is drafted during a period of war.

In short, the risk-to-life argument collapses when analysed. Only a small percentage of the peacetime military is in high-risk occupations, which are the military's most expansionary components. Consequently, rapid promotions and cadre requirements dilute the danger to peacetime professionals. The highly technical Navy and Air Force personnel bear virtually no adverse wartime risk, excepting officer pilots and flight crews. In limited wars, the bulk of the Navy and Air Force are not in the combat theater; those who are tend to be in rear echelons. And in nuclear war, in the absence of mutual counterforce strategies aimed at nuclear strength rather than cities, the military's risk to life is no greater than that of people in large cities. Therefore, the argument against peacetime voluntarism because of undue danger and wartime risk to life does not bear critical examination, except in those cases where the conflict is not large enough to warrant a military expansion, and possibly during the initial stage of a military expansion.

Appendix II-B

The Black Proportion of a Volunteer Force

A practical question of some importance is the black proportion of a volunteer force. Those who argue that a black force would emerge base their case on blacks having a higher elasticity—and therefore a higher enlistment response to wage increases—than whites. Neglected are the facts that (1) black elasticities *decrease* more rapidly than white elasticities as wages increase; (2) there is a limited number of blacks qualified for military service because blacks make up a small part of the population and have a lower qualification rate for military service than whites; and (3) the proportion of blacks can be controlled in any case by adjusting acceptance standards because of the large divergence between the qualified white and black population distributions.

The percentage of blacks entering the military (and reenlisting) can be controlled by adjusting acceptance standards or, more overtly, by quotas. Both have precedents. During the Korean War and earlier, units were often limited to specified percentages of blacks. Since Korea, acceptance standards have been raised and lowered according to demand and supply. The long-term trend has been a steady tightening, until late 1965. The inadvertent effect of these acceptance standards can be seen in Table 2-5. Particularly interesting is that since the abrupt rise in acceptance standards in 1957-58, the percentage of blacks entering the military has been as much as 40% *below* their population share of approximately 12%.

Table 2-5 also shows that blacks are drafted more than their population share, and that their enlistment share in the volunteer Navy, Marine Corps, and Air Force is considerably lower than their population share. This is best explained by Figures 2-4 and 2-5. Figure 2-4 is a bar graph showing the distribution of blacks and whites in the five AFQT groupings. Figure 2-5 sets these distributions in the perspective of population shares. The dashed verticle line at the 31st percentile represents the Army's pre-Vietnam minimum for its enlistees. The other services had slightly lower minimums than the Army, which also had to accept a few draftees scoring as low as the tenth percentile.[112] The dashed verticle line visually indicates three significant points: (1) the ease of controlling black proportions by adjusting acceptance standards; (2) why the black enlistee share has been below its population share; and (3) why black draftee proportions are much higher than their population share.[113]

Calculations based on Figures 2-4 and 2-5 show a basic reason why a black military is unlikely. White youths are 88% of the total, outnumbering black youths by more than 7 to 1. But the number of *qualified* whites to blacks greatly exceeds this ratio. For instance, if the Army's pre-Vietnam enlistment standard is used, qualified whites outnumber qualified blacks 18.3 to 1.[114]

Table 2-5
Non-Whites as Percent of Inductions and Initial Enlistments, FY 1953-1968[a]

Fiscal Year	Total Accessions (000)	Percent Nonwhite[b]		Army				
		DoD	Total	Inductees	Enlistees	Navy	Marine Corps	Air Force
1953	886.1	12.8%	14.5%	14.7%	13.4%	4.3%	8.0%	11.1%
1954	576.3	10.0	10.7	9.9	13.0	4.0	7.8	11.9
1955	622.6	10.6	10.2	8.8	12.7	9.0	5.4	13.5
1956	481.9	11.2	12.2	10.3	15.1	9.5	10.6	12.2
1957	456.7	9.1	10.4	10.8	9.3	3.6	9.5	9.7
1958	376.1	7.9	10.7	13.2	6.4	2.8	5.1	7.1
1959	392.0	7.1	9.3	10.4	8.1	2.4	5.0	6.5
1960	389.4	8.1	10.3	12.3	8.4	3.0	7.9	8.4
1961	394.7	8.2	10.4	14.4	8.2	2.9	5.9	9.5
1962	518.6	9.7	12.6	15.3	9.0	4.1	6.5	8.6
1963	370.4	10.6	14.2	18.5	11.2	4.3	5.5	10.5
1964	471.3	10.4	13.4	14.2	12.2	4.9	8.5	10.4
1965	401.4	12.2	15.2	16.3	14.1	5.8	8.4	13.1
1966	877.8	9.9	12.4	13.0	11.2	3.4	9.4[c]	8.0
1967	751.5	10.6	12.4	13.2	11.2	4.0	9.9	8.2
1968	831.1	12.4	14.2	15.3	11.9	5.3	13.1	10.3

[a]Includes inductions and male non-prior-service enlistments into regular components.
[b]Refers to "non-Caucasian."
[c]Inductees: 12.5%; enlistees: 8.6%.
Source: DD-M(M) 663

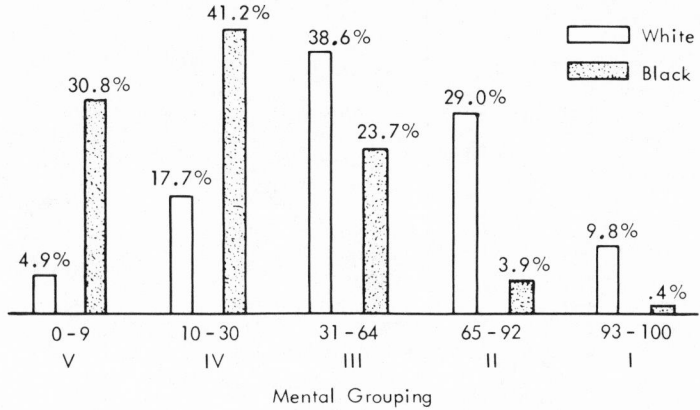

Figure 2–4. Percent of Population Scoring in Each AFQT Grouping. Source: Bernard D. Karpinos, "Expected Distribution of Male Youths, Age: 19–21, by Qualification (Mental Group) on the Armed Forces Qualification Test (AFQT) According to their Educational Attainment, by Geographic Division and Race, 1960" *The Mental Qualification of American Youths for Military Service and Its Relationship to Educational Achievement*, Proceedings of the American Statistical Association, 1966.

Since acceptance standards are unlikely to be as high as the 31st percentile in a volunteer force but would be no lower than the tenth percentile, the ratio of qualified whites to blacks will therefore be between 9 and 18 to 1.

Other calculations showing the low probability of a black military at pre-Vietnam force levels can be based on simple arithmetic. A volunteer military requires approximately 310,000 accessions/year. But during 1970-1975, only 245,000 non-white males will come of military age each year. Of these, only 65,000 will be physically and mentally qualified, assuming the Army's 31st percentile standard. Thus, assuming all enlist, only 21% of the volunteer requirement will be met. Alternatively, if the military were forced to lower its acceptance standards to the legal minimum of the 10th percentile, it would require the enlistment and retention for a twenty-year military career of *every* physically and mentally qualified black to obtain an 87% black military.[115] This figure would, of course, increase with a force smaller than 2.65 million men and with time, due to population growth.

This arithmetic shows the physical limitation of a black military.[116] Economic logic can demonstrate the more likely percentages. The three statistics needed for the economic calculation are (1) black proportions volunteering in the absence of a draft at current military/civilian pay relatives, (2) relative elasticities of the black and white supply curves, and (3) relative reenlistment

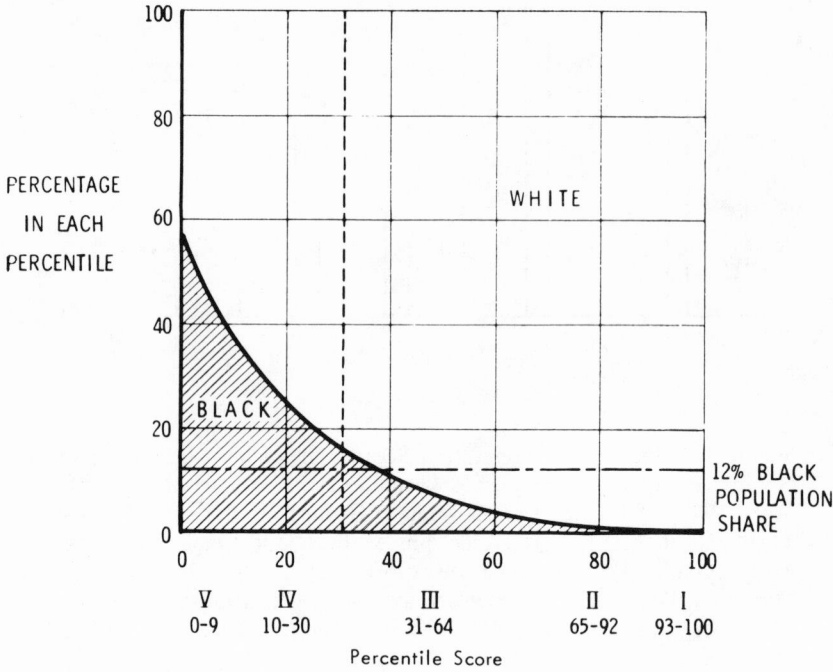

Figure 2-5. Population Distribution by AFQT Percentile Scores.

propensities. Of these, the supply elasticities are the *least* important. Yet this has been the key statistic for those arguing that voluntarism will produce a black military.

The important statistic is the number and relative proportions of those enlisting in the absence of the draft. This number is approximately 250,000/ year. Of these, approximately 225,000 (90%) will be white and 25,000 (10%) will be black, as indicated in Table 2-5. Since a volunteer force requires approximately 310,000 accessions, the recruiting deficit is only 60,000. If we assume that the elasticity of supply is twice as high for blacks as for whites, 47,000 of this deficit will be white and 13,000 will be black.[117] Adding, accessions total 272,000 white and 38,000, or 12.25%, black. A 2.65-million-man ("effective") volunteer force consists of approximately 2.2 million enlistment men. Approximately half are first-termers and half careerists. This gives us a first-term force of 965,000 whites and 135,000 blacks. Now, assuming that the black propensity to reenlist remains twice that of whites,[118] we find a career force of 860,000 whites and 240,000 blacks (21.8%). Summing for the first-term and career segments, we have 1,825,000 whites and 375,000 blacks, or a 17% black enlisted force (versus the present 9-10%).

A sensitivity analysis showing higher relative black elasticities and reenlistment rates does not dramatically change this percentage. The most likely
percentage of blacks in a volunteer military is between 15 and 20.[119] This is
because the key statistic is the 10 percent accession ratio; this figure will not
increase much unless acceptance standards are set considerably below the
pre-Vietnam minimum. Elasticity ratios are intellectually intriguing but relatively unimportant. The black curve is undoubtedly more elastic. On the other hand,
the equation forms of the military supply curves are such that black elasticities
decrease more rapidly than white elasticities as wages increase to attract more
recruits. This is because proportionately more *qualified* blacks volunteer than
whites and blacks are therefore already further out along their supply curve. For
instance, in 1965, Army statistics (Table 2-6) show that medically qualified
Category I-III blacks were 68% more enlistment-prone (and 67% more draft-
susceptible) than comparable whites.

A possible rebuttal of many of these calculations is that increasing educational opportunities will greatly lower black rejection rates. If so, the black-mili-
tary argument partially collapses because the military will become less attractive
to blacks. Two related things to bear in mind are that (1) as blacks improve their
levels, poorer whites will be improving theirs, and (2) percentile qualification
scores are relative. These scores do not change at the same rate as absolute

Table 2-6
**Army Accession Rates of Those Physically Qualified by Mental Category as a
Fraction of the 1965 National Draft Rate (k$'$) and Enlistment Rate (k) of the
Total Population**

	Draftees		Enlistees	
Mental Category	White	Black	White	Black
Group I	.66k$'$	1.49k$'$	.86k	.99k
Group II	1.17k$'$	2.15k$'$	1.64k	2.22k
Group III	1.35k$'$	2.05k$'$	1.68k	2.76k
Groups IV & V	Restricted entry		Restricted entry	

Source: Derived from AFQT categories of Army draftees and enlistees by race 1965,
OASD (M&RA).

$$FAR = \frac{(MG_a) (A_i) (D)}{(MG_p) (1-R_i) (P_i) (P)} \text{, where}$$

FAR = fractional accession rate,

MG_a = mental group percentage specified in Table 2-5,

A_i = percent of Army draftees (enlistees) by race,

k' = $\dfrac{D}{P}$ = draftees (enlistees) divided by population,

MG_p = mental group percentage by race, specified in Table 2-5,

R_i = medical rejectee rate, by race,

P_i = percent of population by race.

increases in educational attainment. (For blacks, from 5.4 median school years in 1940 for ages 25-29 to 11.0 in 1960 for ages 21-25; for whites, 8.7 to 12.3 years.)[120] In fact, the black population in uniform could decrease if the military insists that its technical qualitative requirements are growing even faster than qualitative improvements in the manpower pool. For instance, between 1950 and 1965, when absolute educational attainment was increasing, the military was able to increase preinduction rejection rates for whites from 29.4% to 41% and for blacks from 56.3% to 72.4%.

The position that a volunteer military would be largely black is thus not empirically defensible; in fact, the allegation does positive harm by masking two *valid* arguments. First, a justifiable complaint is that too few blacks are currently admitted to the services. Rather than the 8.2 to 9.5% of the 1962-65 force, a larger percentage would be appropriate, considering their limited socio-economic alternatives. While an exact optimum percentage is subject to debate, 20 to 30% distributed through all services would pose no particular problem and would offer an additional 300,000-500,000 respectable jobs to blacks. If black accessions in 1960-64 had been double their actual number, an additional 20% of the black youth population would have been absorbed into the military. Assuming that many of these would have been blacks likely to have been unemployed, this absorption would have significantly reduced the 24% unemployment rate among 18-19 year old blacks. Seen in these terms, the military's acceptance standards are not only discriminatory, but their benefits of easing the military's training and disciplinary problems are bought at the high social cost of high black youth unemployment.

A second complaint involves the allocation of blacks within each service. Again, due to low mental "achievement," the military frequently assigns blacks to less skilled occupational areas. In 1965 only about 2.4% of black enlistees received the military's highly valued technical training, as opposed to their 10.7% accession shares.[121] Other than post-service economic opportunities, the resulting concentration of blacks in the Army's paratroop and infantry units is objectionable because it can lend weight to the popular argument that blacks bear disproportionate burdens.[122]

Appendix 2-C

Reserve Procurement Alternatives

In appraising reserve alternatives, the same criteria as for the active forces can be used. Several major conclusions follow from this analysis. First, the feared impact on the reserves of eliminating draft pressure is uncalled for and can be viewed as an opportunity to modernize the reserve structure and to remove the inequities and deficiencies associated with the current system of reserve procurement. Second, the budgetary cost of a volunteer reserve range from 175 to 330 million dollars for the current structure and considerably less for an updated structure of considerably fewer but more ready reserves. Third, procurement systems for the reserves and active forces need not be identical and can be designed so that voluntarism's individualistic and conscription's collective values are complementary.

Costs

No rigorous quantitative cost estimate of an all-volunteer reserve, or one operating with reduced draft pressure, is possible at this time. Alleged high cost of a volunteer reserve is based on DoD's earlier $8-17 billion incremental budgetary cost estimate for an all-volunteer military and the high rate of draft inducement among Reserve volunteers.[123] However, a number of qualitative and quantitative factors suggest this cost would not be large: (1) Reserve expenditures for personnel (salaries and benefits) were only $766 million in FY 1968; (2) the incremental budget cost for a pre-Vietnam sized active force is really on the order of $2.1 billion at 1970 wage relatives; (3) a volunteer active force requires considerably fewer accessions, thus increasing the manpower pool available for the reserves; and (4) the high percentage of draft inducement into the reserves is misleading because of the reserve recruitment policy of taking only the best qualified among a queue of potential volunteers.

Two quantitative methods are available to indicate the order of magnitude of the incremental budgetary costs for true voluntarism in the present force.[124] The first method sets an upper limit by assuming that first-term reservists receive the same absolute increases as active-duty first-termers in an all-volunteer military. This procedure yields additional costs of $332 million. Another estimate can be derived from the wage comparability standard with civilian wages. Compensation has to be increased only for the reserve group with less than four years' service to obtain comparability wages. At 1970 wage levels, this incremental cost amounted to only $175 million.

Thus, the incremental budget increase for a volunteer reserve, assuming present strength levels, appears to range from $175 to $332 million/year. The Gates Commission estimate was $240 million.[125] Costs, of course, would be less if the reserve structure were made consistent with present military requirements, a point also made by the Gates Commission.[126] Finally, to the extent that the Nixon Doctrine implies substituting Reserve for active duty forces, reserve costs may increase, but overall costs would be less.

Equity

The most discussed equity facet is the fairness of reserve callups during limited conflicts. Some argue that all reserve callups are inequitable; others maintain that callups ensure wide participation among risk-compensated and draft-dodging reservists. Neither generalization is entirely correct because *ready* reservists in the Vietnam period fell into three broad groupings: obligated veterans (50%), career reservists (10%), and non-prior service reserve enlistees (40%).[127] Consequently, no broad generalization can be entirely accurate. The greatest burden of a callup unquestionably falls on the obligated veterans who have been assigned to reserve units or are called as individual fillers. Recall is tantamount to extending their active duty tour. This can be considered equitable only if everyone is required to serve. Individual inequity for this group can be justified only if the needs of the community were such that its security would otherwise be jeopardized. The small careerist group can be generally considered adequately compensated for its reserve meetings and the risk of being activated. A caveat is that many reserve careerists were recruited under World War II assumptions that the reserves were only the first to go; repetitive callups for limited-war situations were not anticipated, and opting-out now involves a high transfer cost to the individual in the form of nonvested retirement benefits. Thus, of the three reserve groupings, equity can be unambiguously satisfied only by calling up the non-prior-service enlistees; that was the implicit risk of volunteering for the reserves and avoiding regular military service.

Another equity facet is reserve recruitment policies. Because of draft pressure, the supply of volunteers has exceeded demand, inducing the reserves to select the best qualified from the resulting queue. Potential abuse arises because selection is decentralized to each unit and no objective standard of best qualified exists. During periods of high draft pressure, as in 1965-66, cases of favoritism and graft are therefore almost inevitable.[128] Best-qualified is inherently a discriminatory and unfair selection system. Such discrimination aggregates into harmful social class inequity because of the correlation among mental quality, education, and social class. The effects of the queue have been dramatic. During the March 1967 to June 1969 period, 53.4% of reserve enlistees had some college, versus only 17.7% for active duty enlistees; 18.7% of reserve enlistees were college graduates versus only 3.0% for regular enlistees.[129] This discrimination in conjunction with different ethnic AFQT population distributions (Figure 2-5) also largely explains the *Marshall Report's* publicized statistic that 15.5% of whites, but only 2.8% of Negroes fulfilled their military obligation through the Reserves.[130]

Wide Participation

Broad social participation is often cited as a moral justification for reserve callups during hostilities. The underlying rationale is usually neither wide participation nor moralism per se, but the perceived impact on the decision-making process. Advocates believe—as did former President Johnson—that Reserve activation is a disruptive and therefore carefully reasoned act of state with profound external implications and high domestic political costs. Even if the distribution levy among the nation's social groups were similar to the draft's, a callup affects older men and is consequently more burdensome to family life and to the private economy. Another consideration, given the disproportionate political power of rural America in the Congress, is that rural areas are often burdened disproportionately by callups because of their relatively high proportion of reserve units, often manned by the local elite.

While the decision-making process may indeed be affected by callups, two difficulties arise from this tactic. First, the equity criterion is violated. Callups imply some inequity unless only the non-prior-service reservists are called—but such an approach eliminates the differential burden associated with age and hence a major motive for a callup. A second difficulty is that wider social participation and burden-sharing do not automatically follow from a callup. Whether a callup is broadening depends on the reserves' social composition as compared to those entering the wartime forces. For instance, if a lottery were used for the active force and true voluntarism for the reserves, a callup would be less widening than expanding the active forces by the lottery. A reserve callup can also be less widening than Selective Service. During 1965-67, a callup would have been broadening because the better educated were deferred or in reserve units. However, after the tightening of deferment standards in 1968, a callup would have been less broadening than the subsequent drafting of the previously deferred.

Broad participation also serves as a vehicle for achieving a number of communal goals. As long as the individual burdens of duty in the reserves are small, communal benefits can be gained for only a small loss in terms of individual burdens from compulsory service in a militia. Broad participation (1) does or can serve as a social instrument for integrating and reducing the tensions among diverse ethnic and economic groupings; (2) is useful in maintaining law and order during domestic crises; (3) maintains continuity with the American and English heritage of universal service in the militia that has as one of its roles the preservation of individual liberty against the encroachment of a central authority or an errant military; and (4) maintains the Greek notion that citizenship entails obligations as well as privileges.

Other Criteria

Criteria other than military requirements, cost, equity, and the collective benefits associated with wide participation are not particularly relevant for the reserves. The reserves have little, if any, impact on allocative efficiency within the military. The many arguments against free choice based on paternalism, risk of life, and imperfect knowledge are weak. Uncertainty and career interruption are minor factors; the latter being limited to the four-to-six months' active-duty training period.

Relationship Between the Reserve and Active Duty Procurement Systems

The two broad alternatives for recruiting into the reserves are voluntarism and conscription, which may be universal, random, or selective. Reserve and active force alternatives are linked in that (1) occasionally the active and reserve procurement systems may be incompatible and (2) if certain values are emphasized for the regular military establishment, it may be desirable to emphasize other values for the reserves. Thus, conscripted reserve is consistent with a volunteer regular force and has the advantage of offsetting the individualistic values of the latter with the collective values of the former. That is, if voluntarism were adopted in peacetime for the active duty establishment because of its optimizing impact upon individual welfare, an equal vulnerability draft might be considered for the reserves in order to emphasize the collective values of wide social participation, universal obligations of citizenship, etc.

Multiple linkage considerations exist between reserve voluntarism and active force alternatives. If a draft exists for the active forces, voluntarism for the reserves may only cloak implicit coercion. If draft pressure is strong enough to cause manpower supply to exceed the reserves' demand, undesirable consequences can occur unless the resulting selection is random or on a first-come basis. Allowing the resulting selection to be unstructured without explicit rules means opening the system to charges of favoritism. Creating explicit rules based on an index of education or test scores appears fair, but in reality discriminates against the underprivileged minorities. Another linkage is that a well-paid volunteer reserve is inconsistent with a low-paid and drafted active establishment: it would be inconsistent to pay the more burdened low wages while paying the relative unburdened high wages.

Criteria and Alternatives

In appraising alternatives, no single alternative system appears dominant. From the viewpoint of individual welfare, individual equity, and minimizing the economic impact during callups, a truly volunteer reserve relying on positive enlistment inducements is preferable. The arguments against a volunteer reserve are budget cost and the criteria associated with wide social participation. Unless voluntarism became a vehicle to reduce the reserves, a volunteer reserve would be more expensive than conscription. However, the merits of the budget cost argument are questionable when the economic costs already exist and the budgetary costs are not great.

The important argument against reserve voluntarism is its narrowing the burden-sharing and communal aspects of broad social participation. This is particularly important if voluntarism exists for the active forces. If the reserves were also largely recruited by monetary inducements from the same less-privileged social groups as the active forces, several undesirable features would occur. First, callups would no longer ensure wider social participation during crises. For all its inequities, the present system of allowing the reserves to select the best qualified has generally meant that callups are socially widening during wartime. Second, lower class participation in the Reserves would also reduce to some degree whatever impact upon the decision-making process that a callup has. Some would therefore argue that the United States may become involved more readily in foreign military adventures. Third, to the extent that there is some validity to the allegation that a volunteer military leads to professionalism, mercenarism, praetorianism, etc., and is therefore a threat to democratic institutions, desirable countervailing pressures can be exerted by ensuring that the reserves have a more representative, or even upper-class, recruitment basis.

A reserve system based on universal service eliminates the deficiencies of a volunteer system and is by definition equitable in all its many facets. However, even at a low pay, it is budgetarily expensive for the military benefits gained. A more attractive scheme is the lottery, which is not saddled with its economic and budgetary costs and satisfies all universal service's criteria except ex-post equity. A process which randomly assigns nineteen-year-olds ensures ex-ante equity and wide participation. Even the ex-post equity criterion may be partially alleviated by compensating selectees with wages comparable to their age cohort outside the military.

Of the many alternatives, the two dominating systems are true voluntarism and draft by lottery. Each system has strengths the other lacks. If one stresses liberal values, voluntarism is preferable; if one stresses either budget cost or communal values, a lottery is preferable. This conflict of values suggests that a combined system would capture the strengths of both alternatives while reducing their liabilities. Two combining procedures are available. One is to adopt a lottery for the reserves, if voluntarism is adopted for the active forces.

Another is a "bifurcated" military reserve and domestic militia that permits emphasizing the better features of both voluntarism and the lottery. The reserves have domestic military responsibilities, in addition to their national security ones. In our federal system, they act as counterweights to the central government and the regular military. In addition, the states require militia to maintain social order—a function which does not entail high-level combat readiness. On the other hand, external requirements call for a relatively combat-ready reserve. This suggests two reserves: (1) a highly trained reserve to complement the regular military and (2) a second line reserve based on a randomly selected "infantry" militia that is domestically oriented. For the highly trained backup forces, voluntarism is preferable; for the militia, a lottery. Such bifurcation represents a compromise which emphasizes the values of individualism, yet preserves the collective values of wide social participation and the duties and obligations of citizenship.

Appendix 2-D

An Evaluative Example

When each manpower alternative is visualized as a vector with some 17 attributes (criteria) whose relative importance varies according to context, one can readily understand the wide range of disagreement over manpower procurement. This section is an attempt to systematize these relationships by filling in the 459-cell matrix of Table 1-3. Rankings are Excellent (4), Good (3), Satisfactory (2), Poor (1), and Unsatisfactory (0). In combining the rankings, the criteria were unweighted, thus giving each a weight of 1.

Because dominance does not exist, choice among alternatives requires some judgment concerning the relative importance of the various criteria in each of the three contexts. Fortunately, judgment is simplified and no arguments need develop over specific criteria weights, since the clustering of rankings lead to fairly dominating solutions, particularly among the more important criteria. In all environments, the parity pay variants perform better than the exploitative variants. This is because the parity pay variants possess some of the favorable attributes of voluntarism without its defects. Sequential systems rank slightly higher than their corresponding components because of the effect on decision making of "shifting" from one system to another.

The Unweighted Average column of Table 2-8 presents a quick and simplified view of the relative advantage of each alternative. In peacetime voluntarism is clearly preferred to selective service by a distinct margin. Referring to Table 2-7 (which is Table 1-3 filled in) for a dominance check, voluntarism appears to be as good or better than selective service in every way save rejectee equity—a relatively minor consideration—and budget cost. While economically cheaper than selective service, voluntarism is financially more expensive because it is being used in a manpower system designed for the draft. Voluntarism also dominates the lottery, except for budget cost.

During limited war, the preferred choice is the mixed volunteer-lottery system with parity pay. UMT and the pure lottery with parity pay rank equally high with unweighted criteria but rank lower when the five more important criteria are weighted. The mixed volunteer-lottery system ranks higher than the pure lottery because men who desire a military career can volunteer, which reduces labor turnover and training costs. However, this same aspect makes the pure lottery rank slightly better in regard to the Social Class Equity, Social Instrument, and Threat to Democracy criteria. UMT ranks very high in the secondary criteria because of universality and high turnover. It ranks poorly in terms of cost and economic efficiency. UMT also ranks slightly worse than the mixed volunteer-lottery in satisfying manpower demands but slightly better in *ex-post* equity.

80

Table 2-7
Three-Dimensional Military Manpower Matrix of Program Alternatives, Criteria, and Context

System alternatives	Context / Criteria	I Military requirements	Manpower demands*	Industrial production*	II Economic considerations	Economic cost	Budget cost*	Allocative efficiency	III Individual considerations	Ex-ante equity*	Ex-post equity*	Rejectee equity	Pay equity	Uncertainty	Career interruption	IV Social considerations	Social class equity	Social instrument	Conscience, tradition, and law	Threat to democracy	Decision making considerations	V Technical workability
Current mixed volunteer-SS without parity pay	P	S	S		S	G	G	P	P	S	S	S	P	P		P	P	P	S	P	S	S
	LW	G	S		G	G	P	P	P	S	S	G	P	P		P	S	P	S	P	S	S
	FM	E	G		E	E	P	G	G	S	G	G	G	G		G	G	E	S	P	S	S
Current mixed volunteer-SS with parity pay	P	G	S		G	E	S	S	S	G	G	G	P	S		G	S	G	S	P	P	S
	LW	E	G		E	E	S	S	S	U	G	G	P	G		G	S	G	S	P	S	S
	FM	E	E		E	E	S	S	S	G	G	G	G	G		G	G	E	S	S	S	S
Mixed volunteer-lottery without parity pay	P	S	S		P	S	P	E	E	P	P	S	P	S		E	E	S	S	S	S	S
	LW	G	S		S	G	P	E	E	S	S	G	P	S		E	E	G	S	S	S	S
	FM	E	P		G	E	P	E	E	S	S	G	G	G		E	S	E	S	S	S	S
Mixed volunteer-lottery with parity pay	P	G	S		G	E	S	E	E	G	G	S	G	G		E	E	S	G	S	S	S
	LW	E	S		G	G	S	E	E	G	S	G	G	G		E	E	G	S	S	S	S
	FM	E	P		G	G	S	E	E	G	S	G	E	G		E	S	E	S	S	S	S
Pure lottery with parity pay	P	P	S		P	P	S	E	E	G	G	S	G	G		E	E	S	G	S	S	S
	LW	S	S		S	S	S	E	E	G	G	S	G	G		E	E	G	S	S	S	S
	FM	G	P		G	G	S	E	E	G	G	S	E	G		E	S	E	S	S	S	S
Volunteer	P	E	S		E	E	G	E	E	E	E	E	E	E		E	E	E	E	S	S	S
	LW	S	S		E	E	P	E	E	E	E	E	E	E		S	S	S	E	S	S	S
	FM	U	P		E	U	G	E	E	E	E	E	E	E		P	P	P	S	S	S	S
Universal military training	P	S	S		P	P	P	E	E	G	G	E	E	G		E	E	G	P	S	S	S
	LW	G	S		S	S	P	E	E	S	G	E	G	G		E	E	G	S	S	S	S
	FM	E	S		G	G	P	E	E	S	E	E	G	G		S	S	E	S	S	S	S
Universal national service	P	S	G		P	S	S	G	G	E	G	E	E	S		E	E	E	S	S	S	U
	LW	G	G		E	S	P	S	S	E	S	E	E	G		E	E	G	S	S	S	U
	FM	E	G		E	G	P	S	S	E	E	E	E	G		E	E	E	S	S	P	P
Sequential systems	P	E	E		E	S	G	E	E	G	E	E	E	E		E	S	E	S	S	G	S
	LW	E	S		E	E	S	G	G	E	E	E	E	E		G	E	G	S	S	G	S
	FM	E	E		E	G	S	G	G	E	E	E	E	E		G	G	E	G	G	G	S

*Indicates more important criteria.

Table 2-8
Unweighted Criteria Comparison of Various Manpower Alternatives

	E(4)	G(3)	S(2)	P(1)	U(0)	Unweighted Average
Peace Context						
Current mixed volunteer-SS without parity pay	0	1	8	8	0	1.59
Current mixed volunteer-SS with parity pay	1	4	9	3	0	2.18
Mixed volunteer-lottery without parity pay	2	2	9	4	0	2.12
Mixed volunteer-lottery with parity pay	3	6	7	1	0	2.65
Pure lottery with parity pay	2	6	7	2	0	2.47
Volunteer	9	2	5	1	0	3.12
Universal military training	6	2	5	4	0	2.59
Universal national service	4	4	6	2	1	2.47
Sequential systems	9	3	4	1	0	3.18
Limited-War Context						
Current mixed volunteer-SS without parity pay	0	5	5	7	0	1.88
Current mixed volunteer-SS with parity pay	3	4	9	1	0	2.53
Mixed volunteer-lottery without parity pay	2	7	6	2	0	2.53
Mixed volunteer-lottery with parity pay	3	7	7	0	0	2.76
Pure lottery with parity pay	2	9	6	0	0	2.76
Volunteer	6	1	9	1	0	2.71
Universal military training	7	3	6	1	0	2.94
Universal national service	4	4	7	1	1	2.53
Sequential systems	3	8	6	0	0	2.82
Full-Mobilization Context						
Current mixed volunteer-SS without parity pay	5	8	3	1	0	2.94
Current mixed volunteer-SS with parity pay	6	7	4	0	0	3.12
Mixed volunteer-lottery without parity pay	6	6	3	2	0	2.94
Mixed volunteer-lottery with parity pay	6	6	4	1	0	3.0
Pure lottery with parity pay	6	6	4	1	0	3.0
Volunteer	6	2	4	3	2	2.24
Universal military training	10	2	4	1	0	3.24
Universal national service	6	5	4	1	1	2.82
Sequential systems	6	8	3	0	0	3.18

The mixed volunteer-lottery system in the limited-war context dominates the selective service variants except for industrial protection, which is not important in this context. The mixed volunteer-lottery does not dominate pure voluntarism. Voluntarism's difficulty is due to the ethical objection to paying the poor to bear the personal risks of war.

UMT ranks highest in the full-mobilization context. Being universal, UMT is the democratic solution and, by definition, equitable, at least if the medically disqualified but potentially high-income rejectee is levied a special compensatory tax, as in Switzerland. A universal draft of youths 18 to 20 years old is not burdened by industrial protectionism, since few possess a critical skill at this age. The deficiency of wartime UMT is that not enough men exist in the youngest cohorts to meet military requirements, so UMT must be supplemented by drafting older men. But universal service for older groups, which include the nation's skilled and its more burdened family men, is undesirable.

Because UMT (and Universal National Service) cannot provide enough men, and the lottery cannot protect the industrial base, selective service becomes the preferred choice during major wars. Of its two variants, the prevailing non-parity system costs less and is potentially less inflationary; however, this advantage is obtained by a regressive 100% tax rate on the selected, while the higher-skilled nonselected enjoy war-inflated incomes. Equity, therefore, requires the parity pay variant, which can be implemented by deferred compensation and heavier postwar taxation on the nonselected, thus eliminating the short-run inflationary and production incentives problems.

Thus, each alternative has advantages and disadvantages that vary according to context. Where voluntarism is strongest, selective service is weak; where selective service is strongest, voluntarism is unsatisfactory. The lottery meanwhile runs a middle course. This outcome naturally suggests a sequential shift to match each environment with its preferred alternative. The sequential system of voluntarism, mixed volunteer-lottery, and mixed volunteer-selective service in the respective contexts of peace, limited war, and full mobilization, ranks highest in the comparison of unweighted ranking sums in Table 2-9.

Table 2-9
Unweighted System Sums

Current Mixed Volunteer-SS Without Parity Pay	6.41
Current Mixed Volunteer-SS With Parity Pay	7.83
Mixed Volunteer-Lottery Without Parity Pay	7.59
Mixed Volunteer-Lottery With Parity Pay	8.41
Pure Lottery With Parity Pay	8.23
Volunteer	8.07
UMT	8.77
Universal National Service	7.82
Sequential Systems	9.18

3 Deferment Policy: Logic and Issues

A major policy issue of conscription concerns the existence and extent of deferments and exemptions from military service. Deferment policy presumes the selective form of conscription. Voluntarism avoids deferments by self-selection. Universal service and an equal-probability lottery, by definition, exclude deferments. A lottery with deferments and exemptions remains a selective system and differs only in the order and timing of selection. A lottery with *extensive* deferments and a selective system which is explicitly discriminatory thus differs only in form. Selection devices such as drawing by lot or birthday then determine only order and timing; "who serves, when not all serve" is determined by deferment policies and by the military's acceptance standards that reduce the age cohort to the draftable pool. Finally, de facto deferment can come about informally through the induction sequence if the supply of availables (classification 1-A) is greater than the demand. Thus the preferential treatment accorded married men during 1963-65, when they were placed lower in the 1-A induction sequence, was, in effect, an exemption,[1] as was the proviso that student deferees had extended liability to age 35.

The authority and rationale for student and occupational deferment is contained in the preamble to the basic Selective Service Act of 1948, which reads:

Sec. 1(c) . . . privileges of serving . . . should be shared generally, in accordance with a system of selection which is *fair and just*, and which is *consistent* with the maintenance of an effective national economy.

Sec. 1(e) . . . adequate provision for national security requires *maximum* effort in the fields of scientific research and development, and the fullest possible utilization of the Nation's technological, scientific, and other critical manpower resources. (Emphasis added.)

The Selective Service System has interpreted Congressional intent as (1) filling bulk manpower requests, (2) minimizing the economic impact of these levies, and (3) "pressurized guidance or channeling" of individuals into activities deemed to be in the national interest.[2]

For an individualistic society, rationales (2) and (3) are questionable except under the duress of war and social survival. A liberal society has other goals which conflict with rationales (2) and (3), and even (1) if military requirements are inappropriately determined, as some would argue. When peacetime manpower calls become so low that "the maintenance of an effective national economy" is not at issue, then "fair and just" is an inaccurate description of a system that effectively exempts the better-educated upper class. "Maximum effort" is an anachronistic nation-in-arms concept. More relevant in the nuclear age is intensified research and advancement in *limited* specialties. Even the term "maximum" can be criticized as a logical error and an open invitation to gross inefficiency. In weapons system development, "crash" or maximum effort programs have proven to be extremely costly and rarely worth their opportunity costs except for the highest-priority programs. "Critical" is a value-laden term, logically inconsistent with the economy's adaptability, and difficult to define objectively in a highly interdependent, functional, organic society.

SS's student and occupational deferment policies are essentially short-run protectionist schemes appropriate only during full mobilization. They are not "necessary to hold the industrial, agricultural, and social structure of the Nation in balance during either peace or war."[3] In periods other than full mobilization, the economy's invisible hand has ample time to adjust and guide manpower allocation. Unless SS's channeling offsets an existing externality, channeling can only lead to additional labor market imperfections and hence labor misallocation. Without the tautness, sudden demand shifts, and fortuitous windfalls of a fully mobilized economy, controls in the form of either prices, wages, or labor allocation are unnecessary and restrictive. The American economy is demand-oriented; if the demand exists, supply will normally adjust either through labor mobility or new labor force entrants, barring such defects as imperfect knowledge, entry restrictions, imperfect capital markets for human investment, and divergences between private and social benefits and costs. Since SS's protectionist deferment policies are not aimed at solving these allocative restrictions, SS only adds its own externality to an already formidable list of market distortions. A task so fundamentally important as the allocation of the nation's youth should not be self-arrogated by any government agency without (1) explicit authority; (2) meaningful interaction with other interested agencies; (3) specialized and conceptual knowledge of the problems; and (4) some power to reduce the many externalities.

Channelization and Occupational Deferment (OD)

Technically, channelization can be described as a method of indirect labor control designed to guide the flow of *new entrants* into occupations deemed to be in the national interest by some public body. Occupational deferment, on the other hand, is a form of direct labor control designed to guide the stock of *skilled older men* into specified tasks. In the American heritage, direct or indirect labor controls in peacetime are economically unnecessary and are normally considered ideologically repugnant.[4] During full mobilization, when the price system cannot cope with rapidly shifting demands, a valid argument exists for directly allocating the existing stock of skills, but not for channeling, which implies human capital investment to create additional stock.[5]

Student Deferment (SD)

The conventional case for SD is largely protectionism for future technical skills. Other benefits of SD are: (1) encouraging more men to enter occupations deemed critical, (2) obtaining college-educated military officers, (3) protecting universities from fluctuating male student enrollments, (4) preventing military service breaks during the undergraduate period, and (5) precluding double jeopardy for such highly skilled people in short supply as MDs. Detractors of SD base their case on inequity and the disappearance of necessity. Less recognized have been SD's normally negative value during full mobilization and its economic inefficiency during peacetime because of the growth of college output relative to the military's requirements unless the universally condemned pyramiding of SDs by occupational and dependency deferments is continued.

Criteria

The Marshall Commission stated that "without the justification of being in the national interest, the justification originally intended, student deferments have become the occasion of serious inequity."[6] The Harvard group said that "the economic benefits of discriminating among young men are modest, and largely confined to the young men who benefit."[7] Thus, although student deferment has been justified by reference to the national interest, a blue-ribbon panel and a knowledgeable academic group have dismissed its validity. The answer to this apparent paradox is that the context that once justified SD no longer exists. An economic and military case for the present version of SD can only be made if two necessary conditions exist: (1) expectation of an indefinitely long war and (2) a critical shortage of college-educated personnel. As shown in Appendix 3-A, a case can nevertheless be made for non-pyramiding peacetime SDs as a means to ensure wider social participation during wartime.

History

Student deferment began in a period when these necessary conditions existed. Immediately before and during the Korean conflict, (1) a standing army large in relation to the youth cohort base appeared to be an indefinite requirement; and (2) physical scientists were in short supply because of growing and shifting technical demands and the temporary World-War-II supply curtailment.[8] There was, therefore, a case for deferment. Later, when the demand-and-supply imbalances were adjusted and the military labor and industrial output requirement was reduced, these necessary conditions no longer existed, but by then SD had become entrenched and a way of life.

SD was sanctified by the 1948-49 Trytten committees, composed of 27 broadly representative educators and scientists.[9] Though the committees used the dubious procedure of projecting the special political and economic conditions of the period into an indefinite future, they did recognize that their recommendations would be valid only as long as a long period of international stress and continuing shortage of college-educated personnel was expected.[10] Furthermore, the committees conceded that because of the large stock of extant talent, the effect of nondeferment had not been dramatic during World War II and that "the problem of education has in the past seemed always to take care of itself."[11]

Deferment As An Investment

Student deferment is a form of capital investment. During full mobilization, capital is typically depleted in favor of current consumption, except in specified war-related growth industries. In the same way, human capital can be depleted for the war effort.[12] If its very existence is at stake, society may not be able to forgo current benefits for uncertain future returns. If the threat is serious the discount rate for future output may become so high as to render net educational returns negative rather than positive. Replacement of physical and human capital is an appropriate postwar function—a function that both the capital-goods and education industries showed themselves capable of after World War II.

The opportunity costs of faculty, supporting staff, and students are high in wartime. For grammar and grade schools, these opportunity costs are low; the students are too young and housewives can substitute for males needed elsewhere. The costs of wartime student deferment are large and growing faster than the population and the GNP. Using 1965 as an example, the forgone cost to society of student deferment would have been 5.67 million male and female students and a supporting faculty and staff of 495,000; in terms of money, $26.6 billion or 3.9% of the GNP.[13] If 1944's 41.5% of the GNP is taken as the benchmark for the maximum amount of its GNP that society can devote to the war effort, then the curtailment of college education represents a potential 9.4% gain in war-available resources.

In a short war, a demand shift can be met by releasing faculty and students for more essential activities. The annual increment of graduates is too small to significantly affect the total stock, except in those disciplines experiencing a sharp upward shift in demand. A long war is not in itself a justification for student deferment, since personnel can be released after performing a minimum period of military service. The social costs are a partial and temporary interruption in the flow of personnel and a small reduction in their useful professional lives. If the demand shift occurs for only a few fields, and there are enough medical rejectees to fill the void, then no college output interruption need occur, though the quality of the input may be *initially* reduced. Over the long run, quality will not be significantly reduced as the normal input quality returns, except for deaths. If the death rate is high, society has a cruel dilemma. It cannot afford to lose the flower of its youth; yet equity among individuals and among social classes is most important when casualty rates are high.

Scarcity And The Invisible Adjuster

In peacetime, the market system, except for the externalities noted under occupational channelization, can be expected to adjust to the environment and to provide the correct amount of human capital in each discipline. The high psychic and investment return to college education, plus the increasing availability of family funds from higher per capita income, insure adequate supply. As an indication of its strength, during the high-immigration decades 1870-1950, this incentive without draft pressure was enough to induce the number of chemists and engineers to grow 17 times as fast as the labor force.[14] Figure 3-1's semi-log graph summarizes the underlying forces. While the male population between 20 and 24 years old increased by only 100% between 1900 and 1967, bachelor and advanced degrees climbed by 1,400 and 6,371% respectively. Even more interesting, Figure 3-1 shows that World War II, Korea, and channelization have done little to change the pre and postwar rates of growth in degrees conferred. In addition, if lines (Figure 3-1's dashed lines) are drawn between the prewar peak and the postwar trough, the postwar surplus induced by the GI Bill appears to have offset the wartime deficit by a net surplus of 230,000 bachelor and 7,300 advanced degrees, or 11.6 and 1.6% respectively over 1940-1955.

Scarcity, much less equity, is not a credible argument when the percentages of a male cohort earning bachelor's, master's, and doctorate degrees in 1966 were as high as 23.5, 7.1, and 3.1, respectively, and continually rising.[15] Pressure groups caused SD to get out of hand. The Trytten committees advocated limiting deferments to less than 5% of any age cohort through testing and class-standing procedures.[16] Critics who wish broader deferment policies consider such "creaming" an elitist tactic, inequitable to average students. These critics fail to recognize the zero-sum aspect of the draft: "greater" equity among students automatically means less equity for non-students.

Blank and Stigler have shown empirically that the alleged scarcity of scientific personnel does not exist, or represents an economic misunderstanding. By noting the trends in relative earnings, they conclude that supply has actually grown relative to demand.[17]

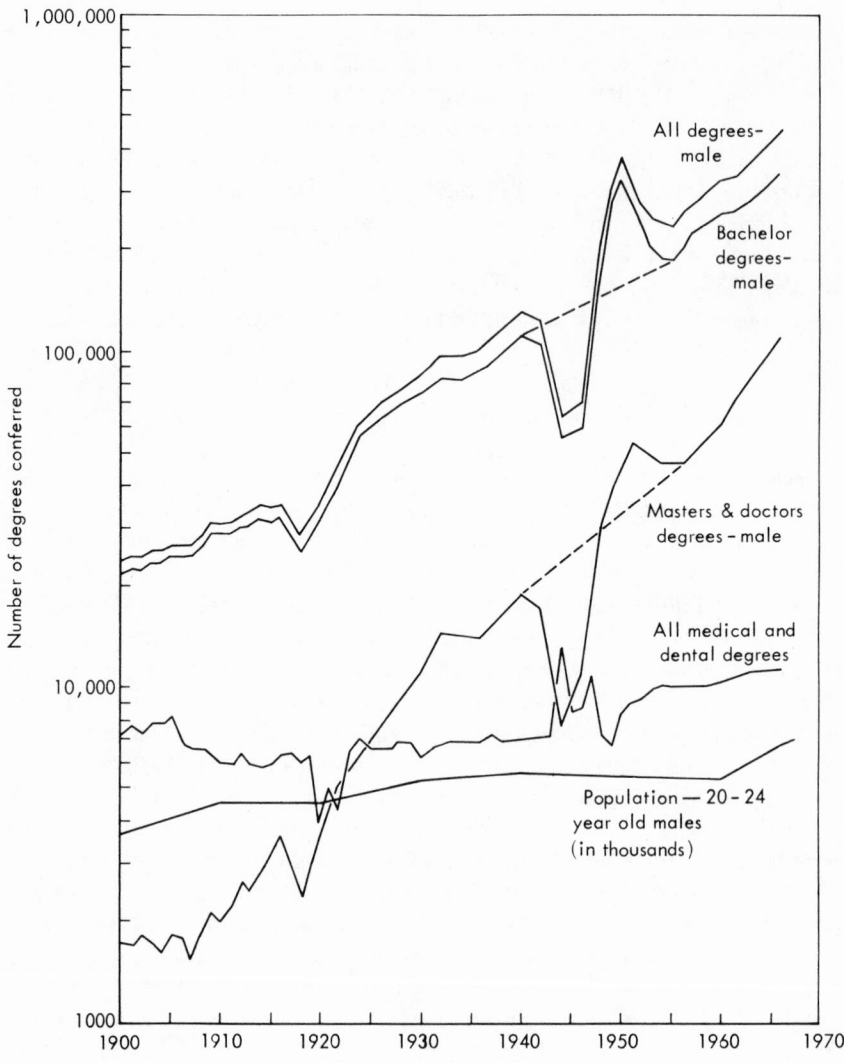

Figure 3-1. Degrees conferred from 1900 to 1969. Source: *Historical Statistics of the United States – Colonial Times to 1957*, U.S. Bureau of the Census. *Statistical Abstract of the United States – 1958, 1960, 1965, 1968, 1971* U.S. Dept. of Commerce.

Even if the draft did interfere with the training of "scarce" scientists, the market would react by training additional scientists to fill the demand. Thus, draft interruptions of education in a peacetime market economy actually increase the available wartime reservoir (assuming no artifical entry restrictions, as in medicine).[18] This exemplifies the fallacy of composition—what may appear hindering to the individual may not be so for society as a whole.

Deferment Issues

Table 3-1 lists the formal deferment classifications. Its breakdown by education indicates the social correlations of deferments and disqualifications and why the middle spectrum bears the heaviest military burden. The lower end is disqualified by the military's mental acceptance standards, while the upper end is deferred by the Selective Service System and the "creaming" policies of the reserves.

Deferments and Deferment Equity

The most important source of deferment is the fatherhood, or dependency category, which does not correlate by social class. Its large size is due mainly to the age creep caused by the Selective Service System's "oldest first" procedure. From 1958 to 1963 the mean age of regular inductees was consistently between 23 1/2 and 24 during the prime family-formation period.[19] As a result, one out of four in an age cohort was able by an essentially discretionary act to avoid military service through dependency and to shift his burden onto others. The draft in peacetime is predictable: marriage and fatherhood can be an avenue of avoidance. Dependency exemptions were designed for full mobilization, when older men with much greater family responsibilities were draft-liable. Such occasions are unpredictable; discretionary choice is therefore not a factor. In peacetime the whole issue of dependency exemptions is artificial. Lowering the draft age to 19 removes most exemptions. The continued existence of dependency deferments then becomes questionable because of the obvious individual advantage of choice and the paternalistic argument that early marriages ought not to be encouraged. Furthermore, in a lottery framework, dependency exemptions can lead to class-correlated exemptions if student deferments are also allowed because of the consequent pyramiding advantage to college men.

The second largest not-available-for-service group is the disqualified. 4-Fs are disqualified for mental and physical reasons; 1-Ys are qualified for service only in time of war or national emergency. Class 1-Y was formed in 1962 to segregate the legally disqualified from those disqualified by the military's peacetime acceptance standards, which are a function of the available supply.[20] To the extent that standards are artifically inflated and exclude many who desire a military career, a low incidence of service for the less-than-high-school group discriminates against them and unnecessarily burdens the qualified.

Though few in absolute numbers at the 26-year age point, the most objectionable deferments are student and occupational deferments. The criticism is at two levels: (1) for allowing students a special scope for choice during wartime even if the overall group burden remains unchanged through postponement; and (2) for the pyramiding of student, occupational, and dependency deferments into service avoidance and low service incidence rates, as shown in Tables 3-1 and 3-2.[21]

Table 3-1

Estimated Military Service Status of 26-Year Age Class[1] by Educational Level, July 1964

Status	Total[2]	Less Than High School	High School	Some College	College
		Number (thousands)			
Total	1,190	495	355	131	154
Entered Military Service (Active or Reserve)[a]	614	247	203	78	62
No Military Service, total	576	248	152	53	92
Available for Service (Class I-A)[3]	13	3	3	1	5
Married	5	1	1	*	3
Unmarried	8	2	2	1	2
Not Available for Service	565	246	149	52	86
Disqualified (Classes I-Y and IV-F)	217	126	43	18	18
Student Deferments (Classes I-S and II-S)	12	–	*	2	9
Occupational Deferments (Classes II-A and II-C)	20	1	1	1	17
Dependency Deferments (Class III-A)	296	116	103	30	38
Other Deferred and Exempt Groups[4]	20	3	2	1	4
		Vertical Percentage Distribution			
Total	100	100	100	100	100
Entered Military Service (Active or Reserve)[a]	52	50	57	60	40
No Military Service, Total	48	50	43	40	60
Available for Service (Class I-A)[3]	1	1	1	1	3
Married	*	*	*	*	2
Unmarried	1	1	1	1	1
Not Available for Service	47	50	42	40	56
Disqualified (Classes I-Y and IV-F)	18	25	12	14	12
Student Deferments (Classes I-S and II-S)	1	–	–	2	6
Occupational Deferments (Classes II-A and II-C)	2	*	*	1	11
Dependency Deferments (Class III-A)	25	23	29	23	25
Other Deferred and Exempt Groups	2	1	1	1	3

Table 3-1 (cont.)

Status	Total[2]	Less Than High School	High School	Some College	College
		Horizontal Percentage Distribution			
Total	95	42	30	11	13
Entered Military Service (Active or Reserve)[a]	96	40	33	13	10
No Military Service, Total	95	43	26	9	16
Available for Service (Class I-A)[3]	92	23	23	8	38
Married	100	20	20	–	60
Unmarried	88	25	25	13	25
Not Available for Service	94	44	26	9	15
Disqualified (Classes I-Y and IV-F)	94	58	20	8	8
Student Deferments (Classes I-S and II-S)	92	–	–	17	75
Occupational Deferments (Classes II-A and II-C)	100	5	5	5	85
Dependency Deferments (Class III-A)	97	39	35	10	13
Other Deferred and Exempt Groups	50	15	10	5	20

[a]Reserve programs account for 14% of the total.

[1]Includes individuals born in calendar year 1938 and who were therefore approximately between 25-1/2 and 26-1/2 years old in July 1964.

[2]Also includes registrants whose educational attainment is unknown.

[3]Includes individuals between 25-1/2 years and their 26th birthday who were still liable for induction until they attained age 26. It is probable that most of the small number of qualified unmarried men in this group were reached for induction before their 26th birthday.

[4]Includes conscientious objectors available for or performing civilian work; officials; certain aliens; ministers of religion and divinity students, etc.

*Less than 500 persons or 0.5%.

Note: Details may not add to total due to rounding.

Source: Review of the Administration and Operation of the Selective Service System. Hearings before the Committee on Armed Services 98th Congress 2nd Session, June 1966, p. 10011.

Occupational deferment in all periods suffers from ex-ante, ex-post, and group inequity problems that are difficult to justify except through necessity. By definition, OD means unequal probability of service. A less obvious implication is that, since military requirements are always stated in the form of perfectly inelastic demands, military procurement has a zero-sum nature and one's gain through deferment is another's loss. Regardless of any altruistic claims about substitute "national service,"[22] OD is inevitably advantageous to the

Table 3-2
Percent of Men Who Served, by Educational Level, in 1964[a]

Education	Men Aged 27-34	Men Aged 26
Eighth Grade or Less	41	
High School Dropout	70	50
High School Graduate	74	57
College Dropout	68	60
College Degree	70	40
Graduate School	27	
Constructed Medical	65	
Constructed Non-Medical	17[b]	

Source: The National Advisory Commission on Selective Service, 1967, op. cit., p. 23 and *RAOSSS*, p. 9931.

[a]Reserve programs account for 9.2% of the total for men aged 27-34 and 14% for men aged 26.

[b]Calculated by using a 65% participation rate for doctors/dentists, who accounted for 20% of graduate degrees during the period. *Historical Statistics*, Series H327-350 and B180-194, and *1966 Statistical Abstract*, p. 138.

deferred/exempted and unfair because it requires replacements. Other than in full mobilization, ODs differ little in substance from the Civil War practice of the wealthy buying out of military service. While others are suffering income losses, career displacements, and perhaps special military burdens, occupational exemptees are not. If society desires to continue these exemptions, a compensatory tax, as in Switzerland, would seem to be the minimum equity adjustment.[23]

The main complaint against ODs is group or social class inequity, since ODs are correlated with education and hence wealth and political power. The vertical distribution in Table 3-1 shows this relationship. For 26-year-olds in 1964, college graduates (13% of the total population) received 85% of the ODs. The probability of a high-school graduate being granted an OD was only 0.2%; with some college, 1%; with a college degree, 11%. Because of this correlation, regardless of intent, occupational exemptions shift the burdens of service from the educated onto the less educated. Such shifting is undemocratic and can strain the social fabric, something society ought to avoid unless it is clearly warranted by the allocative and scarcity pressures of full mobilization.

Although the numbers involved appear few in Table 3-1, SD also causes unnecessary group inequity. The small number of students is because most have graduated by age 26; and before Vietnam and the 1963 de facto marriage exemptions, few undergraduates applied for deferment, because the age creep was causing older men to be drafted and acceptance of SD meant extended liability to age 35. In addition to allowing wartime scope for choice by enrolling in college, SD was part of a selective system enabling college men and those with advanced degrees in particular to pyramid their student, occupational, and dependency deferments into a low military participation rate. Table 3-2 shows that in 1964 70% of college graduates 27 to 34 years old participated in military service. But a breakdown of the really privileged—the graduate-school group—shows an even lower rate of 27% in 1964. If this group is further divided into medical doctor and non-MD graduates, the non-MD rate drops to 17%. The corresponding graduate school rate for 26-year-olds would drop even further as the overall college rate dropped from 70 to 40% for the younger group. Alternatively, if graduate participation rates are assumed a proportionate drop, and given that advanced degrees are about two-ninths of bachelor degrees, the participation rate for 26-year-old college men *not* going to graduate school climbs to 47% in Table 3-2, a more respectable figure but still lower than the 57% for the high-school graduate and 60% for those with some college.

Central vs. Local Determination

During mobilization, when deferments are often necessary, a relevant policy question is whether the resulting labor allocation should be centrally or locally controlled. Selective Service and its defenders argue that only local determination can protect communities from the gross judgments of central authority. They point to the difficulties caused by overt federal involvement in the Civil War and infer that local participation is essential for public acceptance. In rural-frontier America, with its strong fears of government encroachment, local determination was economically and ideologically appropriate. But underlying conditions have changed, and local determination is now less appropriate except, perhaps, in rural Southern regions. Politically, the country has come to accept a greater role for the federal government; increasingly, state and local policies are judged according to their correspondence to national norms. Economically, economies of scale and improved transportation have (1) integrated small communities and submarkets into larger groupings, (2) increased economic interdependence, and (3) improved labor mobility. The relevant labor supply and demand has thus become increasingly national and regional, rather than local. Only a national authority possesses the perspective, knowledge, and means (through work simplification, training schools, etc.) to balance supply with demand. Local determination is simply too fragmented, nonspecialized, and uninformed for this function. There is also the possibility that local boards will abuse or misunderstand their function or simply hoard critical skills for their own locality—a point supported in the Marshall Commission's finding that about half of occupational deferees "were in neither a critical occupation nor an essential industry as defined by the Department of Labor."[24]

Nor does central determination exclude "recourse to judgment," one of the SSS's favorite arguments. A central system can respond to objective criteria, though perhaps not to all the subjective nuances which have caused the present system to be regarded as arbitrary. In fact, as suggested by the previous paragraph, the weight of the judgment argument is now on the side of central determination. "Little groups of neighbors" throughout the country cannot be expected to have the requisite knowledge and perspective for the allocation task. To the extent that the requisite talent exists, a hard-pressed society would be better served by releasing this scarce managerial talent for more productive pursuits. In a centralized system, random processes will occasionally produce excessive statistical variations among regions, but this can be controlled by automatic limiting rules or by ex-post administrative adjustment. But it also has to be recalled that pre-Vietnam deferment and military acceptance standards caused even greater geographical variations.

The final argument against local determination is its ex-ante inequity. A geographical accident—his place of residence—should not affect involuntary restraint of freedom and a young man's risk to life for his country. An offsetting consideration is that though central determination is more impervious to political influence, aberrations and socially correlated determinations that do occur are more visible. This can lead to undesirable social reactions if class discrimination is militarily necessary but difficult to sell politically. Of course, one could also argue that visibility cuts both ways: greater visibility spotlights the "establishment" and reduces the possibilities of manipulating the system for personal and group advantage.

Institution Disruption

An argment for SDs has been that they minimize the impact of the draft on colleges and universities. These institutions find it difficult to adapt to rapidly changing demands. But this is true of all industries; the relevant question is whether the advanced-education industry deserves special consideration. The main concern is protection against abrupt changes in the draft and the availability of young men of college age. Such a consideration does not justify peacetime SD, because the draft's peacetime demands are predictable. Special consideration during full mobilization is also unwarranted, since faculty skills are also needed for direct war-related efforts.

Thus, the argument reduces to pointing out the need for protecting educational institutions during limited war, when the draft's demands have sharply increased and faculty skills are not required for the war effort. Against the desire to dampen cyclical swings in the production and employment of the nation's educational resources are a number of considerations. The most obvious and important is the equity of deferring some and increasing the probability of service and risk to life for others. Another is the relative abundance of scientific talent. If supply outstrips demand, as appears to be happening in the 1970s, then the basis of special consideration for the education industry—namely actual and projected shortages of scientific and educated talent needed to promote the national interest—is undermined. Finally, shielding educational institutions is inconsistent with the positions of (1) those who argue against voluntarism on the grounds that voluntarism leads to social decadence because the wealthier avoid service and (2) those who argue for widespread drafts to broaden social participation in order to dampen tendencies to become involved in foreign adventures.

Procuring College-Trained Personnel

SD ensures an adequate flow of college graduates into the armed forces, particularly into the officer corps. If the draft age were lowered to age 19 or 20 because of high wartime demands or because of the lottery, it is possible that without SD the military's requirement for college-trained personnel would not be met without double jeopardy. SD ensures a draft-liable pool of college graduates, but such a pool is at best necessary only for limited wars. During peacetime, ROTC and voluntarism can be expected to meet the military's officer requirements. During full mobilization, all men (except the elderly) again become draft-liable; a special provision to avoid double jeopardy for the younger cohorts is no longer a consideration. This reduces the question to: Can the military meet its need for college-trained men in a limited war without SD? The factors listed below under voluntarism will assist, but some residue will undoubtedly remain if the lapse of SD means that graduating seniors are no longer draft liable.

But all this neglects the key question of why college graduates are necessary to begin with. Officers with college degrees are needed only in the technical branches and in other branches for later promotion to the higher career ranks. In limited war, expansion is largely in the ground combat arms, where temporary junior officers need not be college graduates. In the Israeli army nondegree men are preferred as combat leaders because they are more aggressive. In our own army it has long been fashionable to note that the noncollege Officer Candidate School (OCS) graduate is a better *junior* officer than his ROTC or West Point counterpart. In limited wars, then, greater reliance could be placed on younger nongraduates by sending the best through OCS. If college graduates are nevertheless preferred, two alternatives to the present SD system exist. One (discussed in Appendix 3-A) is to permit SD in peacetime only, thus automatically creating a large wartime college graduate pool. A second alternative is the geared, sequential combination system, whereby voluntarism eliminates SD and double jeopardy problems in peacetime but puts all young men between specified ages into the draft pool during military expansions.

In peacetime, SD and draft pressure are unnecessary for procuring officers.

The annual peacetime officer input is projected to average 37,000,[25] 41% of whom, survey data indicate, are draft-motivated.[26] The DoD position before the Marshall Commission was:

In the absence of a college student (II-S) deferment policy, officer requirements could probably be met through a major revision of existing officer procurement programs and extensive use of Class I-D deferments. This would involve some difficult (but not insuperable) problems in terms of selection and programming, particularly in view of the very long leadtimes involved in the training of physicians and certain other professional specialists.[27]

Neglected in this admission was the impact on officer accessions of a growing population and a rise in entry pay. Given the projection of a constant-size peacetime military, a large part of the demand-supply imbalance can be expected to be met by volunteers at existing pay relatives by a rapidly increasing college output. From 1955 to 1970, male college and university enrollments were expected to increase from 1580 to 4180-4520 thousand, a 165-186% gain; the comparable 1980 figures are 5900-6900 thousand, a 274-338% gain.[28]

In 1964, draft-motivated officers totaled 41% of the 38,300 officer accessions, or 15,400. Since college enrollment increased 2 1/2 times faster than the male college-age population from 1955 to 1970, colleges are increasingly drawing from less qualified students and from less privileged socio-economic groups, both of whom should find an officer's career relatively more attractive than did earlier college graduates. In the future, the residue of coerced officer accessions should, therefore, be considerably less than the pre-Vietnam figure of 15,400. Student deferment for such a small number would be a small tail wagging a big dog. Few have realized that by 1965 peacetime officer accessions had dropped to only 12.4% of the male bachelor degree output. Indeed, unless deferments are pyramided into de facto exemptions, the draft may swamp the enlisted ranks with college graduates. Though the military welcomes a small percentage of college-trained enlisted men for clerical and other services, a large percentage would be an economic waste and even militarily detrimental, as the military prefers younger, more malleable, men to fill its enlisted ranks.[29] To the extent that large numbers of draftees were college graduates in low-skill slots, the economic value of college deferments versus earlier military service would become *negative*. Student deferment in the future is therefore defensible only with the pyramiding of occupational and fatherhood deferments. This basic policy clash apparently has not been recognized by any of the policy groups who have inconsistently condemned pyramiding while advocating SD.[30]

The DoD statement also overlooked the impact on accessions of pay increases at the most important decision point: entry. Contrary to the testimony of military officers during the volunteer military hearings (but consistent with their actions and their testimony during earlier hearings for pay increases) pay is a major career consideration. Entry pay is particularly important in the competitive placement market. The expectations and time preference of the typical college graduate are high. Finally, officer entry pay has *become* competitive. Officers with less than 2 years' service received an 86.8% increase in basic pay from between 1964 and January 1971, versus a 34.4% rise in the civilian sector. Until the pay increase of 1964, entry base pay had remained constant at $222.30 a month for 12 years and had risen by only $8.55 per month in the 15 years since 1949. Against this 4% increase in money wages, the Consumer Price Index had moved up by 30.2% and civilian money wages by 82.1%. To the extent that higher initial salaries induce nondraft-motivated officer accessions, retention among officers can be expected to increase, which, in turn, will gradually reduce the required annual input as career-motivated accessions flow through the system pipeline.

Procuring Medical Professionals

Related to the preceding section on obtaining college graduates is the military's highly publicized difficulty in obtaining sufficient MDs without draft inducement.[31] With a larger college population, higher pay, scholarships to remove financial constraints, ROTC deferments, etc., only professional medical talent remains a recruiting problem. For MDs, a draft will most likely have to remain for many years unless MDs are given even larger pay supplements over other officers. This shortage, combined with the public's dislike of singling out specific groups to bear the brunt of coercion, has been an important argument against both voluntarism and the equal exposure lottery.[32] In fact, doctors are among the least burdened of the college groups. Doctors in the service receive special pay, practice their specialty, and suffer few of the risk and discipline burdens associated with military life. In 1964 MDs participated slightly less than the total college-educated group aged 27-34 in Table 3-2, because many doctors of this age group were still in medical school and internship during the earlier high-demand Korean period. By 1964 the MD service rate was somewhat higher than the total 26-year-old age group because medical-school output had not kept pace with the overall growth in college degrees conferred (Figure 3-1), while military demand stayed constant for both groups. Thus, only in relation to nonmedical graduate school participation rates have MDs been so far unfairly treated, as shown in Table 3-2. In the future, MD participation rates can be expected to decline more slowly than other groups until medical schools expand proportionately.[33]

Thus, while the MD has not been disproportionately burdened except among holders of advanced degrees, it does appear that medical recruitment cannot be reasonably solved within a voluntary demand-and-supply framework for a number of years. The MD's civilian economic opportunities are too lucrative and the military's demand is too high relative to supply. The fundamental solution is to increase medical-school enrollments and, hence, the supply stock. That supply has not adjusted to demand has been readily explained by many observers. Friedman and Kuznets noted in 1954 that entry was being blocked.[34] In 1967,

Fein wrote that "medicine is one of the few fields in which supply is restricted at the point of entry into the educational system rather than into the profession."[35] An increase in supply would produce two effects. One would be an increase in the number of MDs inclined toward the military. The second effect would be to enhance the attractiveness of a military career, as a greater supply would gradually deflate the relative growth of civilian medical incomes.

A reduction in the military's peacetime demand would reduce the demand-supply imbalance for doctors. The Medical Corps does pool its doctors and uses paramedical personnel extensively;[36] these practices could be intensified. More doctors could be released from administrative chores. Military doctors also assert that larger numbers of dependents and free medical care for them have swamped the medical services, reducing the quality of service and increasing doctors' discontent with military medicine. Rationalizing medical services for dependents by a ration price, as DoD has requested, would relieve this complaint and also reduce the patient load.[37] Demand could also be reduced by further shifting the dependent workload onto civilian doctors through Medicare.

Transformation of the military pay system offers another method of reducing medical demand. Besides ability and experience, the military pay system, through its allowance and fringe benefits, is heavily predicated on an anachronistic "needs" philosophy. The result is that reenlistments correlate with numbers of dependents.[38] A change toward equal pay for equal work would simultaneously reduce the inefficient attraction of family over single men and provide a basis for a rationing charge for dependent services.

Table 3-3
Number of 26-Year-Old Men and Percentage with Military Service Experience

Year (June 30)	Total 26-Year-Old Males (in Thousands)	Never Entered Military Service	
		Number (in Thousands)	Percentage of Total
Actual:			
1958	1,100	770	70
1962	1,110	640	58
1964	1,190	610	52
1966[a]	1,250	580	46
Projected[a]:			
1974:			
3,000,000	1,870	790	42
2,700,000	1,870	640	34

Source: *RAOSSS*, op. cit., p. 10005.
[a]Excluding the impact of Vietnam.

Appendix 3-A

Composite Student Deferment Within a Draft System

The objection to student deferment lies in its high cost in equity for a number of minor and even questionable benefits. Yet, if pyramiding of deferments and wartime scope for choice are prohibited, SD is not inequitable and can even add an important dimension of *wider* social class participation. Ex-ante and group equity are satisfied by eventual exposure and the unequivocal cancellation of deferments during hostilities. That the poor might serve involuntarily at a slightly earlier age in peacetime is not a serious flaw, as long as the college graduate does in fact serve; nor is the drafted graduate's assignment advantage over the noncollege draftee objectionable, for other real advantages accrue to the peacetime enlistee through recruitment options.

A composite deferment system can include the better points of SD with fewer of its weaknesses. A policy of SD in peacetime only is preferable to its outright cancellation—to the student, by increasing his scope of choice as to his exposure date; to the military, by ensuring a smoother officer flow and a larger wartime pool (both quantitatively and qualitatively); to the universities by insulating them from the draft's impact except during hostilities; and, perhaps most important, to society, by ensuring wider social participation during limited military expansions. The weakness of the composite system is economic inefficiency caused by an oversupply of college-educated draftees to the military.

A composite deferment system would allow students and technical trainees in peacetime a choice between lottery exposure with their age cohort (or with a younger cohort upon graduation) and government cancellation of deferments due to hostilities. Two wartime cancellation variations exist. Version A would permit no further scope for choice and would cancel graduate-school defer-ments, thus increasing that year's lottery pool by the new freshman class and the graduate enrollment. Version B would cancel all outstanding deferments, thereby increasing A's pool by the new sophomore, junior, and senior years. Of the two, A is preferable during limited-war expansions because of the military's limited absorptive capacity, while B is preferable during mobilization expan-sions. Version A is, of course, also less disruptive to the universities.

A composite deferment system thus has all the advantages of peacetime deferment and adds a dimension of broader social participation in wartime. Individuals obtain scope for choice as long as one's benefit is not another's loss. Officer availability is enhanced without double exposure. In wartime, an enlarged lottery pool would be available from earlier deferees. Version A's cancellation of incoming freshman deferments and the exposure of the normal graduating class would cause an expanded wartime lottery pool for three years.

Version B's cancellation of all outstanding deferments would greatly expand the lottery pool for one year. A composite deferment system thus provides a larger wartime lottery pool without causing peacetime officer recruiting problems. Random selection will pick an increasing number of college graduates, many of whom would want to opt for officer status. Furthermore, the growth of college graduates relative to wartime officer requirements, in conjunction with the equal probability lottery, would offer an opportunity to increase peacetime ROTC enrollment[39] as graduates perceive that being drafted in wartime forecloses the officer option and increases their probability of serving in the ground combat arms in an enlisted status. Wartime deferment suspensions will not cause subsequent lapses in officer recruitment as long as (1) ROTC is retained and (2) officers are required to complete their tours in order to provide time for the normal pipeline to partially refill.

Another advantage of composite deferment would be an increase in intergenerational equity caused by older cohorts' sharing the wartime burden with the prime-age cohort. More important, wide class participation and its associated decision making benefits would be enhanced as the wealthier classes bore disproportionately high draft rates and were channeled into the expanding ground combat arms during periods of hostility.[40] While this would not ensure proportionate class burdens, the higher rates would be a big step in that direction.[41]

Part II:
The Economics and
Costing Procedures of
Military Manpower

4   Costing Military Manpower

Because military manpower is an institutional complex consuming about half the defense budget and 3% of the GNP, it should be subjected to searching analysis. Unfortunately, most studies have been very narrowly focused. Military manpower's well-advertised difficulties indicate a considerable rate of inefficiency; potential savings are very large indeed.

The big savings lie outside the competence of most economic and systems analysis studies, which focus on obtaining desirable first-order conditions of efficiency. The big payoffs are in using the full range of economic analysis to appraise the assumptions and the structure underlying the military's compensation system and its manpower policies in general. The analysis of military compensation in Chapter 5 indicates that the major problem is structural and the minor problem, inadequate wage differentials. Military compensation is expensive but fares poorly in terms of such criteria as attraction, retention, satisfaction, and its suitability for weeding out ineffective personnel. Another major payoff—not analyzed here or elsewhere—would result from revising personnel policies. These policies are premised upon a now dated nation-in-arms mobilization strategy[1] and detract from forces-in-being necessary for the strategies of deterrence and graduated response.

The purpose of this chapter is to list the procedures, formulas, and supporting data necessary to cost military manpower under varying conditions. These procedures cut through the institutional maze which may otherwise cause significant costing errors. Rather than reproduce the argument developed in detail in the appendixes of the following chapters on compensation and budget cost, this chapter will only summarize these procedures for reference. The exception is the methodology for costing a military billet space, which was not integral to Chapters 5 and 6.

Costing Military Compensation

The complexity of military compensation is indicated by Table 5-2, which shows that military compensation is composed of 25 elements, the first 18 of which are independent of the military's special job-related risks and characteristics.

Pay has often erroneously been considered to be only basic pay, which is 47.4% (column 5) of "Items Comparable to Civilian Compensation." In more recent years, DoD has popularized the term "total income," or salary which includes basic pay, quarters, subsistence, and the tax advantage on the last two items. Even so, this term represents only 69.3% of aggregate emoluments.

Retirement

A major policy issue of current concern, because of its increasingly large cost, is military retirement. The reasons for this large cost are specified in Appendix 5-B.

Those who leave the military with less than 20 years' service get no retirement pay. For those eventually retiring, retirement is a very large element of their total compensation. Based on insurance practices, the budget accrual cost to the government typically runs 80 to 90% of basic pay for each year of service (Table 5-9). The detailed formulas and procedures for this calculation are shown in Appendix 5-D.

A final retirement issue is that DoD underestimates its budget accrual costs for retirement by approximately 53%. The reason is DoD's use of standard actuarial procedures, which do not project future increases in retirement benefits from higher wages, or from increases in the Consumer Price Index for those already retired. This calculation is specified in Appendix 5-D.

Individual Compensation

Table 5-2 gives the aggregate costs for the 25 compensation elements. Individual compensation can be developed from similar breakouts issued annually by the Office of the Assistant Secretary of Defense (Manpower and Reserve Affairs). These sheets list the average cost of each compensation element by rank. Finer detail according to family size or years of service for pay purposes is often available for many elements from supplementary data sheets. The correction to be made in developing costs from these sheets is retirement. These sheets normally allocate retirement costs by the probability of retirement. The correction is that indicated retirement costs need to be multiplied by $\frac{1}{.47}$ to account for the actuarial bias. A more accurate practice is to allocate retirement costs as a percentage of basic pay. If the individual does not reach 20 years of service, his retirement costs are zero; for those retiring, Figures 5-12, 5-13, and 5-14 can be used to multiply basic pay according to anticipated years of service and rank at retirement.

Individual Pay Comparability

A major recurring policy issue is military-civilian pay ratios. To develop pay comparability, the serviceman's compensation is calculated as above, except that only the first 18 elements should be counted as comparable with civilian compensation. The second step is to specify military promotion rates so that a pay profile by age can be developed. Civilian compensation by age and education can be obtained from census data. The section in Chapter 5 on "Graphic Display of Military and Civilian Compensation" indicates the necessary procedures.

Aggregate Pay Comparability

By law, military compensation is now pegged to civil service compensation and civilian wage rates. A quick test for aggregate comparability can be made by summing individual (military and civilian) pay through the time profile. These procedures are developed in Appendix 5-E.

Pay Efficacy

The individual's valuation or perception of benefits received differs from the employer's cost. The ratio of value to cost is the relative efficiency of compensation. Perception can be measured through surveys. These perceptions are graphed in Figures 5-1 and 5-2; the calculations for relative efficiency are developed on p. 119.

Costing Voluntarism

Costing voluntarism is complex. Calculations are needed for four incremental costing components: accession, seniority, retirement, and training. Each has detailed intricacies.

Accession Costs

The intricate aspects of accession costs are calculating long-run (steady-state) demands for volunteers and minimizing the cost of indicated percentage wage increases. Supply projections and elasticity estimates are the remaining steps in accession costing.

Appendix 6-A lists the detailed formulas and procedures needed for projecting requirements. The first step is to determine officer and enlisted strengths for each service from the specified force level. Short-run or transitional demands can then be determined from published DoD Decrement Tables, which are theoretical manpower flows cleansed of such nuisance variables as wartime perturbations. For steady-state requirements, a new decrement table has to be developed, because voluntarism means a new manpower flow from higher reenlistment rates and from replacing draftees with volunteers. The Decrement Table is then massaged to yield a new years-of-service profile for each service. From this profile, a training correction is required, because training requirements are reduced if fewer annual accessions are needed to maintain a given force. If men in end-output operating units are assumed constant, the reduced training requirement can be translated into a total force and an additional accessions reduction.

The final step in calculating accession demands is placing demand on a similar basis with supply. Because of entry restrictions for mental-category-IV individuals, the supply curve is defined for only the top three mental categories. Since each service is required to take a specified percent of mental-category-IV personnel, this percent must be calculated and subtracted from the *larger* requirements figure (Table 6-3) before calculating the deficit.

Survey data indicating the percent of true volunteers among enlistees have been the key element in projecting supply. A time-series projection is then made for true volunteers at low pre-Vietnam wage levels (p. 180). The difference between demand and this supply projection is the accessions deficit. Supply is in terms of mental-category-I-III personnel.

The *percentage* wage increase is obtained by dividing the demand-supply deficit by the elasticity estimate. Considerable uncertainty surrounds these estimates, shown on p. 180, because of limited data and limited pay variation for entrants into military service prior to 1965. Fortunately, steady-state cost estimates for plausible force levels are not sensitive to wide variations in elasticity, for the reasons specified on p. 180.

Translating the necessary *percentage* wage increase into the required *absolute* increase and the *numbers* to receive increases is an essential—and generally neglected—task. Since resulting pay increases are in fully perceived cash, the wage base from which percentage increases are measured must be transformed into equivalent cash for comparability. In addition, the compensation-time stream must be discounted to a present value. The combined effect is the concept of Perceived Present Value (PPVm). The calculation for reducing the compensation time stream to PPVm is specified on pp. 181-182 and Appendix 6-B. The procedures for expanding PPVm wage increases into a time stream are indicated in Appendix 6-D.

The final steps in costing accessions are: determining who receives what absolute wage increase, and summing. Since the existing military wage profile is considerably steeper than in civilian practice, large percentage and absolute increases for first-term personnel do *not* translate into comparable wage increases for career personnel. Rather, the wage profile can be flattened by splicing in progressively smaller wage increases. The procedures for splicing in wage increases to prevent wage inversion (juniors receiving almost as much as seniors) and for summing these increases are specified in Appendix 6-D.

Seniority Costs

Substituting true volunteers for draftees and low-retention-propensity draft-induced volunteers causes a shift to an older, more experienced force. Correspondingly, personnel costs increase. This calculation is developed in Appendix 6-C.

Retirement Costs

Higher reenlistment rates mean higher retirement costs. Because retirement is budgeted on a past-services basis, increased retirement costs do not begin to appear in the budget until 20 years later, when the increased retirement flow begins. However, the proper criterion is a cost-of-doing-business, or accrual, basis. The procedures for this cost are given in Appendix 6-C.

Training Costs

The shift to an older force reduces the continual turnover of personnel through the training system. Assuming strengths in end-output units to be constant, reduced training requirements translate into reductions in force level and consequent manpower savings. This formula is also indicated in Appendix 6-C.

Costing Alternative Enlistment and Retention Policies

The preceding section on costing voluntarism assumed continuation of existing enlistment, retention, and retirement policies. Lengthening term of service before retirement yields only a small net saving; lower retirement and training costs are offset by higher average salaries. Lengthening initial enlistment tours and curtailing reenlistments, however, yield major savings. One such example and the procedures necessary for calculation are described in Appendix 6-F.

Costing a Military Duty Billet for Civilianization[2]

The value of military service is the services of a *billet*; hence, the relevant personnel cost is the total labor cost of a specified slot, or billet, which includes investment in human capital and other miscellaneous costs. In the civilian labor market, employer costs are generally considerably less. Consequently, the choice between civilian and military personnel is affected by these additional costs.

The first step in costing a military billet is to determine individual compensation (above), less proficiency pay and reenlistment bonuses, which vary according to the individual's military occupational specialty (termed MOS in the Army; AFSC, Air Force; and NEC, Navy). Proficiency pay is a flat rate to be added. Reenlistment bonuses require proration among the years contracted.

Training costs vary by occupational specialty and occur throughout the individual's military career. Initial training should be prorated for each year of expected service in "output" billets;[3] subsequent training, for the remaining expected output period. Initial training costs include recruiting costs, training costs, and movement to the first and last duty station. Subsequent training costs include movement costs from the training station to the next duty station.

A number of smaller costs have to be added because of military-civilian differences. (1) Civilians normally remain in one location; military personnel are constantly rotated. A movement cost prorated by tour length therefore has to be added to the military billet. (2) Another cost has to be added because subsistence allowances include only the raw cost of food. "Cook" add-ons can be found by sampling specific units for their cook percentages (as high as 3 1/2% for Army units) and then multiplying by the average cook cost. (3) Civilians pay for local schools through their taxes; for military personnel, the government either conducts free schooling or subsidizes local school districts for military dependents. This cost can be levied by average number of children for each rank E5 and above. (4) Military service entails non-DoD costs such as the GI Bill. This and other veterans costs can be prorated by expected years in a military output billet. (5) Finally, if the choice is between U.S. and foreign personnel, differential tax returns to the U.S. Treasury are involved, as well as possible hardship (combat and R&R) pay for U.S. personnel.

5 Budget Costs and the Military Compensation System

The subject of this chapter—preliminary to the next chapter's budgetary estimates—is the relationship of military pay to the costing of a volunteer military. Military compensation in FY 72 consumed 35% of the military budget, or 2 1/2% of GNP. While not the only motivation for a military career, compensation is an important inducement to enlistment and the easiest to adjust. For simplicity, the estimated cost of attracting volunteers can be viewed as the product of four multiplicands: (1) the elasticity of supply; (2) the recruitment deficit; (3) the perceived wage base; and (4) the number to receive pay increases. The latter two are directly related to the military pay structure; yet they have been neglected by economists who have placed their emphasis on statistical estimates of supply elasticity. The result has been very large cost overestimates. Deriving multiple regression coefficients is a necessary step. Equally important are the three other multiplicands, which reflect manpower demands, the low efficacy and perception of military pay relative to government cost, and the military's very steep pay profile by years of service. If these factors are accounted for, voluntarism need not be prohibitively expensive; nor will its cost increase rapidly under adverse recruiting conditions.

The purpose of this chapter is to show why the existing pay structure allows large wage inducements to be concentrated during the first few years of service, when the increases are most effective for attraction, without creating wage inversion, where juniors receive as much (or almost as much) as seniors. The low estimates in the next chapter of incremental budget costs of only $2.1 to $2.5 billion a year result from taking advantage of this structure by recognizing its theoretical nature and the fact that military wage progression has become very much steeper than in civilian life. These estimates do not require changing the special characteristics of the military pay system. The power of such institutional analysis is demonstrated by the fact that the supply elasticity estimates (for the relevant ranges) corresponded with those in widely published studies whose budgetary means have been $4 to $8 billion.

A secondary purpose of this chapter is to show the low efficacy of the present compensation system. This has two policy aspects. First, if voluntarism is adopted, DoD needs to implement voluntarism by increasing its emoluments. This can be done efficiently and rather cheaply through visible cash increases; or it can become a "goodies" bag with expensive increases in fringe benefits, which enlistees do not often perceive or value and which would do little to attract or retain personnel. Second, if voluntarism became the vehicle for a fundamental restructuring of the pay system, voluntarism could mean *net budgetary savings* as compensation funds were allocated for greater attraction, retention, and satisfaction power.[1]

Overview

If the military did not have to compete in the civilian labor market, the existing system would have much to recommend itself in terms of minimizing military budget costs. During full mobilization, accessions can be obtained at low cost by drafting. In the past, service for the duration has solved the problem of retention and its feedback effect on training costs. For nation-in-arms conflicts, a system of base pay supplemented by (1) "each according to his needs" income-in-kind benefits and dependent allowances, (2) special pays to offset internal differences in risk of life, and (3) retirement accruals for only the cadre makes eminent sense. The system, including longevity pay, has also been cost-effective and equitable for slow-promotion, quasi-isolated, peacetime armies in non-affluent societies.

Unfortunately for the existing compensation system, the conditions for which it is suitable no longer exist. The possibility of nuclear war makes a nation-in-arms situation unlikely. Moreover, modern militaries require hetero-geneous military specialties, many of which are highly sophisticated and in high civilian demand. The social context is also one of widespread affluence. If the civilian pay structure approximated that of the military, where formal monetary wages are only about half of total compensation, the military's problem of attracting and retaining personnel would be largely solved. But civilian pay is less complex and more visible, and the military is only one of many groups competing for labor. Consequently, any attempt by the military to organize a pay system according to its own preferences is doomed to difficulties. Since World War II the most obvious difficulties have been a high turnover of skilled personnel, and the draft, which has been used as a crutch and has hindered thoughtful solutions.

Because it compensates in ways unlike those of the dominant civilian market, military pay is poorly understood and consequently has low attraction and retention power for its cost to the government. Even careerists are dissatisfied, though they actually receive compensation more costly than that of comparable civilians. These deficiencies result from traditional rationales that were formerly acceptable. Their continued use in an inappropriate context means unnecessary government cost and employee dissatisfaction. The deficiencies can be summar-ized as: (1) deferred pay in lieu of entry pay; (2) poorly perceived income-in-kind and contingent benefits in lieu of visible cash; and (3) standardized compensation in lieu of differentials for skills, burdens, and risks.[2]

The first factor—deferred pay substituted for entry pay—is perhaps the most important in a discussion of the cost of a volunteer military. Pay for recruits is far below comparable civilian wages; it is even below the federal minimum wage, which has some status as a social benchmark of minimum fairness. Moreover, until 1965, real pay for recruits continually decreased as inflation eroded a nominal salary that was raised by only $3 per month in 19 years! Concurrently, pay for careerists was continually increased, largely under the circular logic that military pay was inadequate, as evidenced by low retention rates and the need for the draft. The justification for increasing only careerist pay was succinctly stated by JCS Chairman Radford in 1955:

This is not an across-the-board pay proposal. With the size of the Armed Forces at nearly 3 million men, it would be unduly expensive to raise the pay of everyone by even a very modest percentage. Besides, this would result in a large expenditure of money on personnel who have no intention of remaining in the services a day beyond their obligated service period.

This bill is a selective pay increase proposal. It seeks to increase the incentives for career military service. It does this by offering initial pay increases at the expiration of the minimum obligated service period required of the inductee and the officer performing obligated service. There is also a significant increase over present pay levels at other key service points where the individual is faced with the decision of continuing in career military service. Thus, the expensively trained individual in whom the Government has a considerable investment, is offered a monetary inducement which is higher than would be possible by means of an across-the-board proposal.[3]

This pay policy was intended to increase attraction and retention of personnel and, of course, to increase career salaries, which were lagging behind civilian compensation. In reality the policy may have been counterproductive. Though elaborate justifications were developed in congressional hearings and public discussion as to the efficacy of career pay for attracting recruits, such a policy ignores the well-known economic phenomenon of high "time-preference" rates for youths. That is, after discounting to present values, wage increases for senior careerists (and deferred pay in general) have only slight attraction and moderate initial retention power. "Significant" increases at "other key service points" are unnecessary and largely economic rent because of career commitment and the attraction of retirement benefits after 20 years' service.

The policy was counterproductive because of the draft and the selection process used to assign the best enlistees to the expensively trained, skilled, occupational specialties. Draft pressure and other personnel policies were inducing many non-career-motivated enlistments. Particularly since the draft-induced volunteers tended to be better educated and possess higher AFQT scores, low-career-propensity enlistees were displacing higher-career-propensity recruits in the critical skilled specialties. This procedure ensured a higher-quality student in the training programs, but it did little to increase productivity, because of the learning process during the relatively short utilization period[4] and the consequent high turnover. This undesirable situation is an interesting example of interaction between the Congress and the military resulting from myopic economies that fail to allow for long-run behavior adjustments.

The second factor—poor perception or low visibility of benefits—accounts for the dissatisfaction of careerists with military compensation (and hence efficacy in relation to its cost to the government). Visibility raises two crucial points: (1) in costing voluntarism, since pay increases are in fully perceived cash, the wage base from which percentage increases are measured must be transformed into equivalent cash for comparability; and (2) cash wages cost the government less than deferred or in-kind benefits. The first is important only for costing voluntarism; the second holds true regardless of the recruiting system, and means converting in-kind benefits into visible cash whenever possible and substituting immediate for deferred compensation. Reducing the proportion of in-kind benefits means more equal pay for equal work, thus reducing the military's unintentional discrimination against single men—a carryover from the "each according to his needs" philosophy of pay supplements. Removing this discriminatory practice simultaneously reduces the military's relative attractiveness to men with large families.[5] A corollary to paying cash in lieu of in-kind benefits is a continual provision of these services but in a rational *benefit* pricing system for these expensive and presently unrationed in-kind emoluments.

The third factor—inadequate compensation for skill differentials—has received disproportionate attention in analyses of military pay. For costing voluntarism, it is only important if the system is restructured. Though all three factors are in the economist's domain, economists have focused on differential pay because of its ready analogy to the competitive model of the civilian labor market. The model's basic recommendation is that military wages should be discriminating and proportioned to the marginal products of the various military specialties. Given the assumptions of the competitive model, a compensation system can be structured to maximize attraction and retention for its cost to the government; a byproduct is efficient manpower utilization and resource allocation to eliminate the military's incentive for labor intensity and its own performance of many support functions rather than civilian performance because of its underpriced labor. Though the model produces results which in general move in the right direction, the competitive model is no panacea and embodies a number of analytical flaws. The difficulties of the maximizing and comparability models for increasing attraction and retention are specified in Appendix 5-A. The inadequacy of price theory for optimizing behavior in large bureaucratic organizations is another problem, presented in Chapter 2.

System Description

The military pay system is complex and composed of some 25 elements. Table 5-2 displays these elements, their relative size, and their comparison with the civilian sector. Of the 25 elements, only the 17 under I are considered compensation for the purposes of this study. The remaining eight under II are job-related compensatory items associated with the military's special disutilities and cost of doing business. Column 2 shows each item's budget cost in FY 1968. Columns 3, 4, and 5 indicate percentage relationships. Columns 6 and 7 indicate civilian percentages for similar benefits, shown in Table 5-1. The three broad characteristics shown by Table 5-2 are (1) the relatively small amount paid in cash (basic pay, IA); (2) the almost insignificant pay for skill differentials (IB); and (3) the very large amount for retirement (ID).

Basic pay is the item commonly thought of as military salary, and is the item frequently used for comparison with civilian earnings. Other items tend to be labeled fringe benefits; they are difficult to compare and frequently and erroneously assumed to be roughly equivalent to civilian benefits. Since only 47.4% of total military compensation (column 5) versus 87.9% of civilian compensation (column 6) is received in cash, military compensation is relatively less visible and hence often compares unfavorably with civilian earnings. Moreover, the less visible elements loom larger where they least should: junior personnel receive a higher percentage of noncash benefits than their seniors.

These noncash benefits can be characterized as contingent, deferred, and income-in-kind benefits. Contingency can imply economic or market discrimination and hence reduced economic rent. Unfortunately, only 1.2% of total military compensation is economically discriminating (i.e., differential pays); another 2.6% under II discriminates by risk (i.e., risk and hazardous duty pays and SGLI). Economic theory suggests minimizing the remainder: namely the 22.2% going to retirement benefits, the 13.9% disproportionately associated with dependency,[6] and the virtually invisible 3.6% tax advantage (resulting from nontaxable quarters and subsistence allowances). The latter two have no market analogues.[7]

Table 5-1
Cost of Employee Benefits in Addition to Pay as a Percentage of Gross Payroll

1. Legally Required Payments	5.80
2. Payments Based on Time Worked:	
Pension and Deferred Profit-Sharing Plans	2.30
Supplemental Unemployment Benefits	.07
Separation or Termination Pay Allowances	.10
Profit-Sharing Plans	.70
Christmas and Other Informal Bonuses	.40
3. Other Benefits	
Life and Medical Insurance	2.55
Employee Discounts, Meals, and Education	.20
Total	12.12

Source: 1965 Defense Department Congressional Briefing Book.[a]

[a]U.S. Bureau of the Census, *1969 Statistical Abstract,* "Employee Compensation in the Private Nonfarm Economy 1966," No. 338, estimates employer expenditures in addition to payroll as 10.1%.

Table 5-2
Items and Percentage Relationships of Military Compensation (1967)

(1) Item	(2) Cost to Government	(3) As Percent of Basic Pay	(4) As Percent of Salary	(5) As Percent of Military Pay Items[1]	(6) As Percent of Civilian Gross	(7) As Percent of Civilian Pay
I. Military Pay Items Comparable to Civilian Compensation	24,104.7	210.9	144.3	100	100	113.8
A. Salary	16,707.0	146.1	100	69.3	87.9	100
Basic Pay	11,431.9	100	68.4	47.4	87.9	100
Quarters	2,663.7	23.3	15.9	11.1		
Subsistence	1,750.4	15.3	10.5	7.3		
Tax Advantage	861.0	7.5	5.2	3.6		
B. Cash Supplements	463.1	4.1	2.8	1.9		
Normal Reenlistment Bonus	178.5	1.6	1.1	.7		
Differential Pays	284.6	2.5	1.7	1.2		
Variable Reenlistment Bonus	94.2	.8	.6	.4		
Proficiency Pay	147.9	1.3	.9	.6		
Special Pay to Medical Personnel	42.5	.4	.3	.2		
C. Fringe Benefits, Excluding Retirement	1,576.6	13.8	9.4	6.5	9.8	11.2
Dependents' Indemnity Compensation	130.5	1.1	.8	.5		
Death Gratuity	34.1	.3	.2	.1		
Social Security	469.3	4.1	2.8	1.9		
Medical Care[1]	441.0	3.9	2.6	1.8		
Commissary & Exchange[1]	110.2	1.0	.7	.5		
Mortgage Insurance	5.4	.0	.0	.0		
Unemployment Compensation	29.6	.3	.2	.1		
Separation Pays	356.5	3.1	2.1	1.5		
D. Retirement, Current Year Accrual	5,358 [2]	46.9	32.1	22.2	2.3	2.6

II. Non-Compensation Items of Military Pay
   Associated With Special Job-Related Risks
   and Characteristics

and Characteristics	1,424.9	12.5	8.5	5.9
Risk and Hazardous Duty Pays	550.8	4.8	3.3	2.3
SGLI (extra hazard premium)	80.2	.7	.5	.3
Clothing Issues & Allowances	445.9	3.9	2.7	1.8
Personal Money Allowance	0.2	.0	.0	.0
Family Separation Allowance	128.2	1.1	.8	.5
Dislocation Allowance	66.7	.6	.4	.3
Overseas Station Allowance	142.9	1.3	.9	.6
Burial Costs	10.0	.1	.1	.0

Source: *Modernizing Military Pay* (Hubbell Report), DoD, Vol. I, p. 39, November 1967, GPO.

[1] These costs are underestimated by the exclusion of land and capital costs. Recreation is another minor fringe benefit that has been excluded from the table.

[2] The official DoD accrual cost was $2,502.2 million; but this figure underestimates true accrual costs by 53%; corresponding budget disbursement cost was $2,093.5 million.

The 22.2% allocated to retirement is contingent and deferred. The comparable civilian percentage is only 2.3! However, these percentages are noncomparable and the contrast is even starker. Military retirement is nonvested; hence, only the 9.5% who eventually retire receive this benefit.[8] In effect, noncareerists are subsidizing careerists through labor turnover. This phenomenon "washes out" for the 2.3% civilian statistic, since it is an aggregate and not a single "firm" statistic.

The 13.9% associated with dependency is partially contingent and in kind; a small portion is also deferred insurance. In addition, because dependency benefits are correlated with years of service and rank, dependency benefits are more valuable to older than younger personnel. For instance, in 1964, only 17% of EMs in the ranks of E1-E3 had dependents versus 74% for EMs in the ranks E4-E9; the corresponding dependency averages were .31 and 2.36 respectively.[9] Formally, all personnel receive or are eligible for most of these benefits. The distinctions are: (1) married personnel receive larger allowances; (2) married personnel often have an in-cash option and unmarried personnel do not;[10] and (3) benefit size often depends on dependency per se and the number of dependents.

Two other low-visibility compensation items accounting for 7.3 and 3.6% of total compensation are the subsistence allowance and the tax advantage. Schemes such as the Hubbell proposals to include these items explicitly in salary increase their visibility to a full 10.9%. Subsistence for unmarried EMs is a noncash, income-in-kind benefit; for officers and married EMs, a cash benefit. Yet the empirical evidence shows low valuations for both groups. This indicates that the cash allowance is either perceived as a fringe benefit or as a traditional "due" and not a part of salary to be compared with civilian salary. Two characteristics of the tax advantage are its regressiveness and its relative advantage to married personnel. The tax advantage varies from zero for married recruits to 8-11% of total salary for senior generals.[11] The reason is that though senior personnel receive a smaller percentage of their total salary in tax-free benefits, the income tax schedule is progressive. On a nominal accounting basis, the tax advantage appears more valuable to single than to married men, again because of the tax schedule. The crucial caveat, however, is that the total size of the tax-free benefits partly depends on dependency.

A final compensation characteristic is the small 1.2% and 2.6% allocated to compensate for differences in skills and risks/burdens, respectively. Several features of differential pay as practiced are worth noting. First, the effectiveness of proficiency pay (.6% of total compensation) is sometimes attenuated by the individual's uncertainty as to whether he will continue to draw the pay or be shifted to another occupational specialty without a premium. Second, along with the .7% going to the regular reenlistment bonus, differential pay can be called incentive pay, since its purpose is to induce *higher* retention rates at *minimum* cost. This purpose is not being served when (1) reenlistment bonuses are given after the first reenlistment decision, and (2) premium pays rise with rank, as in medical and flight pay. (Due to high time-preference rates, the cost-effective approach would be for premiums to be inversely related to rank or years of service.) Third, differential pay is sometimes offset by slow promotion rates. The Air Force has more men in the skilled occupational areas than the Army and accordingly receives more of the differential pays; however, promotions are so much slower in the Air Force than in the Army that Air Force first-termers average 15% less in *basic pay* and men in the 4 to 7 years of service average 8% less.[12] A fourth form of differential pay, which is difficult to identify, is the faster rate of promotion for the more proficient in a specialty.

The percentages shown in columns 3 and 4 are useful for the comparisons in the next section between military and civilian wage *progression* and wage *levels*. Column 3 shows that when basic pay is used as the index, another 110.9% is accounted for by quarters and subsistence (38.6%), tax advantage (7.5%), cash supplements (4.1%), and what are commonly regarded as fringe benefits (59.5%). Column 4 is a similar comparison using military salary as the index. The point is that comparisons of military and civilian wages have to account for the differences in fringe benefits. Otherwise, arbitrary comparisons of only part of military compensation are made with almost the entirety of civilian compensation. Such biased comparisons are frequent with study groups on military compensation.

Visibility and Perceived Value

Because military compensation is largely composed of contingent, in-kind, and deferred benefits (52.6% versus 12.1% for the civilian sector), military compensation has a problem of relative invisibility. This phenomenon can be termed the problem of *perceived pay*—a theoretical construct describing the individual's subjective evaluation of his compensation benefits. The low visibility and perception of military compensation is shown in Tables 5-3 and 5-4. Table 5-3

Table 5-3
Commercial Credit Firms' Perception of Hubbell Salary

Pay Grade	Basic Pay, Quarters, Subsistence & Tax Advantage	"Salary" Recognized by Credit Firms	Percent of Column One Recognized
E3	$ 3,014	$ 1,462	48.5%
E7	8,081	7,013	86.8
01	6,006	4,249	70.7
06	18,006	17,214	95.6

Source: *Modernizing Military Pay,* p. 38.

Table 5-4
Military Member's Perception of Total Military Compensation

	(1) Perception as Percent of only Basic Pay, Quarters & Subsistence Allowances, and Tax-Advantage	(2) Basic Pay as Percentage of Column 1's Cost	(3) Perception as Percent of all Compensation Costs, Including Retirement
Officers[a]			
4 Years' Service	76	74	–
10 Years' Service	87	77	48
20 Years' Service	90	80	50
Enlisted[a]			
4 Years' Service	76	63	–
10 Years' Service	91	67	51
20 Years' Service	115	73	63
Unmarried Enlistees[b]			
True Volunteers	72	50	65[c]
Draft-Induced Volunteers	68	50	61
Draftees	70	50	62

Sources:

[a]*Modernizing Military Pay,* p. 37.

[b]Rand Survey of Los Angeles Armed Forces Entrance & Examination Station. Questions asked concerned the individual's dollar valuation of eating in the mess hall, barracks sleeping space, retirement, lower prices in the PX/commissary, medical/dental services, and the tax advantage on his in-kind benefits. While not all-inclusive, the list does account for almost all the individually valued items.

[c]Retirement costs allocated on a constant probabilistic basis.

shows that commercial credit firms recognize only a fraction of military salary as pay and that salary itself represents only two-thirds of total military compensation. The percentages are particularly low for younger personnel, whom the government desires to attract to a military career. The problem for a credit firm is that younger personnel tend to be unmarried, and a large percentage of their total compensation is in in-kind benefits which cannot be attached. Another implication is that civilian credit firms do not recognize the rationalized concept of "residual pay," which has been used, speciously, to justify low pay for service entrants.[13]

Table 5-4 shows perception of total military compensation by officers, enlisted men, and unmarried prospective enlistees. That all groups view their pay as mainly basic pay can be seen by the close relationship between perception and the unambiguously visible basic pay component. This is particularly surprising, since most officers and enlisted men with more than four years of service receive most dependency allowances in cash and a large retirement benefit. This means that:

1. the various contingent, in-kind, and deferred benefits receive low valuation;
2. many military personnel seem to consider certain benefits their "due" because of the military's special job-related characteristics (this argument has some validity and accounted for the exclusion of an equivalent 5.9% of total compensation in Table 5-2); and
3. military personnel mistakenly believe that housing, subsistence, etc., are fringe benefits and that their total fringe benefits are equivalent to those of the civilian sector.

Four other points of interest in Table 5-4 are: (1) on a total-cost basis, career officers subjectively value their compensation at half its cost to the government; (2) enlisted men value their pay more highly than officers; (3) fringe benefits are more highly valued as retirement approaches; and (4) unmarried recruit perceptions correspond to those of active service members. Entrants' showing so high relative to four-year men in column 1 is probably due to the Rand survey requiring explicit valuation of the major fringe benefits. In column 3, entrants show high because of this explicit valuation in the numerator and low retirement costs in the denominator.

Tables 5-3 and 5-4 show that military pay is imperfectly perceived and therefore inefficient in satisfying careerists or in attracting potential careerists. Its relevance for costing is that perceived pay is a multiplicand in estimating necessary pay increases for voluntarism or for higher retention rates.[14] Statistically, perceived pay need not be included in the regression equation estimating wage elasticity; but for interpreting and costing the results, the relevant wage base is perceived pay.[15] That is, percentage changes can be measured from any number of wage bases; but for costing, these wage bases must be converted into the same structural form as the pay increase. Specifically, if a pay increase is to be given in fully perceived cash, the wage base must also be transformed to a fully-perceived basis.

As implied by the notion of perceived pay, cost to the government is not identical to value to the individual, although every pay study (except Hubbell's) has treated the items as if they were the same thing. The reasons why perceived pay is so much lower than attributed government costs are (1) restricted choice on many in-kind and deferred benefits; (2) some benefit costs not jointly attributed to the government and the individual; (3) discounting of deferred pays by high individual time-preference rates; (4) imperfect information about many of the benefits; and (5) uncertainty of collection. The ratio of perceived value to cost can be used as an index of pay efficiency. By this criterion, civilian pay efficiency is ≥ 87.8% (civilian pay divided by gross civilian payroll); military pay efficiency is variable but averages 50-60% for careerists and slightly more for noncareerists who receive no retirement benefit. Income-in-kind benefits lead to low perception through the fringe benefit analogy and restricted choice. Harry Gilman has explained the latter:

A pay package that has many unrationed income-in-kind items of pay may be expected to have a lower value on the average than one that consists entirely of an equal amount of cash. This is true because the former package controls, *in part*, the individual's pattern of consumption. Cash, on the other hand, may be spent by the individual on the goods and services he most prefers. Consequently, in order for the two pay packages to be equally attractive, the one with the income-in-kind components would almost certainly have to be more costly to the Government than would payment in cash.[16]

In-kind benefits prevent the consumer from maximizing his satisfaction by moving along his budget line to higher indifference curves; conversely, free choice would permit servicemen equal satisfaction at less government cost. This does not mean, however, that the government should convert all in-kind benefits into cash. An operating military requires conformity to certain practices and consumption of specific in-kind benefits. For example, barracks provide the essentials of shelter to the individual (although he might prefer to live elsewhere), while maximizing troop response at a low cost. Other examples are the government's legitimate interest in the balanced diet and health of its troops. Such examples indicate that joint preferences need to be satisfied and that the costs should be *jointly* attributed to the individual and to the government as a cost of doing business. Whether income-in-kind benefits are analyzed from the value or cost perspectives, their costs should not be fully attributed to the individual.

The low perception of deferred pays can be readily explained by low present value. A dollar discounted 10 to 20 years at time-preference rates of 20 to 28% is worth only a few pennies in present value and has virtually no attraction power.[17] This implies that arguments justifying major pay increases for careerists only, under the guise of attracting and retaining young men, are specious. Retirement benefits, of course, are even less efficient.[18] Table 5-5 shows discount rates for various ages and categories of Air Force Personnel (5-5a) and for high-skill Navy first-termers (5-5b). The tables conform to a priori expectations as rates diminish with age, education, and sums involved. For young men (17 to 24) in their initial tour, both tables show similar discount rates of 20 to 28%.

High individual time-preference rates, collection uncertainty, and restricted choice suggest that retirement benefits and steep wage profiles are not effective in attracting and retaining young men. The single exception is the "star" phenomenon, whereby a few at the top are paid high wages to attract the most gifted, as well as to serve as a beacon for the many who will never make the top. Yet the pay policy since 1955[19] has been increasingly steeper wage profiles and retirement benefits increasing approximately 50% faster than military salary because retirement benefits are a function of the CPI and basic pay.

Contingency is another factor reducing perceived pay; 36.7% of compensa-

Table 5-5
Time-Preference Rates

Table 5-5a
Median Annual Interest Rate Used by Air Force Personnel in Discounting Future Payments (1953 Air Force Survey)

Age Group	Officers	Enlisted	Total
19 and under	·	28.3%	28.3%
20-24	8.9%	20.2%	19.2%
25-29	8.9%	18.3%	14.0%
30-34	7.5%	11.5%	9.4%
35-39	6.3%	11.1%[a]	8.9%
40-44	6.5%		7.4%
45-49	6.7%		8.5%
50 and over	6.7%		10.6%

[a]Ages 35 and over.

Source: R.L. Chaney, "Discounting by Military Personnel by Various Ages."

Table 5-5b
Relative Preference of Navy Enlisted Men in Last Two Years of First Enlistment for Reenlistment Bonus in an Immediate Lump Sum Payment or in Monthly Installments over a Four-Year Period (by Median Interest Rate)[b]

Group	Minimum Preference in Monthly Payments to $800 Lump Sum	Minimum in Monthly Payments to $1600 Lump Sum
All	23.0%	16.8%
By Reenlistment Intentions		
Plan to Reenlist	31.0%	19.6%
Do not Plan to Reenlist	23.0%	16.8%
Undecided	19.0%	15.4%
By Family Status		
No Dependents	23.0%	15.4%
Dependents	23.0%	18.2%
By Year of Service		
3rd year	26.0%	16.8%
4th year	20.0%	16.8%

[b]Survey was limited to the high skill ratings of electronics equipment maintenance and electronics equipment operation.

Source: DoD OASD (M) *Defense Study of Military Compensation,* Washington, D.C., 5 October 1962.

tion is contingent in some way upon dependency, retirement, or proficiency pay. Contingency connotes an element of uncertainty; it therefore implies a probability distribution ($p \leqslant 1$) that reduces the valuation of benefits, many of which are further diminished by their in-kind and deferred nature. The argument for contingent benefits is that a given wage fund can be disbursed more discriminately and hence more effectively. But if the discriminatory criterion is noneconomic, perversions can occur. For military compensation, only 1.9% of total compensation (plus 2.6% for risk) is based on economic discrimination to induce higher retention rates or to distinguish skill differentials. Discriminatory payments based on dependency rationales have the undesirable attribute of attracting and retaining men likely to have large families. On their account the services incur greater expenses because of, for example, an intensified demand for medical care, larger change-of-station costs, and larger dependent enclaves abroad. Thus, while discriminatory benefits based on an economic criterion reduce economic rent and promote efficiency, discriminatory practices based on "to each according to his needs" do not address these topics and increase government cost by favoring family men. This conclusion would not be valid only (1) if the private economy had a similar compensation ("to each according to needs") policy, in which case the military policy would be neutralized; and (2) during wartime, when older family men are also required and volition is not a factor.

Because of the complexity of military compensation, imperfect knowledge also partially explains the individual's low perception of military pay. For instance, prospective entrants and even many service members are unaware of the tax advantage or find its calculation too difficult. Another slippage is that the tax advantage is based on poorly perceived benefits. An educational campaign could increase perceived pay and pay efficiency without restructuring military compensation. However, while imperfect knowledge is undoubtedly a factor, particularly among younger men, the problem of low perception even among long-term careerists is so general that more seems to be involved than this factor alone. The most effective solution to the problem of imperfect knowledge will also help solve that of low perception: a larger cash salary in lieu of the many income-in-kind, contingent, and deferred benefits. An educational campaign has a low probability of success; in any case, it would be desirable only if the present system were considered preferable to proposals to restructure compensation.

A final possible factor—somewhat akin to imperfect knowledge—in the problem of low perception is that income-in-kind benefits have become traditionally associated with military life and have evolved into inherent "rights" or "just dues." The solution is, again, a larger cash salary.

Graphic Display of Military and Civilian Compensation

Figures 5-1 through 5-7 compare military and civilian wage levels according to age and education. For purposes of comparison all enlisted men are assumed to have completed high school; all officers, 4 years or more of college. *Civilian pay* is defined as the mean earnings of high-school and college graduates, as taken from the 1960 census and corrected for changes in weekly earnings for a constant workweek from 1959 to 1968.[20] *Gross civilian payroll* is civilian pay plus 12.12% to account for civilian fringe benefits (column 7, Table 5-2). Among military careerists, the *median officer* is a lieutenant colonel retiring after 22 years' service; the median enlisted man is an E7 retiring after 20 years' service.[21] This distinction implies a specified rate of promotion and government annuity contribution.

Military basic pay is the cash salary all military personnel receive. *Military salary* is defined as the cash equivalent of basic pay, quarters and subsistence allowances, and the tax advantage. Only married personnel now receive these allowances in cash or in the even more advantageous form of subsidized on-post family housing. *Gross military pay* includes all cash and fringe benefits, as measured by cost to the government. The differences between the median individual's salary and gross pay (column 4, Table 5-2) are the additional 2.8% of salary from cash supplements, the 9.4% from fringe benefits, and a very large 63.9% of salary (adjusted for turnover) that the government implicitly contributes to a retirement fund for a lieutenant colonel who will retire after 22 years' service (the comparable contribution for an E7 with 20 years' service is 63.1% of salary). Finally, *perceived pay* is the recipient's subjective valuation of his gross military pay at each point in time as determined by survey data.

The limitation of the comparison between civilian and military wages below is that in general it overstates the civilian-military pay ratio; that is, corrected for similar populations and other effects, military pay looks even more attractive in comparison with civilian pay than Figures 5-1 and 5-2 indicate. The first and most obvious reason is that the comparisons assume that all officers are college graduates and all enlisted men are high-school graduates. In point of fact, in the pre-Vietnam force only 72.3% of officers were college graduates and only 81.6% of enlisted men were high-school graduates.[22] Second is the relative quality of military and non-military personnel among noncollege and college graduates. The draft and high mental acceptance standards have ensured an abnormally high quality of enlisted accessions, particularly enlistees. Rapid promotion (hence pay and prestige) in the enlisted ranks for good performance has also induced some of the better personnel to remain in the service, even though initially these men may have had a low career-propensity. A result of unsatisfactory overall retention rates has been command pressure on unit commanders to show higher reenlistment rates; this implies low selectivity, which adversely affects the quality of the NCO corps. Military sources have indicated in the past that virtually all applications for extended duty have been accepted.[23]

The draft has had less effect on officers. Graduate-school deferments pyramiding into occupational deferments and dependency exemptions have permitted many of the brighter college graduates to avoid service.[24] Furthermore, differential rates of promotion based on performance do not exist for junior officers until the rank of major, so that better officers do not receive differential enticements to offset their differential civilian opportunities. Another qualitative indicator is the casual observation that ROTC enrollment and academic prestige of the institution are inversely related. Third, and even more serious, is the opting-out problem after the initial tour of service, for many are draft-induced.

A fourth limitation derives from the nature of the census data. The census surveys to some extent underestimate earnings "because of the tendency to forget minor or irregular sources of income."[25] On the other hand, moonlighting by military personnel was completely excluded in these comparisons. Available statistics indicate that 20.1% of stateside enlisted personnel moonlight during a month versus 4.6% for civilians.[26]

Three biases of census data make military pay *appear* less favorable. (1) The census data cover "money earnings only" and exclude in-kind benefits, a factor mainly relevant for farm and certain service workers who are generally not college or high-school graduates. (2) The military earnings are for fully employed men, whereas civilian earnings are weighted down by the unemployed and part-time employed. Some military men object to comparisons of fully employed military men with partially employed civilians. However, the fact is that civilian earnings are less because of unemployment. Moreover, excluded from the income comparisons is the fact that military men have greater economic security and therefore suffer less from the debilitating psychic effects of unemployment. Finally, the comparisons would not be significantly changed by placing civilian earnings on a fully employed basis because of the low unemployment rates of older, largely family men. (3) The hours worked are different. The typical civilian workweek is slightly over 40 hours. The military workweek for both officers and enlisted men is considerably longer and only partially offset by more liberal vacation policies. One can argue that much of the overtime is "makework," or is not socially useful. However, this is an anti-system argument: the individual has no option. In any case, this serious distortion has been excluded for lack of data.

A final consideration is that census data cover individuals, not families. The earnings potential of military wives is reduced through frequent moves and concentrated oversupply near military bases, which are often remote.[27]

Figure 5-1 compares the earnings profile of the representative lieutenant colonel and the average civilian with four or more years of college. The dotted line represents civilian pay; the dashed line represents civilian pay plus fringe benefits. The other lines represent military pay. The bottom broken line represents the basic pay the typical officer receives (at 1968 wage scales) as he progresses from second lieutenant to his retirement rank of lieutenant colonel. The military salary line is basic pay plus quarters and subsistence allowances and the tax advantage. The three gross salary lines represent military salary plus fringe benefits, including retirement, which has been calculated at three different

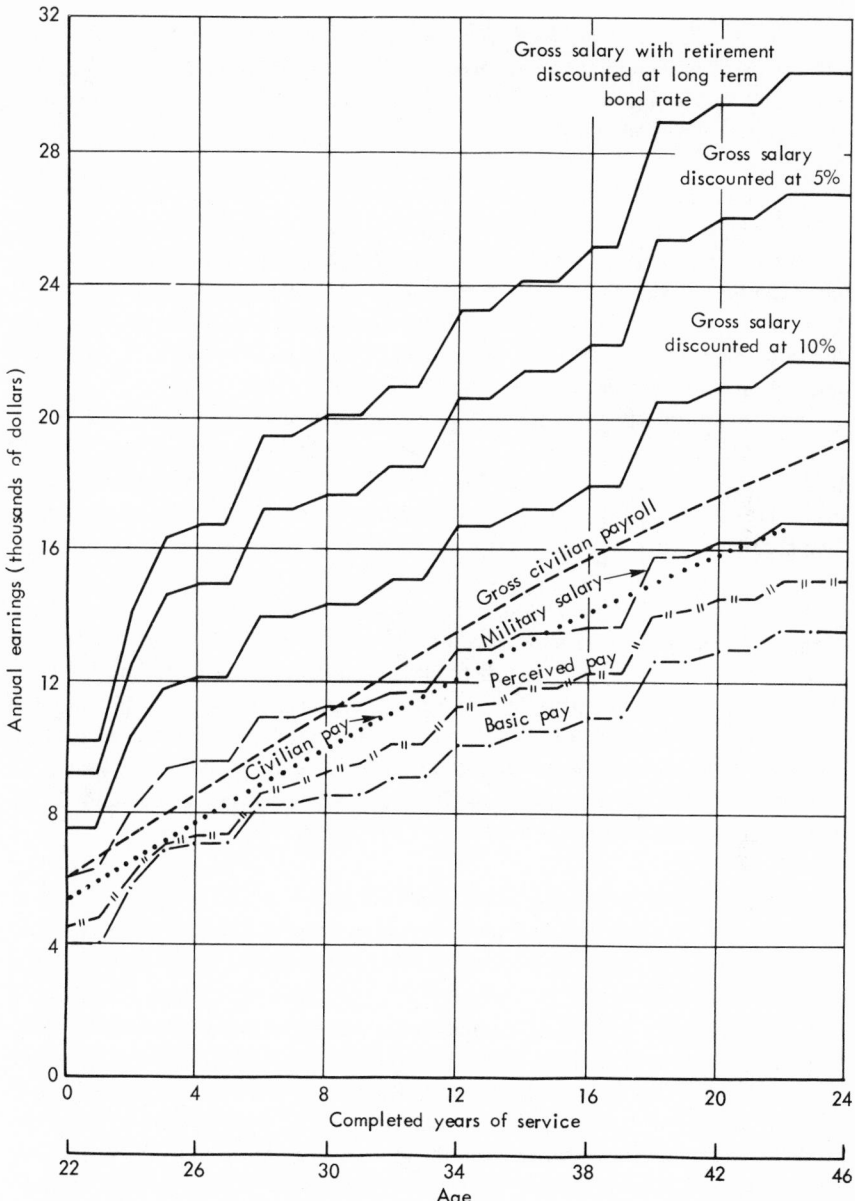

Figure 5-1. Mean College Graduate Earnings Profile Versus Representative Military Career Officer (1968).

interest rates. For calculating actual government costs, the correct comparison is the top line, with computations based on the long-term bond rate.[28] The line marked "Perceived pay" represents the typical officer's valuation of his total emoluments. The points of interest are:

The basic pay line is always below the civilian pay line; the percentage difference is particularly great for the entry years.

Military salary, defined as basic pay, quarters and subsistence allowances, and tax advantage, is almost always greater than mean college earnings.

When cash supplements and fringe and retirement benefits are included, gross military salary greatly exceeds mean civilian earnings for any of the plausible interest rates for accruing retirement contributions.

Most significant is that though officers gross considerably more than their civilian counterparts, their *perceived pay* is always less than civilian pay and even military salary. That is, in subjective valuation terms, as opposed to government cost, the officer consistently views himself as doing less well financially than civilians.[29]

Figure 5-2 is a similar comparison for the representative enlisted man. Because so many enlisted men are unmarried and only 9% of accessions become careerists, Figure 5-2 makes the distinction between the unmarried noncareerist and the married careerist. Figure 5-3 displays noncareerist compensation in more detail. The important point is that the gross pay for the typical recruit is about half that of the civilian for the first two years of service.

For representative enlisted careerists, the following similarities and differences as compared to officers exist:

1. Basic pay always remains below civilian pay.
2. Military salary is almost always less than mean high-school civilian earnings.
3. Gross military salary again greatly exceeds gross civilian pay.
4. Although military salary is generally lower than civilian pay, enlisted men perceive a progressively larger percentage of their total compensation as retirement approaches. That is, at the 4th year of service their subjective valuation of their total compensation package is considerably less than both military salary and civilian pay. By the 14th and 17th years respectively, the perceived pay line has crossed over the lines representing military salary and civilian pay. This is somewhat surprising; one would expect enlisted men to possess less knowledge and to value their fringe and retirement benefits less than officers. For an E7, these non-salary benefits were 2.8% of salary in cash supplements, 9.4% in fringe benefits, 63.1% in implicit government contribution to the retirement fund (versus 63.9% for the officer), and, excluded from the calculations, 8.5% in "non-compensatory" benefits associated with the military's job-related disutilities.

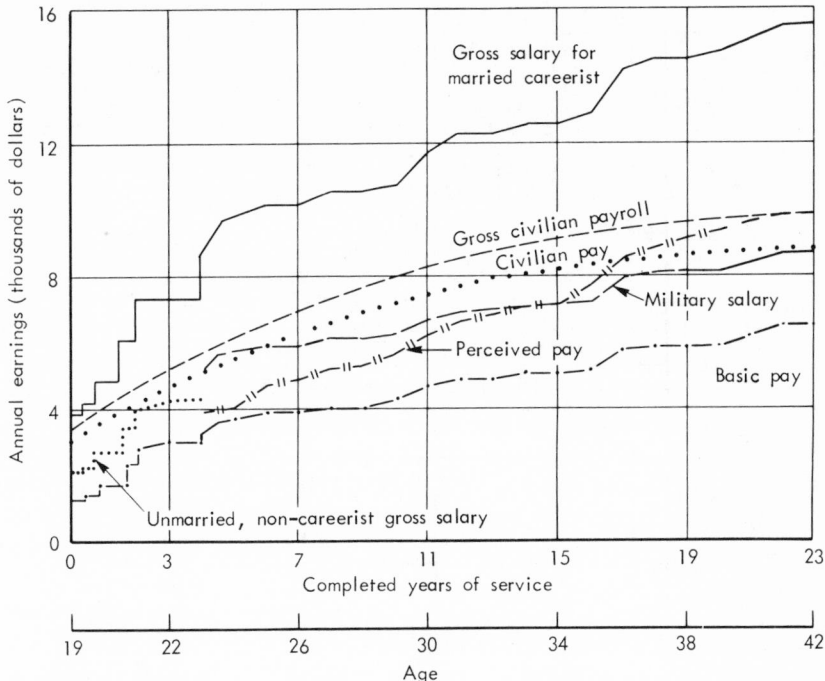

Figure 5-2. Mean High School Graduate Earnings Profile Versus Representative Typical Career EM (1968).

First-term enlistee compensation is compared with gross civilian payroll for comparable high-school graduates in Figure 5-3. Figure 5-3's distinctions are that (1) percentage costs are disaggregated and specifically delineated, and (2) retirement benefits are calculated on a probabilistic basis rather than on the dichotomous distinction of who does and does not retire and receive these nonvested benefits.[30] Its salient point is that unmarried enlistees—who are 90% of entrees and the very group the services desire to attract—earned on a government-cost basis for their 4 years of service considerably less than comparable civilians and even less than the federal minimum wage during the first 2 years. The few who were married averaged slightly more than the minimum wage but still less than comparable civilians. The 1967 minimum wage line shows what a large pay raise unmarried recruits would have had to receive between 1964 and 1967 just to achieve minimum wage standards. However, in the five-year period from 1964 to 1969, pay and allowances for recruits increased by only 22% (though the more visible base pay increased by 31%); civilian earnings meanwhile maintained their spread by rising 19%. (An impor-

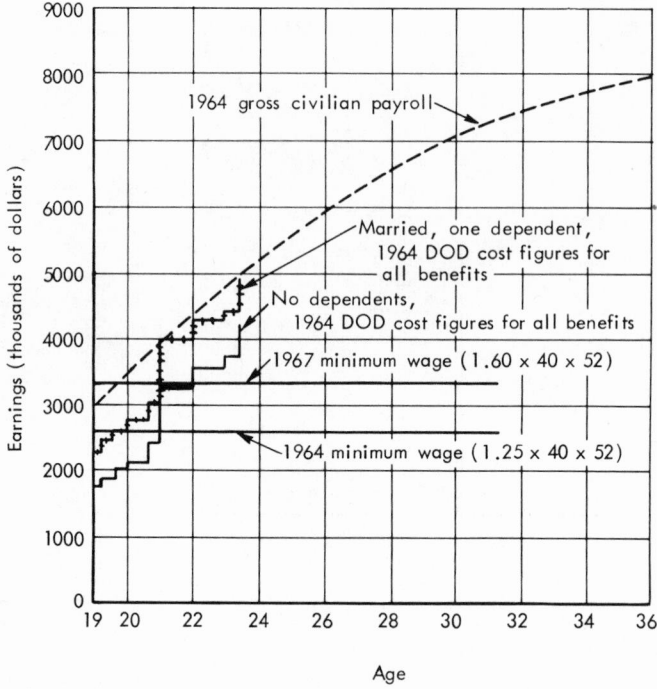

Figure 5-3. 1964 Gross Salary for First-Term Enlisted Men. Source: "Comparison of Military and Job Corps Compensation," *DOD Congressional Briefing Book*, April 1965.

tant caveat in Figure 5-3 is that comparisons are in terms of government cost, not the enlistee's subjective valuation.)

Figures 5-4 through 5-7 show the counterclockwise pivot around the entry wage of basic pay that has occurred since 1946.[31] Figures 5-4 and 5-6 graph monthly earnings as the typical serviceman progresses from his entry to his exit rank. Figures 5-5 and 5-7 are a semi-log graph of the same data to show earnings growth. The dotted line in all four graphs is the comparable civilian salary growth, for the reader's perspective. This trend is most pronounced for enlisted personnel. The five influences shaping this profile since the beginning of World War II have been:

1. The egalitarian increases of 1942 and 1946, in response to populist pressures that flattened the wage profile;
2. The military's feeling, after 1946 and extending up through the mid-fifties, that recent wage increases had adversely affected military incentives by primarily benefiting junior personnel;

3. The short-lived influence of the 1948 Hook Commission, which, operating in an all-volunteer context, advocated pay comparability at all levels, including recruits;

4. The 1956-57 Cordiner Committee recommendations, which reflected the then dominant military opinion as espoused by Admiral Radford. This has been the strongest influence up to 1964, and was only contained, not reversed, by the McNamara rationales afterwards. The argument was that pay increase from the "wages fund" should be concentrated on careerists for retention (and fairness); entrants need not be given increases, since draft pressure would maintain their flow, and fairness for entrants need not be considered, since they were merely fulfilling their military obligations and were receiving valuable training;

5. The McNamara rationale that military pay, as in the new civil-service practice, should be reviewed annually for comparability with civilian wages and quadrennially for more searching reappraisals.[32] This influence, combined with populist war pressures which favor short-termers, has caused a flattening for officers since 1964 and a slight flattening for enlisted men since 1965.

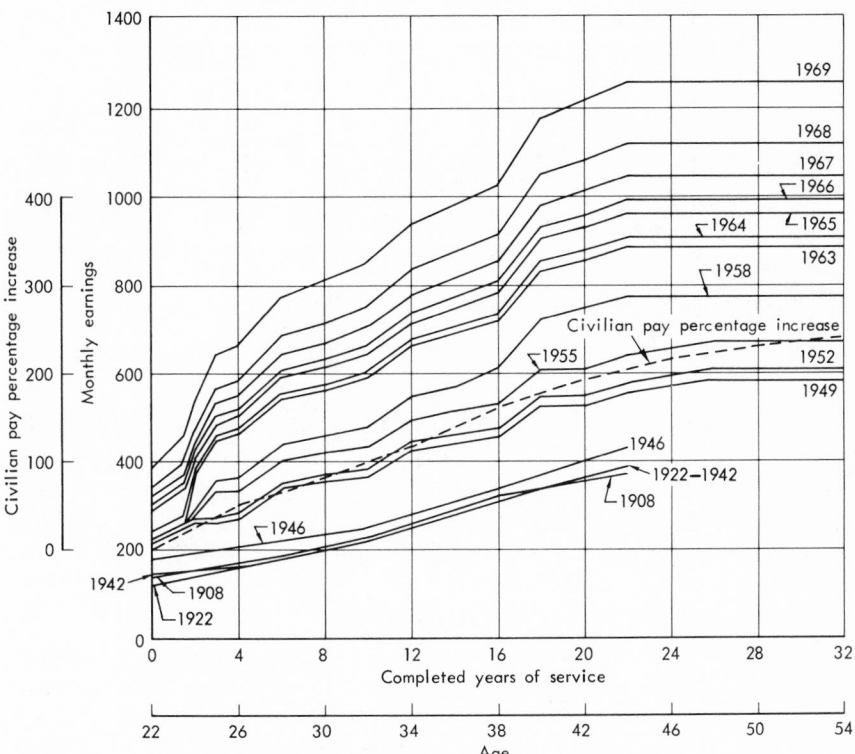

Figure 5-4. Basic Pay Progression, Lt. Colonel.

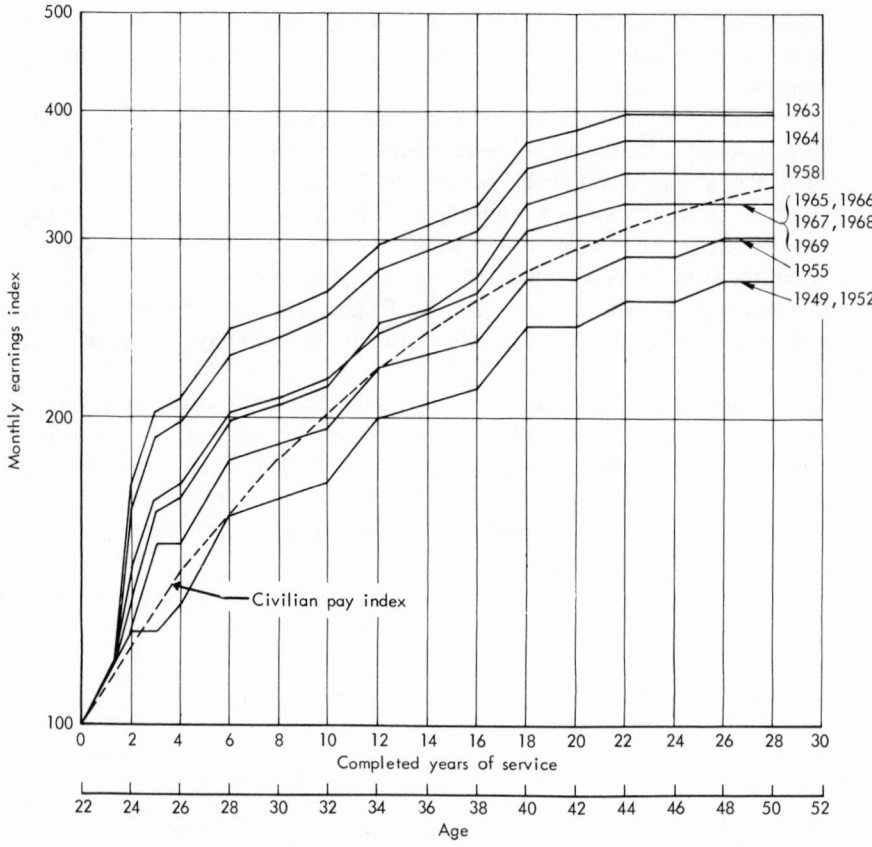

Figure 5-5. Military and Civilian Pay Index, Lt. Col. and College Graduate.

Figures 5-4 and 5-6 show two groups of pay increases: 1908 to 1946 and 1949 to 1969. The focus is on the latter. The former is of interest in showing that the earnings of the officer and NCO corps have slipped considerably relative to civilians; it has *no* analytical significance as to how much officers and NCOs should be paid. Table 5-6 shows that per capita income in current dollars increased by 327% between the 1907-11 period and 1946; officer incomes increased only slightly; and NCOs, by 100 to 200%.

The civilian pay index on all four graphs is an abstraction showing civilian pay progression. The interesting features of Figure 5-4 are the sharp increase in pay after two years' service starting in 1955 and the paucity of pay increases before 1963. These pay scales are shown on semilog graph paper in Figure 5-5 to show

Table 5-6
Percentage Compensation Increases of Selected Military Ranks, 1907-1946

Rank[a]	Percentage Increase 1907-1946
Second Lieutenant	57.3
Lieutenant Colonel	30.0
Brigadier General	11.2
E4	218.2
E7	116.7
Per capita income	327 [b]

[a]Comparisons for officers were made on the basis of pay and allowances; NCOs only by basic pay rates. "Illustrative Examples of Pay Rates for Military Personnel, 1907-1968," OASD (M&RA), Actuarial Consultant, November 8, 1968.
[b]Series F 1-5, "Gross National Product, Total and Per Capita, in Current and 1929 Prices: 1869 to 1957," *Historical Statistics of U.S.*

percentage increases. The interesting features readily displayed by the semilog graph are:

1. The wage profile slope—its flattening during World War II (not shown), its sharp climb from 1949 to 1963, and its flattening since the 1963 pay raises.
2. That the wage progression since 1955 has been considerably steeper than civilian progression for the first six years of service due to the low entry wage. Thereafter the two slopes are roughly similar up to the twenty-second year—the last year a lieutenant colonel receives a pay longevity increase and the year when most will have retired. However, the inclusion of fringe benefits, as can be seen by comparing the military salary and civilian pay lines in Figure 5-1, causes a flattening of the officer's total compensation profile to approximately the same as the civilian's overall progression.

The phenomena working against entrants in Figures 5-4 and 5-5 are even more salient in Figures 5-6 and 5-7. In Figure 5-6 the disparity between the pay of men with less than and over two years' service is even greater. The semilog graph of Figure 5-7 shows the same general features as for officers except that wage progression for enlisted personnel has remained near its 1964 apogee. Again, the steepest slope occurs during the initial six years, due to a low entry wage; thereafter, the slope flattens but remains steeper than the high-school graduate's earnings slope.

The result of the pay policies followed from 1949 to 1964-65, essentially pivoting the basic pay profile line counterclockwise about the entry wage, has been a steady erosion of the entrant's purchasing power in absolute as well as relative terms. Table 5-7 shows this erosion in terms of real wages deflated to

Table 5-7
Purchasing Power of Monthly Base Pay At 1967 Consumer Prices

	1946	1964	% Change 1946-1964	1968	% Change 1946-1968	1971 (1 Jan)	% Change 1946-1971	% Change 1964-1971
Recruit	128.21	83.96	−34.5	98.18	−23.4	113.19	− 11.7	34.8
Private	136.75	92.36	−32.5	108.83	−20.4	125.29	− 8.4	35.7
E7	366.67	413.67	+12.8	477.06	+30.1	548.57	+ 49.6	32.6
E9	366.67	617.76	+68.5	712.28	+94.3	819.32	+123.4	32.6
2nd Lt.	307.69	259.63	−15.6[a]	329.37	+ 7.0	378.66	+ 23.1	45.8
Lt. Col.	740.39	976.53	+31.9	1075.05	+45.2	1236.30	+ 67.0	26.6
4-Star General	1253.56	1969.54	+57.1	2168.52	+73.0	2493.78	+ 98.9	26.6
4-week average gross earnings in manufacturing	296.21	443.36	+49.7	470.29	+58.8	465.21	+ 57.1	4.9

[a]At its nadir, this percentage was −21.3 in 1963.

Sources: Illustrative Examples of Monthly Basic Pay Rates for Military Personnel 1908-1965, OASD, 17 August 1965, and 1968 and 1971 (Jan.) Monthly Basic Pay Rates. *1971 Economic Report of the President*, Tables C-30 and C-45, pp. 232 and 249.

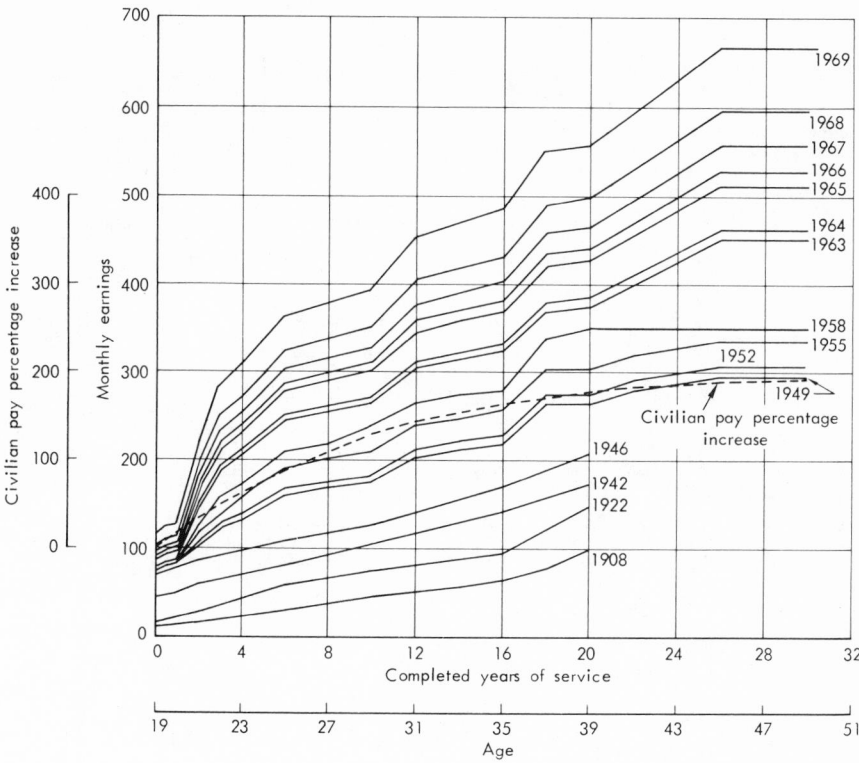

Figure 5-6. Basic Pay Progression, E-7.

1957-59 consumer prices. From 1946 to 1964 real wages for the recruit and second lieutenant actually *decreased* by 34.6 and 15.7% respectively, while wages for nonentrants continuously increased, though lagging substantially behind civilian increases except for the most senior officer and enlisted grades. In other words, inflation continually eroded the value of entrant wages while others in the military and civilian sectors were receiving wage increases reflecting both inflationary and productivity gains.

Since 1964 military wages have risen considerably faster than civilian wages, as indicated by the last two columns in Table 5-7. While not restoring the military's position relative to civilians in 1946 and earlier, the increases have more than restored wage comparability between military careerists and civilians as determined by mean earnings, *exclusive* of retirement benefits, which disproportionately favor the military. Two important caveats are: (1) although military wages are more than comparable in cost, their visibility is not; and (2) entry pay remains very low and unattractive to potential recruits.

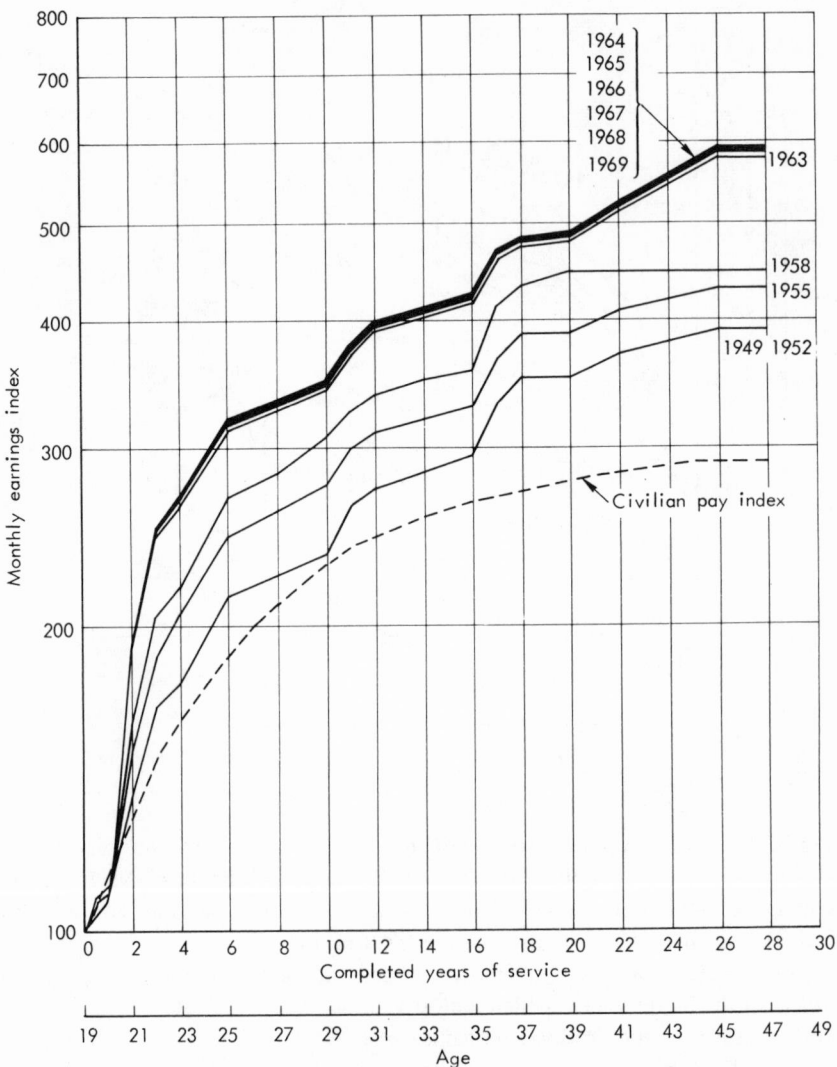

Figure 5-7. Military and Civilian Pay Index, E-7 and High-School Graduate.

Appendix 5 - A

Models for Military Pay Reform

The topic of military pay has plagued every administration since the close of the Korean War, when it became apparent that the services were losing valuable technicians trained at government expense.[33] Proposals to reduce this deficiency can be generally divided according to whether compensation is viewed as income or the price of a person's labor. With their bent toward the criterion of economic efficiency, economists have been critical of the compensation system, have generally emphasized the price aspect, and have recommended changes in the pay structure in order to reward by differential skills, as in the private sector. Others, whose views have predominated, have generally not been critical of the compensation system and have focused on the income aspect of compensation, with its implied criterion of fairness in comparison with civilians. The concept of wage comparability manifests this concern with fairness; a prominent example is the recent Hubbell Report, *Modernizing Military Pay*, which recommended, among other things, that military salaries should be raised because they are said to lag behind civilian wages.

Both emphases suboptimize and have internal deficiencies. As applied in practice, both models have suboptimized by implicitly accepting existing personnel philosophies and their derived policies, which are generally similar throughout the services. It is quite apparent, though, that Air Force requirements differ from the Army's. Yet because of the Army's large size, its special recruiting difficulties, and its legacy to the Air Force, Army requirements have generally determined DoD policies. This immediately implies a trade-off between the benefits to be gained from removing constraints[34] and the political disadvantages of dissimilar policies, which could prove difficult for the public to comprehend. To gain higher-level optimization, a searching reappraisal of underlying personnel philosophies is necessary. This is quite important in environments where the rationalizing impact of market forces is absent; customary practices and bureaucratic resistance to change over time often account for greater inefficiencies than any improvement in marginal costs could cause when underlying practices remain *unchanged*.[35]

Price Models

Economic models employ the logic of maximization. Its most straight-forward application is a constrained maximization problem whereby an Effectiveness Function

135

(1) $E(X_1, \ldots, X_n)$,

where X_i are the inputs, is to be maximized, subject to a budget contraint,

(2) $B(X_1, \ldots X_n) = 0$.

A mathematically well behaved function is also assumed, meaning

(3) $E_i > 0$ and
(4) $E_{ii} < 0$.

That is, a small increase in an input (3) leads to positive increases in effectiveness (i.e., marginal product) but at a diminishing rate (4).[36]

The most convenient maximization expression is the method of Lagrange multipliers,

$$(5) \ L = E(X_1, \ldots, X_n) + \lambda \left(B - \sum_{i=1}^{n} p_i X_i \right)$$

where p_i are the input prices. Upon partial differentiation of L with respect to each input and setting the result equal to zero, we finally derive the first-order maximizing condition,

$$(6) \qquad \frac{E_1}{p_1} = \frac{E_2}{p_2} = \frac{E_n}{p_n} \ .$$

The literal translation is that effectiveness is maximized when the marginal products of each input are proportional to input price.

The model in principle serves as a guideline for increasing military effectiveness at least cost. As an abstract intellectual exercise indicating the desirable characteristics of a pay system, the model is extremely useful. As a practical guide of how to implement the best possible system in an imperfect world, the model has serious internal flaws. First and foremost, its first-order maximization condition requires knowledge of an effectiveness function. This is beyond the state of the art. Yet knowledge of this function is so fundamental that economic models based on the maximization logic founder on this reef. The model unsuccessfully tries to avoid this deficiency by substituting Replacement Cost (RC) for Effectiveness (E). That is, E_i of equation (3) is used as a measure of E in equation (1), and training costs which dominate RC are used as a measure of E_i. This substitution makes the model cost minimizing which, in this case, is not the converse of maximization.

The economic model represents itself as a maximizing decision rule. But maximization cannot occur if marginal products are *assumed*, as implied by the RC substitution. Maximization requires that management be able to adjust the numbers of an input or the derived demand blade of the scissors to the supply price blade, to use Alfred Marshall's well-known analogy. More bluntly, substituting E_i for E implicitly assumes the validity of existing operating practices, which is contrary to the premise of maximization. Second, substituting RC for E_i in (6) leads to the decision criterion,

$$(7) \quad \frac{RC_i}{p_i} = \frac{RC_j}{p_j} \; ,$$

that retention and higher pay for the specialty with the higher ratio are preferable up to the point where increases in p_i bring an equality condition. Even when abstracting from fixed speciality requirements, equation (7) does not lead to decisions moving in a maximizing direction unless the side conditions,

$$(8) \quad E_i \geqslant E_i \, (RC_i) \text{ and}$$

$$(9) \quad E_i = \propto (RC_i),$$

are satisfied. Equation (8) means that without knowing the true marginal product, there is no assurance the condition holds, and pay increases are in fact given to the right specialties (i.e., $E_i \geqslant RC_i \geqslant \lambda \, p_i$). Equation (9) is an even more serious limitation; the equality condition only holds if marginal productivity and replacement costs are proportionate for all specialties. Unless proportionality exists, there is no way of assuring that a constrained budget is being allocated properly among the specialties.

The question is now: What is the likelihood of an incorrect decision? The answer is: Very likely. Since equation (7) is really developed from only one blade of the scissors, it implies only cost minimization of stated requirements. It is not at all improbable that many skilled occupational areas may be overstocked, and hence have lower marginal products than some less-skilled specialties. Furthermore, because it cannot be assumed that marginal products and training costs are proportionate, there is no assurance that the equalities of equation (7) indicate the preferred specialties for higher pay and retention. For example, DoD policy before Vietnam was predicated on the belief that reenlistment rates for the low-skilled occupational specialties such as the combat arms were satisfactory and even too high, but retention for the technical specialties was too low. In peacetime, as long as the combat arms productivity did not need testing and technicians performed a measurable output, DoD policy led to cost reduction. But if increased infantry productivity can be translated into infantry reductions, then differences in infantry productivity can be translated into large manpower reductions through a support slice multiplier, which in the case of Vietnam, was 9 to 1.[37] Thus, as a simple example, doubling the productivity of an infantryman potentially permits a reduction of 10 men, some of them expensively trained technicians.

A second flaw in the straightforward maximization model is that its reward mechanism is oriented toward those with skills and excludes consideration of differential risks and burdens within the military. In the market economy, these disutilities are reflected in the input's supply price. In the military sector, the point of departure has been a politically constrained common wage, which is an inadequate measure of a speciality's supply price.[38] The supply curve of military personnel, therefore, does not meet the assumptions of the competitive model. The result is that the economic model's wage increases are based solely on marginal product, which means in practice skill differentials that are determined by reference to training costs or comparability with the civilian sector. Hence the marginal equivalency conditions of equations (6) and (7) are incorrect, since p_i is a biased estimate of the true supply price. And, of course, neglect of burden differentials, which has an emotive content for the military, has been the source of the services' dislike of a compensation structure based on skill differentials.[39]

A third flaw in the maximization model is its implicit assumption that wages paid in accordance with marginal products will solve the perennial problem of insufficient recruitment and retention of first-term personnel. Using present institutional practices as the starting point, differential wages do imply a movement in the direction of greater micro cost-effectiveness. But it does not follow that this is also the way to solve the overall macro problems of attraction and retention. If military compensation is valued by its recipient at only a fraction of its cost to the government, then mileage can also be gained by focusing analytical attention on the "body" of military pay rather than just on the margins, as implied by the maximization calculus. Policy analysis requires an array of analytical tools and approaches; the standard maximization calculus is but one, though its elegance has tended to mesmerize its users and conceal underlying difficulties.

The Becker Model

A final flaw of the straightforward maximization model is its failure to take account of the services' human capital investment; it is necessary to distinguish between training that is specific to the military and training that has general applicability. This leads to what might be called the Becker model of military compensation. The military labor market is one of the few labor submarkets which permit contractual labor agreements.[40] This allows the military to invest more heavily in human capital; civilian firms are reluctant to undertake such investment because they find it difficult to recoup their direct and indirect training costs. Failure to include training costs as a part of compensation can lead to what has been termed

a conspicuous example of an organization that both pays at least part of training costs and does not pay market wages to skilled personnel. It has had, in consequence, relatively easy access to "students" and heavy losses of "graduates."[41]

The Becker model corrects for this deficiency by noting the extent to which a firm can recoup its training costs. Specific training useful only to the firm implies a lower wage than general training. For general training, a firm has to pay employees their marginal product to prevent their leaving (i.e., E_i = Opportunity Cost); since the firm cannot depress later earnings to recoup its costs, it depresses earnings below marginal product during the training period. For specific training, a firm can pay its employees less than their marginal product (i.e., $E_i > OC$) as long as the wages paid are at least as great as can be earned elsewhere, where this training has no market value. The firm can therefore recoup costs and does not need to depress initial earnings as much. The firm imparting specific training has an incentive to retain its employees because of its investment; the employee has an incentive to stay because specific training implies that his marginal product is higher with the firm than elsewhere. The firm's wage policy should therefore be to pay a wage between the employee's marginal product and his opportunity wage; hence, specific training implies only moderately depressed earnings during the training period. Becker's summary is:

When the final step is completed, firms no longer pay all training costs nor do they collect all the return but they share both with the employees. The shares of each depend on the relations between quit rate and wages, layoff rates and profits, and on other factors not discussed here, such as the cost of funds, attitudes toward risk, and desires for liquidity.[42]

The Becker model's implication for the services is that specialties in high civilian demand, e.g., data-processing, ought to receive a higher wage than such specifically trained specialties as the combat arms if only because of the general/specific training dichotomy. The model also implies that men receiving valuable general training should receive a smaller initial wage than specifically trained personnel. This conclusion is based on the assumption that other conditions are equal; to the extent that recruits for the general specialties are of higher quality, with better civilian opportunities, their initial wage should reflect a higher supply price and the wage differences for the training period between specific and general training would be less.

While the Becker model is an improvement over the straightforward maximization model, it still has some of the latter's faults. It still is not a maximizing process; it still founders on the difficulty of measuring marginal productivity; it still tends to neglect disutility differences, except where comparable civilian differences can be measured; and it still uses a micro technique to solve a problem that also has macro deficiencies.

Wage Comparability Model

Comparability with civilian wages has been the standard by which most military pay increases have been justified since World War II. Comparability focuses on the income aspect of military compensation through the notion of fairness. As a method of attaining fairness, comparability can be supported by Professor Pigou's paraphrase of Alfred Marshall that

wages are fair relatively to wages in industries in general, if . . . , they are about on a level with the payment made for tasks in other trades which are of equal difficulty and disagreeableness, which require equal natural abilities and on an equally expensive training. As between persons . . . , fairness implies wages which . . . are proportioned to efficiency.[43]

This definition, to be fully satisfied, implies wage differentials according to differences in disutilities and skills among the occupational specialties; it also suggests that wages for enlisted men ought to be somewhat lower than wages for comparable civilian trades to recoup the government's cost of training.

Though comparability focuses on equity, comparability also suggests that compensation efficiency depends on the degree that the Pigou-Marshall definition is satisfied. Wage differentials that discriminate according to skills and burdens are cheaper than nondiscriminating wages that pay all personnel at the same rate. Individuals in specialties with greater skills or risks, all other things being equal, command a higher supply price than those with fewer burdens or skills. A high common wage set to satisfy the supply price of the more burdened and skilled means large economic rents for others; a lower common wage reduces economic rents, but may increase total costs through rapid turnover of the more skilled and burdened specialties. A discriminatory wage policy minimizes economic rent and those costs associated with turnover by tailoring wages to the supply prices of the various specialties.

Wage comparability as a criterion for reforming military compensation retains some of the major liabilities of the maximizing model. This is not a startling conclusion, since the Pigou-Marshall definition is developed from an economic model which assumes an equilibrium condition whereby marginal products are equal "in industries in general." If firms were not in equilibrium they would either have an incentive to expand or contract their employment. A hidden assumption of the comparability standard is that the military's marginal product is at least as great as the civilian's. The comparability model has the operational advantage of being able to avoid addressing the virtually intractable productivity problem. It does this by focusing on the supply blade of Marshall's demand and supply scissors and argues that fairness to the individual requires wages similar to those of civilians of comparable attributes. Implicit in this argument is that the individual has no control over the management system and should not be held responsible for its deficiencies. "Fairness" in the comparability model is a long-run concept different from the normal economic concept, which usually deals with short-run opportunity costs. This is because of differences in the individual's labor mobility. Military careerists are immobilized in the short run by their commitment to a career with its specific human capital investments and its nonvested retirement benefits; civilians are much less constrained. Hence a difference in the definition of fairness is appropriate. It is also apparent that military careerists are easy to exploit in the short run; in the long run, this can be myopic, because lower-quality personnel gradually replace higher-quality personnel who slowly leave the system.

The exclusion of the demand blade means that the wage comparability model does not provide a maximization process for modernizing military pay. At best it can minimize costs within the imposed requirements, just as the maximizing economic models operate in practice. Both models recommend differential pay, with the distinction that economic models derive this conclusion through the notion of economic efficiency and the mechanism of marginal productivity; comparability models, through the notion of fairness and the mechanism of supply price. A second limitation of the comparability model is in its implicit assumption, as in the maximizing model, that comparable wages will solve the perennial problems of insufficient recruitment and retention of first-term personnel. This assumption breaks down on the perceived-pay problem unless the term "comparability" is broadened to include comparable visibility with civilian earnings. On the other hand, the wage comparability model does not suffer two other limitations of the straightforward maximizing model. Whereas the formal economic models gloss over the differential risks and burdens internal to the military, the comparability model explicitly recognizes them. Second, the comparability model, as in the Becker model, may take account of investments in human capital. In this regard the Becker model is preferable for its more explicit account of the behavioral implications of human capital investment.

In principle, the attributes vector of the wage comparability model is superior to the economic models. In practice, this conclusion does not follow. The economic models break down analytically because of the infeasibility of deriving productivity estimates; wage comparability models break down in their specific application to the military sector. The former cannot be corrected, at least within the current state of empirical economics; the latter can. The comparability model has been constrained by the military's preference for a compensation system that rewards according to needs, burdens, and responsibility—all factors correlating with years of service and hierarchical rank. Comparability has not been conceived to improve internal mechanisms of military compensation; rather, comparability has been used solely as a means to raise the *level* of military pay. Thus, while the comparability model is a rationalizing tool as well as a wage-level seeker, its application to military compensation has been restricted to wage-leveling, and consequently its utility has been diminished.

The second difficulty in applying the wage comparability model is that the various blue-ribbon commissions and study groups on military compensation have forgotten that comparability is a requirement for the *entire* profile.[44] This common oversight is understandable, given the draft's supply of entrants and the difficulty of obtaining a larger wages fund from Congress. However, comparability for only the career portion of the force will inevitably cause distortions and ultimately prove inefficient and self-defeating. The relevant manpower system is dynamic, not static. Reenlistment bonuses and higher pay at a decision point, while an important incentive to increase retention and satisfaction of the *given* force, do little for initial attraction.[45] The inevitable result is a first-term force composed of many reluctant volunteers with low reenlistment propensities. This effect is compounded by the military's tendency to offer the most expensive training to the more educationally and mentally qualified—those, unfortunately, with the lowest reenlistment propensities. Survey data show that the percentage of draft-induced volunteers is higher in the higher mental categories[46] and that retention propensities vary inversely with draft-inducement.[47] This behavior can be explained, exclusive of valuable training received, by the better-qualified having the better civilian opportunities. Thus, a major causal factor behind low retention rates is the service's own recruitment policies.

The often-heard argument that low retention rates are caused by industry's competitive bidding can thus be viewed as a rationalization of only partial validity; however, its continual repetition and belief can lead to lower retention rates through expectations which are subsequently unsatisfied. Two additional factors undermining this rationalization are: (1) many of the skilled specialties are specific to the military and have little market value; and (2) as the Hubbell group found " . . . for the most part, military members who have left active duty are not employed in civilian occupations that are similar to their military occupations."[48] Hubbell's examination of DoD loss tapes disclosed that only "professional and technical personnel in the higher educational levels [i.e., college-trained officers], such as doctors, lawyers, chaplains, and engineers, tended to work in civilian occupations that were directly comparable to their military specialties."[49]

A third critical difficulty is that comparability is an operationally difficult standard. In a market economy, comparability for each specialty occurs through the mechanisms of labor mobility and market demand and supply. These mechanisms do not exist within the military, nor do they adjust between military and civilian labor markets. Moreover, the military forecloses virtually all entry movement except at the entry level.[50] Lack of mobility compounds the problem that, while some military specialties have a readily identifiable civilian analogue, others obviously do not. This would be a source of concern if the comparability model were strictly followed for each specialty. However, comparability as practiced has been defined as comparability between military rank and levels of similar civilian responsibility.[51] This places any conclusion on a dubious conceptual foundation; yet the conclusions of all the DoD-sponsored groups using the comparability model have been predicated on matching military and civilian occupational hierarchies.[52]

The basic difficulty is that hierarchical levels are not comparable because the hierarchical levels of the military (and civil service) are not determined by objective market forces but by self-interested groups. Comparisons between military and civilian personnel occupying apparently similar jobs can be deceptive. Military personnel are often in charge of more human and capital assets than corporate managers; but it does not follow that military managers should therefore be paid as much.[53] The reward criterion is not assets in one's charge, but discretionary managerial authority. The military manager is hemmed in by rules and regulations; furthermore, there is no question of organizational survival (in peacetime). On the other hand the civilian manager, even in many of the large corporations, is subject to the uncertainties and vicissitudes of the marketplace and its objective standard: profits.

Moreover while countervailing market forces determine civilian hierarchical levels, the military's are arbitrarily self-determined. Additional military levels can be created by fiat, as in the proliferation of additional headquarters. The private sector has countervailing market forces to help ensure that its positions are neither over nor understated. Market demand controls overstating tendencies; union pressures and individual opportunities elsewhere contain understating pressures. No such pressures exist in the government sector. Rather, in the civil service and military, an upward bias to overstate positions exists as management becomes, in effect, a union to upgrade its positions in opposition to a Congress and a politically appointed Executive that lacks the indomitable will of market demand and the requisite detailed information to contain the uplifting pressures from below. This hierarchical bias is one reason why the Hubbell group found military salaries lagging behind civilians' compensation, when in fact civilian salaries lag behind the military's.

Summary

The road to improving the effectiveness of military compensation is one strewn with hidden obstacles. The models commonly espoused for modernizing military pay are inadequate for their task even on their own terms. All three lead at best to rough decision rules to reduce the costs of a specified force. The two economic models are too formal and lack operational content. The comparability model is less pretentious and actually preferable, but it has been misused and its implications have not been fully appreciated. But even if these models were maximizing and did not have internal deficiencies, they would, at best, lead to low-level suboptimization. The constraints which decree this suboptimization come in two packages: pay visibility, and the manpower philosophies that drive service personnel policies.

Appendix 5 - B

Military Retirement

Retirement is the second largest component of military compensation; it averages 57-65% of a careerist's military salary and is almost as large as his basic pay.[54] On a gross basis, retirement accounts for 22.2% of the services' compensation costs, as against only 2.3% for employer in the private sector. No comparison of military and civilian compensation, therefore, can exclude a retirement comparison.[55] The retirement system can be briefly described as follows:

Retirement Eligibility	20 or more years of active federal service.
Calculation of annuity	2.5% for each year of active federal service times terminal basic pay.
Annuity	50 to a maximum of 75% of terminal basic pay.
Employer-Employee Cost Sharing	Employee does not make an explicit contribution toward costs of the retirement system.

Annuity is not vested until retirement eligibility is attained.
Military service is covered by Social Security.
Annuity is adjustable to maintain real purchasing power.

Two special features of military retirement costs are its unfunded status and its underestimation of economic accrual costs. The economic costs of doing business include present costs of accrued future benefits. Formal budget procedures do not take such costs into account. On an informal basis, DoD does make an accrual estimate. However, its accounting procedure is static and based on current wages; it excludes the effect of wage increases and the consumer price index, to which retirees' benefits are linked to maintain constant purchasing power. The result is a 53% underestimate of actual government cost.[56] More serious is the fact that retirement costs are unfunded and paid on an annual disbursement basis for *past* services rendered that have been less than DoD's low accrual estimates. Because the military expanded from a small pre-World War II base, retirement disbursements have been relatively small, though growing rapidly (at a rate of 13.2% a year from 1957-69) as the World War II retirement exodus began. The military has thus been given a large hidden subsidy since World War II, and defense management has had little incentive to cost manpower as an economic system or for revising the retirement structure.

However, events are about to force changes. Table 5-8 shows that estimated

145

Table 5-8
Projected DoD Retirement Costs[a]

FY	(1) Cost[a] ($M)	(2) Percent of Military Personnel Budget[b]	(3) Retired Pay Disbursements Growth Index	(4) GNP[b] Growth Index	(5) Retired Pay Accrual[a] Growth Index
1969	2,450	11.8	1.00	1.00	1.00
1975	4,344	16.5	1.77	1.27	1.55
1985	8,174	21.0	3.34	1.87	2.92
2000	17,350	24.8	7.08	3.37	7.59

Source: Office of the Secretary of Defense, *Modernizing Military Pay*, Vol. IV, pp. 2-31, 2-32, and 10-11, columns 1 through 4.
[a]Assumes a force level of 2.64 million; basic pay increases of 12.6% in FY 70 and 5% thereafter; and CPI increases of 4% in FY 69, 3% in FY 70, and 1.5% thereafter.
[b]Assumes a growth rate of 4%.

disbursement for past services rendered is growing rapidly and becoming a larger share of the military budget, increasingly constraining future defense managers. Thus while the budget is assumed to grow at 4%, disbursements grow at an average rate of 6.5% (though at a decreasing rate as the growth in the total number of retirees slows as the year 2000 is approached).[57] Changing the accounting system to a "normal" or accrual basis is also of no avail. Its growth rate is an even greater, though constant, 6.6%.

The reason why both the disbursements and accrual rates are so high is because military pay raises to match civil-service increases are given in the form of basic pay. Since basic pay is only a fraction of total military salary, concentrating pay raises in basic pay causes it, and therefore military retirement benefits, to rise faster than the corresponding civil-service increase. The implication is that if military wage increases are continually concentrated in the form of basic pay to match civil-service increases as existing law requires, future defense managers will be increasily hampered. Nor are increases in non-basic-pay elements more than a palliative solution; these elements can absorb inflationary price increases but not increases reflecting civilian productivity increases without becoming meaningless. Moreover, such increases have low visibility and hence low efficacy. A very important implication, therefore, is that the present compensation structure will not long withstand the pressures that are building.

Retirement Objectives

The stated objectives of the retirement system are:

(1) Management Effectiveness. (a) assist in attracting and retaining the kinds and numbers of qualified members required; (b) provide a socially acceptable

method of removing some members who must be separated to insure main-tenance of a young and vigorous force. (2) Just treatment of members. Provide, after many years of faithful service, some degree of financial security that is understood, assured and protected against the inroads of future inflation.[58]

How well are retirement objectives met? Available evidence suggests that these objectives are not adequately satisfied by the existing retirement system. The system becomes even more questionable if the key assumption behind many military manpower policies, namely the desirability of a "young and vigorous" force, is appraised.

Retirement benefits do assist in attracting and retaining military personnel, but inefficiently. The deferred and uncertain nature of the compensation begets low attraction, low retention, and even low satisfaction of careerists for each dollar of government cost, as explained earlier. Yet while these attributes discourage first-term personnel, nonvesting locks in a careerist as the retirement point is approached.[59] Moreover, nonvesting before completion of at least 20 years' service causes several adverse behavior patterns within the services. First, since the services follow an "up or out" promotion policy to insure promotion progression for a "young and vigorous force," individuals tend to avoid innovative activity, since deviations from standard solutions and practices can lead to errors and accusations of poor judgment, which can become the basis for nonpromotion and hence for administrative separation from the service before retirement. Such separation means a substantial monetary loss for the individual, since separation pay is only a fraction of the present value of the retirement benefit.[60] This loss reinforces the tendency towards subservience to superiors and rigid adherence to doctrine inherent in any military's hierarchical struc-ture.[61] Second, nonvesting places commanders in an awkward position. Their empathy for their subordinates makes it difficult for them to recommend separation for subordinates who have been good men but because of the "up or out" policy have been promoted beyond their level of competence; yet commanders cannot permit such individuals to degrade the unit's effectiveness. This has led to the assignment of unsatisfactory personnel to low-prestige functions. While such assignments may lower the efficiency of the low-prestige, noncombat functions, forced separations would be even more costly because of their adverse impact on morale and the further reinforcing of adverse hierarchi-cal tendencies. One reason why the military has resisted civilianization programs is that they would remove these havens for unsatisfactory military personnel and force a harsh choice between nonvested separation or retention in a "line" unit. Finally, nonvesting strengthens a commander's control over his career subordi-nates, thus increasing the possibility of abuse of position and authority—a factor a democratic society is particularly sensitive to.

These factors would seem to argue for a system that permits vesting. Vesting has the desirable economic attribute of contributing to economic efficiency through labor mobility. Its undesirable economic attribute is that it reduces a firm's incentive for human capital investment. From the military viewpoint, vesting is probably not desirable. First, vesting for first-term enlistees is equivalent to a negative reenlistment bonus. Many young servicemen, particularly family men,[62] hesitate to leave the military because of financial uncertainty; an opting-out bonus would reduce this constraint. In addition, an opting-out bonus reduces the attractiveness of reenlistment bonuses. A second potential argument against vesting is higher budget costs; however, this depends on the extent of vesting and the method of calculation.[63] The critical argument against vesting is the relatively greater attractiveness to the services' better personnel, who generally have the better civilian opportunities. This undesirable effect is reinforced by the services' incentive and reward system, particularly for officers. The military promotion system can best be described as a modified seniority system. It provides only limited recognition and earlier promotion for its most promising personnel. The result is that promising personnel are not provided sufficient money and psychic income differentials to offset their better civilian opportunities. Vesting career officers would also undermine programs which send officers back to civilian universities for advanced degrees.

The other objective under management effectiveness is that retirement be a "socially acceptable method to insure maintenance of a young and vigorous force." Retirement per se meets this criterion. Its deficiency is associated with nonvesting, which makes it difficult to force men out of the service before retirement is vested at 20 years' service. The real question, however, is the desirability of maintaining a young and vigorous force, and thereby forcing many retirees into a second career.[64] "Young and vigorous" implies a high-turnover labor force, but the Air Force and the Navy must operate and maintain expensive technical equipment. Such equipment implies a need for an older, more stable, labor force with accumulated technical skills. A "young and vigorous" force is necessary only to provide fighter pilots and the ground combat arms of the Army and the Marine Corps. These elements comprised only 13% of the pre-Vietnam force. Yet this small segment drives the entire personnel system. One reason is that most general and flag officers and virtually all three-and four-star officers are drawn from and have generalized from this small segment, which has traditionally formed the core of the military.

The final retirement objective is "just treatment" of members. Large annuities have been justified as ensuring a reasonable post-service income for those forced to retire after 20 years and begin a second career. A rationalization has been that military annuities are not much higher in absolute monthly payments than Civil Service benefits. This is true in terms of monthly payments; it is not true in terms of present value of benefits at time of retirement. However, both these criteria mask the relevant question of cost to the government for services performed. By this criterion, military retirement benefits are much higher, because the median retirement age is 20 years earlier than in civilian life. This means a relatively short input period (into the retirement fund) and a long period of withdrawals. The typical military retiree adds to the fund for 21 years and draws out for 31.2 years; the typical civilian contributes for 40-46 years and has an expected life at time of retirement of only 12.8 years.[65]

Assuming the need for a young and vigorous force and the consequent retirement of most careerists soon after 20 years' service, relatively large and costly annuities can be justified on the grounds that the government has a paternalistic responsibility to ensure that retirees do not suffer psychic and monetary income losses upon retirement. In general, retirees have not fared well in the civilian sector. Up until the early 1960s most officers and many EM believed they were in high demand by the civilian economy. However, since the increased supply of retirees starting in 1960 who did not have the advantage of reaching high rank by being in the military before the World War II expansion, these expectations are no longer widely shared by military personnel except those with civilian professional skills.

A 1963 DoD survey disclosed that the median civilian earnings of officers and EM after one to three years in the civilian job market were only $6,130 and $4,690 respectively. A 1964 BSSR survey of retirees after six months disclosed median incomes of $7,785 and $4,730 for officers and EM, respectively. The BSSR survey showed that the median income of officers with college degrees was $9,490; for EM with high-school degrees, $4,815.[66] By comparison, in 1964 the mean income for a comparable 44-year-old civilian college graduate, excluding fringe benefits, was $14,049; for a comparable 40-year-old civilian high-school graduate, $7,400. Thus, according to the higher 1964 survey, retired officers and EMs (excluding the retirement cushion) were earning only 67% and 65% as much, respectively, as civilians of the same age and education. These data, of course, exclude the psychic disappointment to many retirees of an unsatisfactory second career.

Many reasons account for retirees' poor showing, such as the "culture shock" of different organizational and career patterns after age 40, the non-transferability of specific skills, discriminatory seniority practices (operating even within the Civil Service), imperfect knowledge of opportunities, and poor placement procedures. Perhaps most important, is the fact that certain behavior patterns hamper the retiree; they cluster with other retirees, often around geographically remote military installations with their medical and other facilities. This preference often forecloses viable employment due to low demand for, and an oversupply of, retiree skills. Thus, to a certain extent, low post-retirement earnings are a result of the retiree's own actions and his attempts to gain fringe benefits which are available to him from using military facilities.

Income Maximization and Pay Inversion

A feature of the retirement system is that officers with skills in demand in the civilian market can make more money by retiring after 20 years' service and adding a civilian salary to their retirement pay.[67] This induces a quality drain after the 20-year vesting point. The services may force the less desirable out, but many of the best select themselves out. This leaves the middle group and a fraction of the better-qualified individuals who visualize psychic income from promotion into the star ranks.

Associated with early retirement's maximized future earnings are undesirable pay variations caused by the individual careerist's retirement date. Figure 5-8 (Gross Salary at Year of Retirement by Rank) and Figure 5-9 (Gross Salary of Selected Officer and Enlisted Ranks Retiring with Different Years of Service) show these variations. In most cases, early retirement in a given rank is more expensive to the government; the exceptions are due to longevity increases upon 22 and 26 years of completed service. This causes two types of pay inversion (juniors' receiving as much as seniors). The first type occurs only in the ranks of colonel and above. During his last year of service, an officer in a higher grade with more years of service often receives less than one in a lower grade with fewer years of service. For example, in Figure 5-8, a colonel retiring at his 27th year earns as much as a brigadier general retiring after 34 years. The second type of pay inversion (Figures 5-9 and 5-11) is more subtle and involves retirement accruals' swamping rank differentials. During each year of his military career, the average lieutenant colonel of 22 years' service will earn considerably more than the outstanding officer who later is promoted to high rank. Thereafter, the disadvantages narrow only slightly, as the basic pay advantage of being

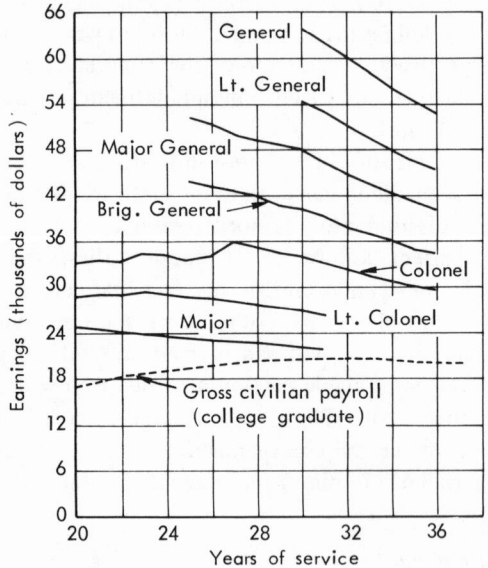

Figure 5–8. Gross Salary at Year of Retirement, by Rank (Entry Age 22) (1968).

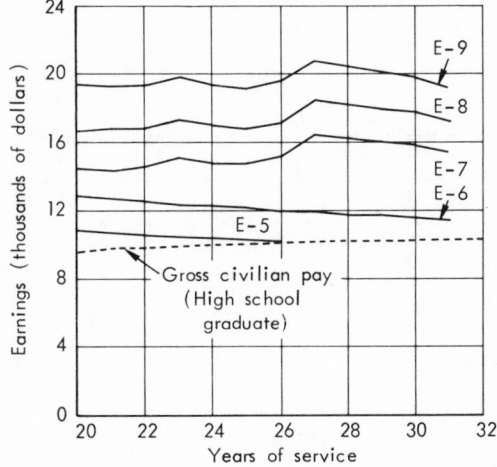

Figure 5-9. Gross Salary at Year of Retirement by Rank (Entry Age 19) (1968).

outstanding and gaining more rapid promotion varies from 3.7% at 12 years to 19.6% at 22 years. This gap thereafter diminishes and becomes reversed as the outstanding officer receives a series of rapid promotions into and within the general officer ranks. Within a given rank, these two phenomena are demonstrated in Figure 5-8 by the example of a four-star general who retires after 30 years; he earns $63,789 during his retirement year, versus $52,753 for the 36-year general. The former has earned a larger retirement accrual, which is equivalent to an *additional* 40.7% of basic pay for each year of comparable service.

In conclusion, the retirement system inadequately satisfies its objectives, is extremely expensive, causes wage inversions, and induces undesirable behavior patterns. Moreover, the retirement system is being used to support a management effectiveness objective which appears to be more appropriate for an expansionable cadre military of World-War-II vintage than a modern military with complex technical equipment. This implies that analytical studies of retirement alone are at best suboptimal without an appraisal of the fundamental assumptions and philosophies that underlie the military manpower system.

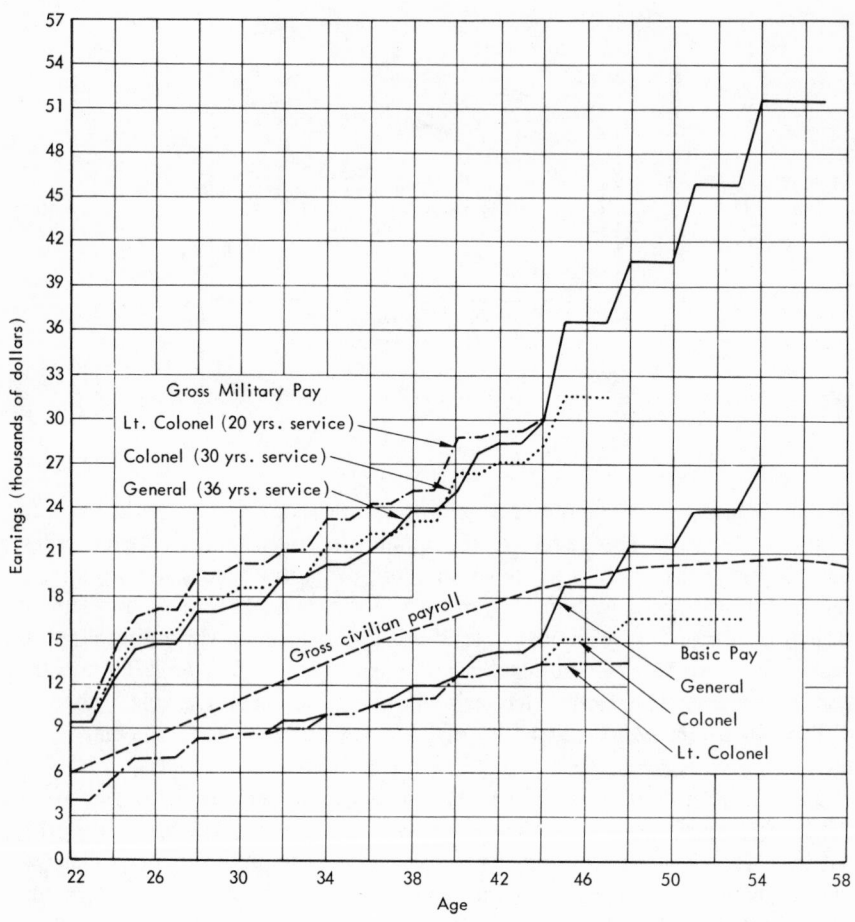

Figure 5-10. Basic Pay and Gross Military Pay for Selected Terminal Officer Ranks (1968).

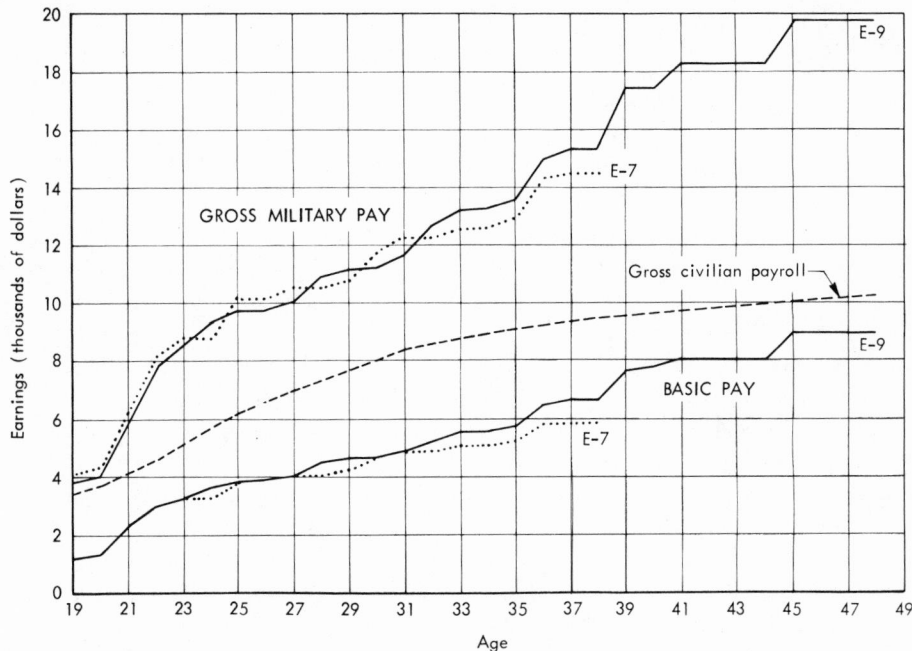

Figure 5-11. Basic Pay and Gross Military Pay for Selected Terminal Enlisted Ranks (1968).

Appendix 5 - C

Annuity Cost Model[6][8]

This appendix describes the methodology and results of computing retirement benefits to be paid to military persons in terms of a percentage of their basic pay.

When a military person retires, he has received one income stream, his basic pay for each year of service, and he is about to receive another, his retirement benefits until death. The present value of his retirement benefit stream is computed by summing for each year after retirement the product of the yearly retirement benefit, the probability of survival to that year, and a discount factor for that year.

The retirement pay percentage is computed as that percentage which, when multiplied by his basic pay for each year and an interest factor, yields at retirement the present value of his retirement benefits. Another way to view the retirement percentage is in terms of the retirement cost to the government as a percentage of the retiree's basic pay. The equations for calculating the retirement percentage are described here, results are shown, and the sensitivity of the results to various parameters of the equations is examined.

Methodology

The value upon retirement of a retiree's basic pay income stream, B, can be represented as

$$B = \sum_{n=1}^{s} \left[b_{r,s,n} \cdot (1+i)^{(s-n+.5)} \right]$$

where

n = the year of service (a retiree's first year of service corresponds to $n=1$),
s = the number of completed years of service at retirement,
r = rank of retiree at retirement,
$b_{r,s,n}$ = the basic pay in year n of those retiring with rank r and years of service s, and
i = interest rate at which basic pay is assumed to accumulate.

Basic pay is summed in yearly increments from the first year of service to the last. Note that the first year is compounded for $S-.5$ years and the last year for

155

.5 years. It is assumed one's pay is earned midway through each year and compounded to the end of the last year of service.

The analysis was done for those retiring in FY 1968. The basic pay for each year was obtained by assuming a typical promotional pattern given one's rank and years of service at retirement. The actual pay for each year as determined by the assumed rank and longevity for the year was used. For example, a lieutenant colonel/commander retiring in FY 1968 after 23 years of service was assumed to hold the rank of captain/lieutenant during his tenth year of service, FY 1955. The basic pay for a captain/lieutenant with 9 full years of service in FY 1955 was $5,054. Thus, $b_{r,s,n}$ equals $5,054, for r equals lieutenant colonel/commander, s equals 23, and n equals 10.

The present value of the retiree's expected retirement benefits, R, is

$$R = \sum_{y=a+s+1}^{109} \left[b_{r,s,s+1} \cdot 0.025 \cdot t \cdot (1+c)^{(y-a-s-1)} \cdot p_{y,a+s} \cdot \left(\frac{1}{1+i}\right)^{(y-a-s-.5)} \right]$$

where

   y = the age of the retiree,
   a = the age of the retiree upon entry into the service,
   t = years of service if $s \leqslant 30$, or 30 if $s > 30$,
   c = the percentage increase in the Consumer Price Index, which is used to
       adjust retiree benefits to maintain constant purchasing power, and
$p_{y,a+s}$ = the probability that a person retiring at age $a+s$ will live to age y.

Retirement benefits are summed from the first year after retirement until the retiree reaches age 109, when the probability of surviving reaches zero. Retirement pay each year equals his basic pay at retirement times 2.5% times years of service (or times 30 if years of service is greater than 30) times the percentage increase in the Consumer Price Index (CPI). Since the retiree has served for s complete years, he is serving during his $s+1$ year of service upon retirement. Thus retirement pay is computed from his basic pay at $s+1$ years of service. The assumption is made here that he retires immediately after serving s years. The CPI factor is equal to $1+c$ raised to the power corresponding to the number of years after retirement. It is assumed that the retirement pay for the year of retirement is not inflated by the CPI factor. For the next year, retirement pay is increased by c percentage. For that year, the retirement factor is

$$(1+c)^{[(a+s+2)-a-s-1]}, \text{ or } 1+c.$$

Expected retirement pay is obtained by multiplying the retirement benefit at a given age by the probability of surviving to that age. Probabilities of survival are derived from current *United States Life Tables.*[69] Mortality statistics for total males are assumed to apply. The probability of survival to age y when retiring at age $a+s$ is computed as the number of survivors of age y divided by the number of survivors of age $a+s$, out of 100,000 persons born alive. It must be pointed out that the mortality statistics are based on persons dying from 1959 through 1961. If longevity is greater for males retiring in 1968 than for those dying in the period 1959-1961 (due to medical advances), then the retirement pay expression presented here understates the true expected retirement pay.

To obtain the present value of this expected retirement pay, it is discounted at the interest rate, i. The interest rate, CPI percentage increase, entry age, years of service, and rank, were assumed to be parameters. That is, they were allowed to vary over significant ranges of values. The effects of varying the parameters are discussed later.

The retirement pay percentage, X, was derived such that the value at retirement of the sum of X times the retiree's base pay each year until retirement equals the value at retirement of his expected retirement income stream. This can be expressed as

$$\sum_{n=1}^{s} \left[(X \cdot b_{r,s,n}) \cdot (1+i)^{(s-n+.5)} \right] = R,$$

or

$$X \cdot \sum_{n=1}^{s} \left[b_{r,s,n} \cdot (1+i)^{(s-n+.5)} \right] = R.$$

Because

$$B = \sum_{n=1}^{s} \left[b_{r,s,n} \cdot (1+i)^{(s-n+.5)} \right],$$

$$X \cdot B = R; \text{ and}$$

$$X = R/B.$$

Results

The retirement percentage for lieutenant colonel/commander (O5) and sergeant 1st class/chief petty officer (E7) retiring after 20 to 31 years of service is shown in Figure 5-12. The illustration shows, for example, that the cost to the government of the retirement pay of a lieutenant colonel/commander with 23 years of service is roughly equivalent to 80% of his basic pay each year.[70] The retirement percentage is quite sensitive to years of service for both ranks. As one

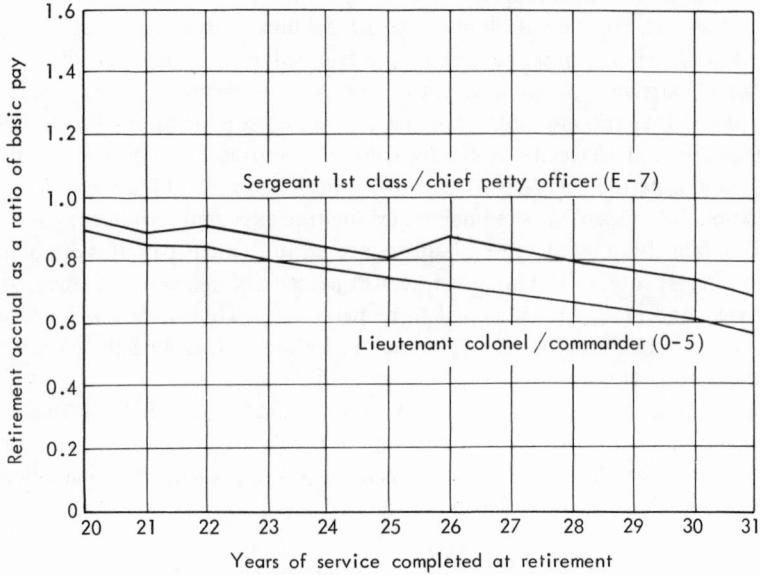

Figure 5-12. Ratio of Retirement Accrual to Basic Pay as Affected by Years of Service Completed at Retirement.

stays in the service longer, his basic pay stream increases. His retirement stream also increases for a while, although at a slower rate because he becomes older. After a certain number of years of service, the retirement stream begins to decrease.

Figures 5-13 and 5-14 indicate, for both officers and enlisted men, how the retirement percentage is affected by the retiree's rank. For colonel/captain and below, 23 years of service, the DoD median for officers, was assumed. For comparison, 30 years of service is shown for all officers. Enlisted men were assumed to retire after 21 years, the DoD median for enlisted men.

To obtain the values for Figures 5-12, 5-13, and 5-14, typical values were chosen for the interest rate, percentage increase in CPI, and age of entry. The typical value for interest rate was 3.63%, the average long-term U.S. government bond rate from 1950 to 1968. The effect of using other interest rates is shown in the next section. The typical value for the percentage increase in CPI was 2.06%, the average rate from 1950 to 1968. An entry age of 22 was chosen for officers assuming entry immediately from college. For enlisted men, 19 was used under the assumption that they enlist within a year of completing high school.

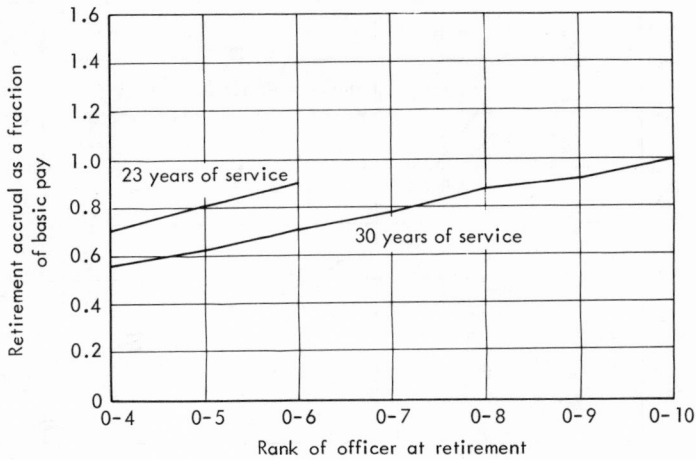

Figure 5-13. Ratio of Retirement Accrual to Basic Pay as Affected by Rank of Officer.

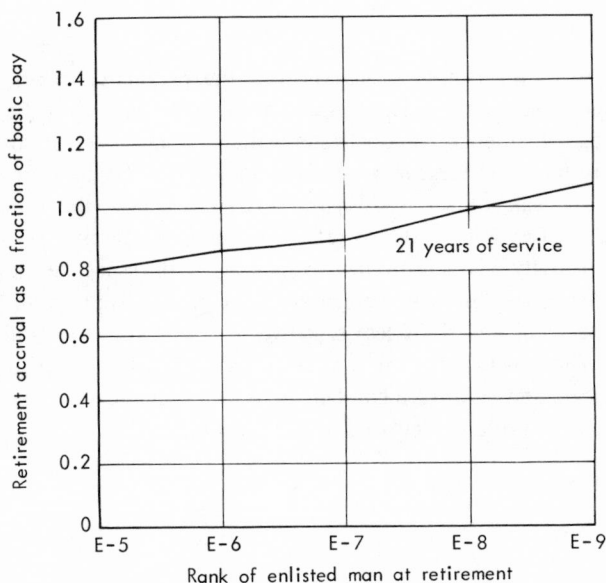

Figure 5-14. Ratio of Retirement Accrual to Basic Pay as Affected by Rank of Enlisted Man.

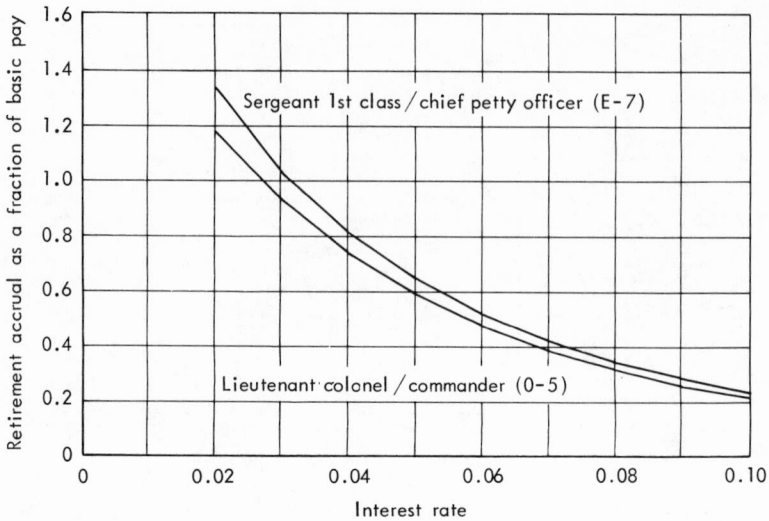

Figure 5-15. Ratio of Retirement Accrual to Basic Pay as Affected by Interest Rate.

Sensitivity

The sensitivity of the results to variation of the parameter values was tested. Each parameter was varied independently to show the effect on the retirement pay percentage. Lieutenant colonels/commanders were assumed to retire after 23 years of service, and sergeants 1st class/chief petty officers were assumed to retire after 21 years of service. Figure 5-15 shows how the retirement pay percentage decreases as the interest rate increases from 2% to 10%. Figure 5-16 shows the sensitivity of the retirement percentage with respect to the percentage increase in CPI. The retirement percentage is quite sensitive to both the interest rate and increase in CPI. It is less sensitive to age of entry, as is illustrated in Figure 5-17. The sensitivity of the retirement pay percentage is roughly the same for both officers and enlisted men. This is to be expected, since the retirement pay percentage for both is calculated by the same method.

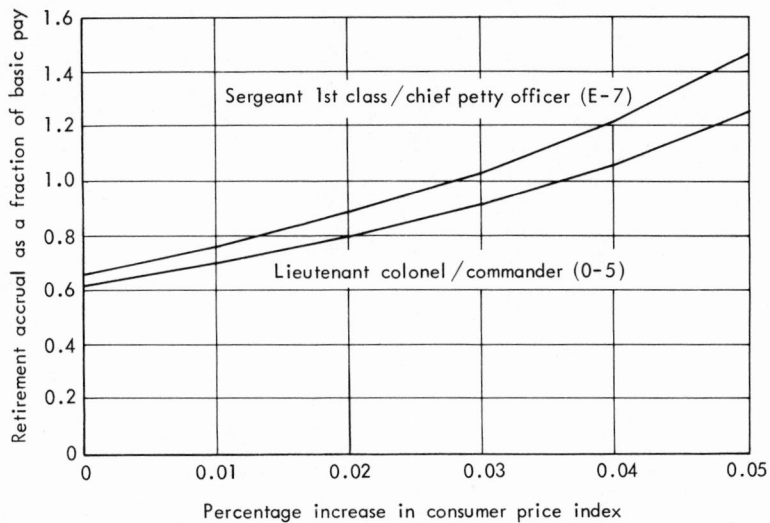

Figure 5-16. Ratio of Retirement Accrual to Basic Pay as Affected by Percentage Increase in Consumer Price Index.

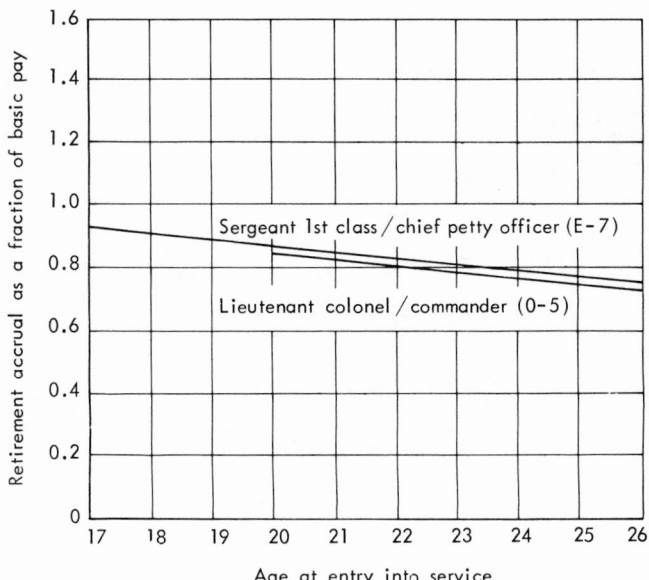

Figure 5-17. Ratio of Retirement Accrual to Basic Pay as Affected by Age at Entry into Service.

Appendix 5-D

The DoD Accounting Cost Underestimate of Retirement Compensation

Though military retirement is unfunded, DoD does make estimates of economic accrual for internal use. Its underestimate of these accrual costs is explained by the fact that it follows standard actuarial procedures, to wit:

An actuarial valuation of a retirement system is a statement of the probable future cost of the system. Unless otherwise stipulated, it is based on the present retirement provisions, the present pay scale, and the present outlook for persistency in service to retirement. It reflects the dynamic situation rather than merely the current (and transitory) situation.[71]

This procedure was designed to insure the solvency of insurance companies and protect against false statements of profits based only on current operations. For DoD, the practice is static, since it does not reflect continual rises in retirement benefits, which grow as the product of current basic pay increases and expected CPI increases after retirement.

This same phenomenon accounts for the recurring deficit in the civil service retirement fund. Accounting for the true accrual costs requires projections of future wage and CPI increases. In the following calculations, the rates were assumed to be identical to historical rates for the current force. The assumptions behind these calculations are listed in Appendix 5-B.

The DoD accrual cost for a given force can be estimated by the formula,

$$(1) \qquad \sum_{j=1}^{2} A_j \sum_{l=0}^{30 \,\&\, over} B_{ji} N_{ji} \;,$$

where

    i = completed years of service
    j = 1 for officers; 2 for enlisted men
    B = Basic pay
    N = number of personnel
    A = DoD acturial estimate of retirement cost as a function of basic pay.

The true approximation is

$$(2) \qquad \sum_{j=1}^{2} F_j \sum_{i=0}^{30 \,\&\, over} B_i N_i P_i \;,$$

163

where

P = probability of retiring

F = government cost as function of basic pay.

The complex calculation is F, which is derived from the estimate of retirement costs in Appendix 5-C as a function of basic pay for individuals who retire with certainty from military service. Table 5-9 weights these derivations by rank and years of service for those retiring as 0.806 for officers and 0.886 for enlisted men. Table 5-10 summarizes the costs for officers and enlisted personnel for a force standardized to 2.65 million with FY 1968 pay scales. Basic pay totals $7,094.7 and $2,535.6 million for enlisted men and officers respectively. Multiplying these by 0.2300 and 0.2376 respectively[72] yields the DoD estimate of $2,234.2 million.[73] The true approximation is $4,787.5 million. Thus DoD underestimates by approximately 53.3%.

Table 5-9
Retirement Cost Factors

Rank	Average Completed Years of Service	Percent of[1] FY 63-64 Retirees	Basic Pay Factor
O10	36	0	0.587
O9	35	0.1	0.589
O8	34	0.4	0.608
O7	33	0.5	0.607
O6	28	11.3	0.777
O5	22	31.9	0.846
O4 to W1	20	55.7	0.793
E9	25	3.1	0.915
E8	24	8.1	0.901
E7	21	32.6	0.895
E6	20	27.7	0.907
E1-5	20	28.4	0.847

[1]"Number of Retirements from Active Duty by Active Duty Pay Grade and Service," FY 63, FY 64, OASD(M), 12 April 1965.

Table 5-10
Retirement Cost Summations

A. Enlisted

(1) Completed Years of Service	(2) Average Strength* (thousands)	(3) Average Basic Pay**	(4) Cost Col. 2 X Col. 3 (millions)	(5) Probability of Retire- ment***	(6) Cost Col. 4 X Col. 5 (millions)
0	478.5	1440	689.1	.091	62.7
1	441.6	1973	871.2	.098	85.4
2	292.4	2762	807.7	.146	117.9
3	192.0	3009	577.9	.221	127.7
4	84.5	3401	287.2	.497	142.7
5	73.4	3515	258.0	.568	146.6
6	68.8	3797	261.1	.604	157.7
7	62.9	3864	242.9	.658	159.8
8	55.7	4106	228.9	.740	169.4
9	50.9	4210	214.3	.808	173.2
10	47.9	4393	210.5	.856	180.2
11	45.9	4424	203.0	.892	181.0
12	44.4	4655	206.8	.918	189.8
13	43.4	4691	203.6	.937	190.8
14	42.5	4904	208.5	.953	198.7
15	41.8	4970	207.9	.965	200.7
16	41.3	5127	211.7	.973	206.0
17	40.8	5291	216.1	.980	211.8
18	40.4	5423	219.2	.985	215.9
19	37.8	5582	211.1	.989	208.8
20	23.9	5776	137.9	1.000	137.9
21	16.4	5947	97.3	1.000	97.3
22	11.8	6264	74.1	1.000	74.1
23	8.9	6384	57.0	1.000	56.9
24	7.1	6508	46.3	1.000	46.3
25	5.9	6668	39.1	1.000	39.1
26	4.9	7504	36.4	1.000	36.4
27	4.0	7627	30.4	1.000	30.4
28	3.3	7758	25.6	1.000	25.6
29	2.7	7324	20.8	1.000	20.8
30	–	–	–	–	–
Total	2315.8		7101.6		3891.6
Corrected Total	2313.6		7094.7		3887.8

Table 5-10 (cont.)

B. Officers

(1) Completed Years of Service	(2) Average Strength* (thousands)	(3) Average Basic Pay**	(4) Cost Col. 2 X Col. 3 (millions)	(5) Probability of Retire- ment***	(6) Cost Col. 4 X Col. 5 (millions)
0	43.7	4108	179.7	.179	32.2
1	43.2	4294	185.4	.181	33.6
2	34.9	5524	192.9	.223	43.0
3	22.8	6855	156.3	.340	53.1
4	17.0	7623	129.7	.454	58.9
5	14.5	7734	112.3	.531	59.6
6	12.9	8074	104.4	.595	62.1
7	11.9	8030	95.8	.644	61.7
8	11.3	8360	94.1	.681	64.1
9	10.8	8394	90.5	.710	64.2
10	9.4	8878	83.1	.816	67.8
11	9.1	8916	81.1	.838	68.0
12	8.4	9370	78.9	.904	71.3
13	8.3	9352	77.2	.920	71.0
14	8.1	9842	79.9	.938	75.0
15	8.0	9914	79.2	.946	74.9
16	7.9	10368	81.5	.959	78.2
17	7.7	10464	81.1	.970	78.7
18	7.7	10782	82.6	.979	80.8
19	7.6	10549	80.0	.985	78.8
20	6.5	10882	70.6	1.000	70.6
21	4.3	11100	48.0	1.000	48.0
22	3.7	11815	43.3	1.000	43.3
23	3.1	12045	37.9	1.000	37.9
24	2.7	12393	34.0	1.000	34.0
25	2.4	13028	31.1	1.000	31.1
26	2.1	14157	29.0	1.000	29.0
27	1.8	14122	25.4	1.000	25.4
28	1.5	14388	22.2	1.000	22.2
29	1.3	14819	18.6	1.000	18.6
30	1.8	16210	29.8	1.000	29.8
Total	336.4		2535.6		1666.9

*1965 Multiple Decrement Tables for Department of Defense.

**"Average Annual Basic Pay All Personnel on Active Duty, 30 June 1968 by Length of Service for Pay Purposes." OASD (M&RA) Actuarial Consultant, 16 December 1968.

***"Percentage of Military Personnel on Active Duty, 30 June 1965 Expected to Continue on Active Duty until Retirement by Length of Active Service," OASD (M), Actuarial Consultant, 2 August 1966.

Appendix 5-E

The Hubbell Report on Modernizing Military Pay

The great virtue of the Hubbell Report is its recognition that the primary deficiency of military compensation is in its low visibility. A second virtue is its specification of military retirement as a problem area, though its own solution was a marginal adjustment of retirement benefits that failed to attack the root cause and was inconsistent with its own retirement objectives. Apart from these two features, the Report's recommendations are analytically dubious. It is even possible that implementation of the Hubbell proposals would even make a military career *less* attractive to prospective recruits.

The difficulties of the Hubbell recommendations are caused by the career-force perceptions of its authors. The Report's primary aim is to improve career attractiveness; a secondary aim is to increase the services' ability to manage career profiles more effectively by strengthening the individual's desire to remain and providing the military with a fairer means of forced egress. But the utility of its *specific* proposals (as opposed to generalities) toward these objectives is dubious except for those already career-committed.

The first and most serious deficiency is the Report's double standard, biased in favor of careerists. It claims that "fairness and equity" to all parties are the solution to the perennial attraction and retention problem.[74] In fact it assumes away half the problem in an obscure footnote:

As long as noncareer personnel are for the most part citizen-soldiers discharging a civic obligation, the question of rates and methods of pay needed to attract and retain an all-volunteer noncareer force does not arise.[75]

This manifests the pay policy enunciated by Admiral Radford in 1955. Yet it is the central nexus of the retention problem; for as long as the services depend on draft-induced volunteers for their expensively trained specialties, retention in these specialties will remain a cause for concern.

To justify its argument that "the noncareer enlisted force (52% of all personnel) is appropriately compensated both in method and amounts,"[76] the Hubbell group has revived an old military pay concept, that of "residual pay." This concept compares the residual or free-cash position of military personnel with that of comparable civilians after subtracting for all the income-in-kind and low-price benefits associated with military service. That is, the cost to the individual of shelter, subsistence, haircuts, etc., is subtracted from cash salary and the residual compared for military personnel and civilians. In this way, first-term enlistees are shown to be paid 33% more than civilian high-school graduates of similar age.[77] The procedure is dubious. It implies that (1) civilians

167

would buy the same bundle of goods, such as weekly haircuts; and (2) the goods compared, such as a barracks bunk in an isolated locality and an urban apartment, have equivalent utility. The criterion may be valid in a Spartan economy, but not in a modern industrial society. The "residual pay" notion is also inconsistent with the Hubbell comparability comparisons for the career force; that is, many items are considered compensation for noncareerists but not for careerists.

A second difficulty of the Hubbell Report is that its claim of improved retention and higher career selectivity is vitiated by its vesting provisions. Vesting retirement benefits is often desirable for reasons of equity and labor mobility. However, vesting also reduces the firm's incentive for human capital investment. The adverse features of vesting for the military are that (1) vesting for junior personnel, in particular, amounts to a negative reenlistment bonus and removes the financial constraint which induces many to reenlist; and (2) vesting is most attractive for the military's best personnel, who generally have the better civilian opportunities. A corollary is that vesting will not necessarily increase command incentive to use forced separation more extensively. Forced separation before retirement is still unfair to the individual, because the combined total of Hubbell's vested retirement benefits and separation pay are much less than the discounted present value of the individual's retirement at 20 years, as shown in Table 5-11. The reason is because the vesting benefits are based on a 6.5%

Table 5-11
Financial Loss Due to Forced Egress[1]

	Hubbell Proposals			
Years of Service	Vesting Pay	Proposed Hubbell Separation Pay	Lump Sum Annuity Fund Discounted at 10%	Difference
10	$ 2,197	$ 9,784	$ 93,904	$ 81,923
15	5,900	17,573	151,223	127,750
19	11,320	24,988	221,390	185,082
20	–	–	243,529	–

[1] Based on 1968 pay scales for an officer who would have retired as a lieutenant colonel with 20 years' service.

retirement contribution, which is only a small fraction of the retirement benefit's total cost. A surprising feature of Hubbell's vesting is that it does not imply higher government costs. This is because the 6.5% of salary that is the individual's retirement contribution increases salary visibility by almost that amount at no cost to the government. This is done by the simple accounting device of switching from a poorly visible unfunded account to a fully visible sum that is to be included in a visible salary and then deducted, as is the civilian practice. The government's out-of-pocket costs are from those not retiring; but this cost is more than offset by increased wage visibility for all personnel and the increased visibility accruing to careerists at no cost to the government.

A third serious deficiency of the Hubbell recommendations is that their comparability calculations are erroneous. The Report alleges that as of *October 1967* military salaries lagged $824.3 and 925.1 million (i.e., 6.2 and 6.9%) respectively behind civil service and civilian salaries.[78] Part of this is due to Hubbell's definition of salary. The Report arbitrarily defines a military salary which excludes the cost of all differential pay, fringe benefits, and the great bulk of retirement benefits. For the representative career officer and enlisted man, these benefits are 70% of his Hubbell-defined salary as opposed to only 12.1% of civilian compensation. With so much of military compensation excluded from comparison, the Hubbell salary ought to be smaller than comparable civilian salary. But the startling fact is that aggregate military income as defined by Hubbell for the career force actually exceeds aggregate mean income of college (for officers) and high-school (for EM) graduates. This can be seen by comparing Tables 5-12 and 5-13. The manpower base for both tables is the 30 June 1967

Table 5-12
Military Personnel Cost with Military Salary (1967)

	Rates
Officers	
(1) Number of Officers:	$361,824^1$
(2) Adjusted Average 1 October 1967 Military Salary	$ 11,528^2
(3) Officer Cost:	$4,171,107,000
Warrant Officers	
(1) Number of Warrant Officers:	$22,670^1$
(2) Adjusted Average 1 October 1967 Military Salary	$ 9,694^2
(3) Warrant Officer Cost:	$219,763,000
Enlisted Careerists	

(1) Military Salary $= \dfrac{1.065}{.6815} \displaystyle\sum_{i=4}^{30~\&~over} B_i N_i$, where

  $i =$ Completed years of service
  $N =$ Number of enlisted men
  $B =$ Basic pay
  $.6815 =$ Basic pay for career enlisted as percent of total "salary."[3]
  $1.065 =$ Explicit retirement contribution.

(2) Career enlisted cost:	$6,827,571,924
Total Career Force at Military Wages:	$11,218,221,924

[1]"Number of Military Personnel on Active Duty, 30 June 1967 by Pay Grade and Length of Service for Pay Purposes," OASD (M&RA), Actuarial Consultant, 5 February 1968.

[2]Office of the Secretary of Defense, op. cit., p. S-10. Includes basic pay, quarters & subsistence allowances, tax advantage and 6.5% of salary for a retirement contribution.

[3]Ibid., Table 3-9, Composition of Average Annual Regular Military Compensation by Pay Grade, p. 45.

Table 5-13
Military Personnel Cost with Civilian Salary (1967)

Rates

Civilian Salary Costs for Officers:

(1) $CS_O = 1.312 \sum\limits_{i=22}^{51 \ \& \ over} S_i N_i$, where

   i = Civilian age corresponding to completed years of service.[1]

   N = Number of officers.[2]

   S = Mean earnings of college graduates by age from 1960 census.[3]

   1.312 = Increase in average gross weekly earnings from 1959 to October 1967 in Total Non-Agricultural, Private, Table B-30, *1969 Economic Report of the President.*

(2) Total civilian salary cost: $3,746,438,461.

Civilian Salary for Warrant Officers:

(1) $CS_W = 1.312 \sum\limits_{i=20}^{49 \ \& \ over} S_i N_i$, where

   S_i = mean earnings of professional, technical, and kindred workers.[3]

(2) Total civilian salary for warrant officers: $243,031,420.

Civilian Salary for Career Enlisted:

(1) $CS_E = 1.312 \sum\limits_{K=23}^{48 \ \& \ over} S_i N_i$, where

   S_i = mean earnings of high-school graduates by age.[3]

(2) Total civilian salary for career enlisted: $6,220,280,799

Total Career Force at Civilian Wages: $10,209,750,680.

[1] Entry age was assumed to be 22 for officers, 20 for warrant officers, and 19 for enlisted men. Costs are, of course, sensitive to the entry ages chosen. In 1964 the median age of all male enlisted accessions was 19.2; 25.9% were less than 18-1/2. "Percentage Distribution of Non-prior Service Male Accessions, By Age and Education, All Services, Enlisted," OASD (M), 2 September 1964. Higher entry ages would make civilian wages more costly and reduce the military's earnings advantage.

[2] "Number of Military Personnel on Active Duty, 30 June 1967 by Pay Grade and Length of Service for Pay Purposes," OASD (M&RA), Actuarial Consultant, 5 February 1968.

[3] *Present Value of Estimated Lifetime Earnings,* Technical Paper 16, Bureau of the Census, Washington, D.C. GPO, 1967, pp. 9-11.

force. Careerists for this calculation are defined as officers, warrant officers, and enlisted men with 4 or more completed years of service. This differs from Hubbell's definition only in that his career group includes an undetermined number of E4s and E5s with 2 to 4 years of service. At military salary rates, military personnel cost $11,218.4 million; at civilian rates, $10,209.8 million. Thus, rather than lagging 925.1 million or 6.9% behind cohort parity, military pay for *careerists* was $1,008.7 million, or 9.9% more than cohort parity in 1967. Furthermore, this gap is even larger when one considers fringe benefits and the four pay rises since October 1967, which amounted to 24-33% in regular military compensation[79] as compared with only 19.1% for civilians as of 1 January 1971.[80]

The difference in estimates occurs because Hubbell's wage comparability is based on salary comparisons of arbitrarily determined hierarchical levels; mine, on mean earnings by age and education. The major discrepancy in estimates suggests that either (1) the military's and possibly the civil service's hierarchical levels have been overstated relative to civilian levels; or (2) the military (and civil service) as a group bears greater responsibility and hence deserves a higher hierarchical level and its concomitant compensation.

6

The Budget Cost of a Volunteer Military[1]

Introduction

While economists would generally regard budget costs as an inaccurate measure of real cost, budget costs are politically relevant and important. Costing voluntarism is intricate and involves more than econometrics, because the military is an institutional complex that differs in many ways from the more familiar civilian labor market. Analogies to civilian models can be misleading. Moreover, previous cost estimates have omitted certain plausible cost savings, thereby accentuating the bias against voluntarism. This chapter considers such savings in an effort to remove the bias.

A volunteer military with the combat effectiveness of a 2.65-million-man draft-induced force may be attained in peacetime for an additional budget cost of $2.1 to $2.5 billion in the long run. These costs appear similar to those recently estimated by the President's Commission on an All-Volunteer Armed Force, but the Commission estimates focus on the short-run costs of voluntarism, and do not fully examine long-run cost implications.[2] This chapter's findings contrast sharply with previous volunteer studies whose estimates range between $4 and $17 billion.[3] My costs are lower because all of the following factors are considered in my methodology:

1. Increased retention in a volunteer force.
2. Use of the draft or the Vietnam phaseout to reduce the high short-run costs of a transition to voluntarism.
3. Reduced training activity in a volunteer force.
4. The theoretical construct of perceived pay.
5. A steep military wage structure caused by low entry wages.
6. Enlistment bonuses.
7. Rapid youth population growth since 1964.
8. Use of the same proportion of mental-category-IV (below average) enlistees as before Vietnam.
9. Recognition that category-IV men are in excess supply.
10. Discrimination among services to overcome the Army's recruiting disadvantage.

Conversely, no previous study considers the increased cost implications of all of the following:

1. Cost estimates based on 1970 wage levels.
2. Higher retention rates of a volunteer force, which increase compensation costs as the average soldier achieves more seniority.
3. Increased retirement costs due to higher retention rates.
4. The DoD underestimate of retirement accrual costs.

Besides considering the collective impact of these fourteen points on the cost estimates, this chapter shows the sensitivity of such estimates to the youth unemployment rate, the supply elasticity of volunteers with respect to military pay, the proportion of enlistees who are true volunteers, the retention rate of volunteers, two definitions of military wages, and the force size. The cost estimates are relatively insensitive to plausible changes in these variables because of the cost-retarding impact of effects 1 through 10. In most cases considered, the annual cost increments necessary to establish voluntarism are below $2.3 billion.

This chapter's estimates have several limitations. First, published estimates of the budget cost of voluntarism, except for the recent Presidential Commission Report, are based on pre-Vietnam data. Although data from the Vietnam period contain offsetting "nuisance" variables, information as of 1969 indicates that increased anti-military attitudes on the part of young people have not appreciably influenced the subset of true volunteers from which the services recruit. Second, this chapter's cost estimates are based on existing institutional constraints. Changes in military compensation, recruitment, and retention policies can lead to major cost savings and increases in combat effectiveness. I have accepted existing policies since their change is a major problem and study in itself. Third, I have not considered the possibility of savings from the following factors: productivity increases caused by the rationalizing impact of market wages, capital-labor tradeoffs, and a more experienced force; "womanization" and civilian contractual performance of some military functions; reduced veteran benefits for peacetime volunteers; tax rebates from larger entrant wages; and, since the Army drives the cost of voluntarism, the possibility of shifting overlapping functions from the Army to the other services.

Methodology

Considerable uncertainty surrounds the 1970 projection of volunteers generated in previous studies. Such projections are used only as a basis of comparison for the eight alternative cases considered here. Fortunately, total budget costs do not vary widely among the cases, even though we assume two unemployment rates and calculate wage costs under different assumptions about the responsiveness of volunteers to wage changes. Therefore, it is not necessary to know the "true" case in order to conclude that a volunteer military is cheaper and more flexible than previously believed.

Initial manpower requirements depend on the desired force size and the overall personnel retention rate of this force. Manpower supply depends on the population of young men and the relative advantages they see in military and civilian life. These advantages depend in part on the military wage rate, a control variable enabling the military to offset the disadvantages associated with service life. The size of the volunteer deficit and the responsiveness of supply to wage changes basically determine the added cost of attracting volunteers. With these things in mind, the estimating methodology is separated into three processes, described in the next three sections:

1. A projection of the annual *demand* for military manpower requirements that will sustain a 2.65-million-man effective force.
2. A projection of the 1970 *supply* of volunteers in the absence of the draft.
3. A calculation of the wage change necessary to balance demand and supply.

Long-run costs and savings associated with voluntarism are also calculated for alternative assumptions about the youth unemployment rate and the responsiveness of volunteers to pay increases.

To clarify the analysis, the cost estimates are divided into four major elements: (1) increased wage costs for new recruits, (2) increased wage costs due to the greater seniority of a volunteer force, (3) increased retirement costs, and (4) savings from reduced training activities. This study also differentiates between the short-run transition costs to achieve voluntarism and the long-run steady-state costs. Failure to account for this distinction has caused some public confusion. Short-run transition costs are less than steady-state costs, though the transition can be expensive if an abrupt change to voluntarism is made without using the draft as a cushion or without taking advantage of a post-Vietnam force phasedown. A phase-in period during which military wages are increased is also desirable in the uncertain post-Vietnam period. For example, changing youth attitudes or a continuing threat of limited wars may vitiate the most careful analysis of past data on military supply.

In order to present the argument as clearly as possible, the body of the text is brief. Detailed calculations are relegated to the appendixes. In a series of sequential calculations, Appendix 6-A describes the annual accessions needed for a volunteer force. Appendix 6-B outlines the perceived present value of a second lieutenant's pay as an example of how a young man views the compensation benefits of service life. Appendix 6-C describes the longevity, retirement, and training costs associated with a volunteer force. Appendix 6-D illustrates the methodology in calculating the costs of a volunteer force. Appendix 6-E compares my cost estimates and methodology with those of the 1970 Presidential Commission. Appendix 6-F discusses the cost implications of alternative enlistment and retention policies.

Projecting Manpower Requirements

Military force levels and retention rates determine the annual manpower inflows necessary to stock the force. The flows, in turn, are a basic element in the volunteer cost equation. In this study a fixed-force level of 2.65 million men was assumed, the size of the pre-Vietnam force and the force level used in most other cost studies of voluntarism. (Appendix 6-D briefly considers a 3-million-man military.) Based on pre-Vietnam experience, a 2.65-million-man effective force would consist of 333,000 officers and 2.32 million enlisted men. Excluding perturbations caused by wartime expansions, such a force requires an average annual inflow of 43,500 officers and 498,600 enlisted men *if the draft and current below-market wages for new enlistees are continued.*[4]

Enlisted Men

If the services increase wages, true volunteers will replace draftees and draft-induced volunteers; average retention rates and average enlistment periods will rise and the inflow required to maintain the given force level will fall. The average first-term reenlistment rate of eligible men from 1958 to 1965 has been 25.3%.[5] Not all are eligible to reenlist for various moral, mental, and physical reasons, so that a 498,600-man inflow leaves only an average strength of 84,500 at the five-year point, as seen in Table 6-1. (Eligibility standards are assumed unaffected in the switch to voluntarism.)

Table 6-1

Enlisted Men: Years-of-Service Profile for a 2.65-Million-Man Effective Force (In thousands)

Years of Service	Type of Force	
	Draft-Induced[a]	Volunteer[b]
Entry	498.6	312.9
1	478.5	299.3
2	441.6	276.5
3	292.4	260.1
4	192.0	181.0
5	84.5	106.0
12	45.9	58.4
16	41.8	53.3
20	37.8	48.5
21	23.9	30.7
25	7.1	9.1
29	3.3	4.4
30	2.7	3.4

[a]1965 Multiple Decrement Table for the Department of Defense, Office of the Actuarial Consultant, DoD.

[b]After a 5.9% training reduction. See Appendix 6-A for an expanded discussion.

The volunteer force profile may now be constructed. Oi derives a first-term reenlistment rate for true Army volunteers (those who would volunteer without the draft) of 33%;[6] the corresponding DoD rate is 36%.[7] The initial retention rate with voluntarism is therefore assumed to increase from 25.3 to 36%. Subsequent rates are assumed unchanged because the force is essentially a volunteer military after the first tour of duty—three years for the Army and four years for the other services. At the end of his second tour, an individual is largely locked in by his training, some of it specific and nontransferable, and by the growing attraction of retirement benefits.

Assuming an initial 36% reenlistment rate and the historical retention profile (Table 6-10, Appendix 6-A) thereafter, an annual inflow of 332,700 men is sufficient to stock a 2.32-million enlisted force. This new recruit flow is only 67% of that required for a draft-induced force, so the portion of the force engaged in training activities may be cut with no loss in combat effectiveness. On this basis a further force reduction of 5.9% is calculated in Appendix 6-A. The smaller enlisted force contains only 2.18 million men and requires only 312,000 yearly volunteers to maintain its size.[8]

Officers

Officer requirements for the volunteer force are based on Oi's estimates. During 1960-1965, accessions of 37,300 per year were required to maintain an officer level of 340,000. The volunteer force benefits from higher officer retention rates and requires only 34,200 accessions per year to maintain its officer stock of 336,000.[9] When training manpower savings are subtracted, the yearly officer flow falls to 32,200.

Army Requirements

The Army has the most difficulty in fulfilling its requirements. If, in a volunteer military, other services were to pay the same recruiting wages as the Army, non-Army recruits would receive more than is needed to induce them to enlist, and they would be in excess supply. Supply and demand projections should reflect the Army's special difficulty and have been therefore broken down into Army and non-Army.

Replacing draftees with longer-term and higher retention rate volunteers causes Army requirements for a 2.65-million-man military to drop from 217,000 to 124,000 annual accessions. This reduction in Army training and training support activities permits a 9.6% overall reduction in Army strength levels,[10] while operating units remain at constant strength. Army accession requirements then drop from 124,000 to 112,100 in the steady state. Officer demands also fall 9.6%, from 12,000 to 10,800. These Army figures appear in Table 6-3, along with non-Army demands.

The foregoing are requirements for a given force level; higher levels would require proportional changes in annual accessions in the long run. Rapid buildups for war are another matter. In principle, voluntarism could be maintained for limited wars, although sharp wage increases would be necessary, unless patriotism and a sense of adventure stimulated enlistments. But sharp wage increases in wartime could easily cause administrative and morale problems, and some people would object to wartime voluntarism for a number of ethical and philosophical reasons. However, the question of flexibility is not an objection to voluntarism if the draft is maintained in operational readiness for use in military expansions.[11]

Projecting the Supply of Volunteers

This section considers the supply of volunteers without a draft. In 1965 the DoD study of a volunteer military projected the FY 70-71 enlistments shown in Table 6-2A, without a draft and with the 1963 military-civilian wage ratio.[12] Consistent with recruiting history, the DoD projections include mental category IV proportions of 20% (Army), 10% (non-Army), and 14.2% (DoD). But category IV men queue up to enlist even at current low wages. They are in excess supply and should be subtracted from both supply and demand before calculating the wage increase necessary to equate the supply and demand of mental category I-III volunteers. Table 6-2B shows enlistments left after subtracting category IV personnel.

Table 6-3 compares the long-term demand requirements of a volunteer force

Table 6-2
Enlistments for a 2.65-Million Effective Volunteer Force in 1970 (In thousands)

Service	Enlisted Men[a]		Officers
	14.9%	11.5%	
A. Categories I-IV			
DoD	317.0	272.0	27.0
Army	106.0	91.0	9.0
Non-Army	211.0	181.0	18.0
B. Categories I-III			
DoD	274.7	235.7	27.0
Army	84.8	72.8	9.0
Non-Army	189.9	162.9	18.0

[a]Assuming two unemployment rates for enlisted men.

Table 6-3
Recruiting Deficits for a 2.65-Million Effective Volunteer Force in 1970
(In thousands)

| | Enlisted Men | | |
| | (1) | (2) | (3) |
Measure	14.9%	11.5%	Officers
Department of Defense			
1. Total requirements (Appendix A)	332.7	332.7	34.2
2. Requirements after 5.9% training reduction	312.9	312.9	32.2
3. Requirements for categories I-III are 85.5% of (2) for enlisted men only[a]	270.3	270.3	32.2
4. Supply of categories I-III[b]	274.6	235.6	27.0
5. Deficit	0	34.7	5.2
6. Percentage deficit[c]	0	14.7%	19.3%
Army			
7. Total requirements (Appendix A)	124.0	124.0	11.9
8. Requirements after 9.6% training reduction	112.1	112.1	10.8
9. Requirements for categories I-III are 80% of (8) for enlisted men only[a]	89.7	89.7	10.8
10. Supply of categories I-III[b]	84.8	72.8	9.0
11. Deficit	4.9	16.9	1.8
12. Percentage deficit	5.7%[d]	23.3%	20.0%
Non-Army			
13. Total requirements (Appendix A)	208.7	208.7	22.3
14. Requirements after 3.8% training reduction	200.8	200.8	21.5
15. Requirements for categories I-III are 90% of (14) for enlisted men only[a]	180.7	180.7	21.5
16. Supply of categories I-III (DoD-Army)	189.9	162.9	18.0
17. Deficit	0	17.8	3.5
18. Percentage deficit	0	10.9%	19.5%

[a]Assumes that 20% of Army enlistments and 10% of other enlistments are category IV.

[b]Altman and Fechter, op. cit., p. 25, Table 5, corrected for category IV proportions at 1963 relative wages.

[c]Altman and Fechter project deficits of 58% and 88% for enlisted men, depending on the unemployment rate, and 37% for officers. They do not consider the higher retention rates of a volunteer force, however, and thus greatly overstate their requirements.

[d]Oi, op. cit., p. 48, estimates a 60.1% deficit, but overstates Army requirements and ignores the use of category IV personnel.

with the supply projection for 1970, assuming no draft pressure and 1963 military-to-civilian wage rates. The recruiting deficits are shown under two unemployment rates. The Army deficit is the largest and drives the cost of attracting volunteers.

The DoD forecasts are necessarily speculative.[13] Fortunately, the budget-cost estimates that follow are not especially sensitive to changes in the supply projections. Yet the forecasts are intuitively plausible because they can be approximated by assuming that the estimated true volunteers of 1964 increase proportionately with population growth to 1970.[14]

Table 6-3 indicates that recruiting deficits will appear, but the supply forecasts assume no change in the ratio of military-to-civilian wages. To determine the responsiveness of volunteers to increased military pay so that deficits can be eliminated, elasticity of supply (ES) estimates of DoD volunteers were derived from time series data. This concept is defined as the percentage increase in volunteers divided by the percentage increase in the ratio of military-to-civilian wages.

Published elasticity estimates have been slightly greater than unity. Fechter and Altman's initial point estimate was 1.17; Oi's, 1.36; and the Gates Commission's, 1.25.[15] Their estimates, however, were based on misspecified equations. For goodness of fit, these estimates were derived from a functional form corresponding to the upper end of a Pareto distribution. But potential volunteers are known to be drawn from the lower and middle ranges of the income distribution. The functional form of their estimates led the above authors to rationalize decreasing elasticity, even though economic theory suggested that because perceived military wages for entrants were so much below comparable civilian wages, a threshold might well exist where a region of increasing elasticity existed (though the supply curve's slope would still be positive). A second misspecification occurred in the explanatory variable: its elasticity estimates were for across-the-board wage changes rather than for only the desired first term increases.

Klotz, building on Fisher's work,[16] found an across-the-board elasticity of 1.44 (versus Fisher's .74), based on a more theoretically correct lognormal income distribution which has regions of increasing and decreasing elasticity.[17] Klotz's estimate of first-term supply elasticity was .9 for DoD and slightly less for the Army.

The cost calculations of this chapter are based on Army and DoD ES estimates of 1.0 and 0.5. This brackets the conservative Klotz estimate of .9 and gives a measure of cost sensitivity to elasticity estimates. The elasticity estimates used for the cost calculations are thus *lower* than those used by the Presidential Commission and earlier studies. However, costs are not particularly sensitive to elasticity estimates for a *steady-state* military of less than 3 million men for two reasons: (1) the relatively small recruiting deficit due to population growth, and (2) the pay increases that the present compensation structure can absorb for first-term enlistees before wage increases have to be passed across the board to all personnel.

Bonuses and the Correct Pay Variable

If the recruiting deficit and the elasticity of supply are known, the percentage increase in military wages necessary to eliminate the deficit can be calculated. But the absolute wage increase implied by this percentage depends on the beginning wage level. This level, in turn, depends on the definition of the pay variable.

The perceived present value of first-term pay is the theoretically correct pay variable to achieve the desired volunteer force, for several reasons.[18] First-term enlisted income is low for the first two years and then jumps about $900 at the two-year point, as shown in Table 6-4. The four-year pay profile rises more quickly than the comparable civilian pay profile.[19] Also, young men have a high time-preference, valuing present income much more highly than future income because they aspire to reach a certain life style quickly. They manifest the high time-preference by their willingness to borrow at high interest rates. More concretely, survey results indicate that 18- and 19-year-olds have a 28% subjective discount rate, which apparently falls to about 7 to 10% when they reach middle age.[20] Because some enlistees are over 19, the entire enlistee age group is assumed to discount future income streams by only 25% in the following analysis.

Discounting and the present value attained by this process must be refined even further. Pay must be perceived before it motivates enlistment, and the enlistee apparently does not perceive, or value, his pay to be as high as his defined "total income," which includes base pay, cost of food and housing, and a tax advantage on these items.[21] Quite plausibly this may be due to ignorance, restricted choice, or low appraisal of the worth to him of military food, clothing, shelter, and other such benefits. In any case, his appraisal is much less than the cost value calculated by the DoD accountants.[22]

The perceived present value concept incorporates both the undervaluation of pay by enlistees and their discounting of future income in order to arrive at a wage definition that is most relevant for enlistee behavior. Table 6-4 shows that

Table 6-4
Annual Military Incomes of Enlisted Men in 1963

Year	Total Income	Base Pay	Pay Volunteer Perceives
1	$1830	$1055	$1550
2	$2143	$1382	$1880
3	$2991	$2002	$2650
4	$3344	$2433	$3030

in 1963, first-year base pay for enlisted men was $1,055, DoD-defined total income was $1,830, and perceived pay for *all* the military's cash, income-in-kind, and deferred benefits was only $1,550. Perceived pay for the remaining three years of service was obtained by applying the same discount as for the first year.[23]

Chaney's study leads us to apply a 25% discount to the stream of perceived pay (PP).[24] We calculate perceived present value (PPV_m) for four years of service in 1963 as

$$PPV_m = \sum_{i=0}^{3} PPi/(1 + .25)^i = \$1550 + 1500 + 1700 + 1550 = \$6300.$$

Wage increases given to first-termers between 1963 and 1968 caused the discounted perceived pay to rise to $7971 by 1968. With a 10% across-the-board wage increase between 1968 and 1970 we have a PPV_m = $8800 in 1970.

From Table 6-3, both the first-term elasticity definition ES = % V/% PPV_m and the assumption ES = 1 for first-term wages indicate that wage increases of 0 and 14.7% are necessary to balance the DoD's category I-III demand and supply in peacetime at 14.9 and 11.5% unemployment, respectively.[25] But military wages for the *first two years* of service have already risen 30.3% between 1963 and 1968, as opposed to only a 21.8% rise for manufacturing earnings so that relative wages for draftees have already increased 7%.[26] Thus, even at the low youth unemployment rate of 11.5% in 1970, military wages apparently need only be increased 14.7 − 7 = 7.7% if ES = 1. For example, using an $8,800 base, we have a PPV increase of $678.

Nevertheless, wage increases are allocated to give all entrants into the military a 14.9% increase in PPV, which amounts to $728 in cash each year for the first two years of service.[27] This is to bring all enlistees up to the standard of the federal minimum wage; it also fills in the existing gap in the enlisted wage profile for those with less than two years of service. In most cases, this increase suffices to close the recruiting deficit. In cases where this amount was insufficient, Army and non-Army volunteers could be distinguished and a discriminating Army enlistment bonus could be paid up to an arbitrarily determined maximum limit of $2,000 for enlisted men.[28] If the amount with this procedure were still insufficient, as it was for Army recruits in the most adverse combination, the enlisted wage profile could be flattened to the civilian practice by splicing the remaining PPV increases into the wage profile.[29] These procedures permit potentially large increases in volunteer wages, while still maintaining interrank wage differentials and no wage inversion (where juniors receive almost as much as seniors, causing expensive across-the-board wage increases to all military personnel).

The Cost of Voluntarism

The elements influencing the budget cost of a volunteer military are presented in Figure 6-1. Manpower demand (accession requirements) depends on force levels, reenlistment rates, and the length of enlistment contracts, whereas supply depends on draft pressure and the relative attractiveness of military life. Draft pressure disappears and manpower supply falls with the advent of voluntarism. Also, substituting volunteers for draftees and draft-induced volunteers lengthens the tour of duty and causes a higher reenlistment rate. Smaller inflows can then maintain a given force size.

A recruiting deficit remains. It is eliminated by military wage increases equal to the product of the percentage deficit, the elasticity of supply, and the fraction of military compensation that the enlistee perceives (a function of the compensation structure). The wage increment, when multiplied by the inflow of required volunteers, is defined as accession costs.

The short-run transition costs from conscription to voluntarism for a 2.65-million draft-induced force can be high. Before the higher retention rates and longer enlistment contracts of volunteers took effect, manpower losses would be 499,000;[30] accessions would need to equal this amount for two years to maintain the force. The initial recruiting deficit would therefore be large, as would the initial wage increase required to attract volunteers.

Transition costs and the problems associated with extraordinarily high entry wages can be reduced by a transition plan combining voluntarism with the draft for two or three years. This would not only maintain force flexibility for Vietnam contingencies, but would also provide the data base to test the accuracy of statistical supply projections.[31] Wages then need only to be increased enough to attract the target inflow of 312,900 enlisted volunteers and 32,200 officers (Table 6-3). Any required residue would be drafted and paid the volunteer wage.[32] Because no savings or additional costs result from training savings and a costly shift to an older force, transition costs involve only the accession costs of a yet unreduced flow of entrants. Assuming a draft assist, these transition costs appear on line 1 of Table 6-5, which summarizes short-run and long-run costs for eight alternative cases depending on the elasticity of supply (ES = 1.0 or 0.5), youth unemployment rate (14.9% or 11.5%), and definition of the relevant wage variable (PPV or DoD "total income"). Three judgmental constraints were imposed in this costing: no enlisted man receives less than the federal minimum wage; enlistment bonuses are used, but do not exceed $2000 for enlisted men and $4000 for officers; and the Army may receive a differential enlistment bonus. Short-run costs do not exceed $1,580 million, and are usually closer to $1,000 million because of discriminating Army enlistment bonuses, the small recruiting deficit implied by the steady-state volunteer target, and the PPV concept.

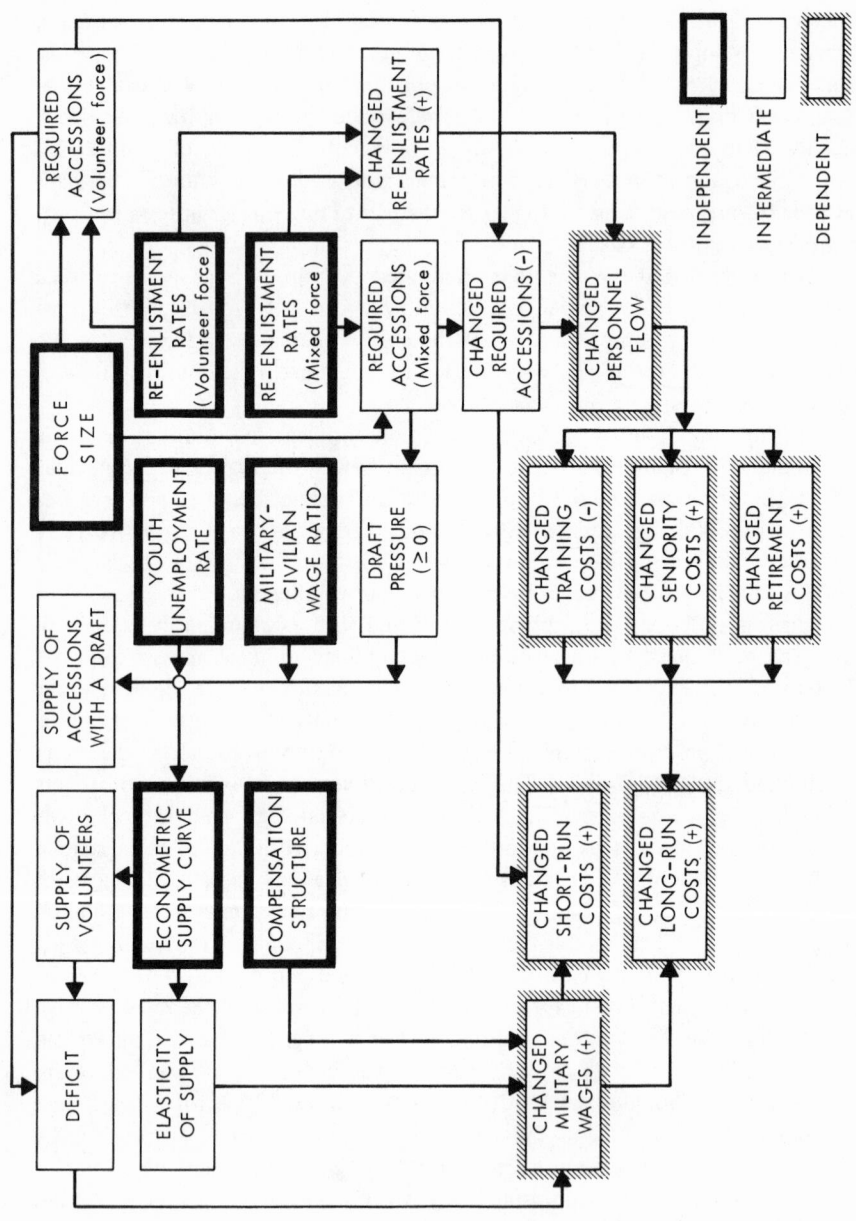

Figure 6-1. The Interaction of Cost Elements.

Table 6-5

Cost Increases to Establish a Volunteer Force[a] (in $ million)

	Perceived Present Value				DoD Total Income			
	1.0		0.5		1.0		0.5	
Costs	14.9	11.5	14.9	11.5	14.9	11.5	14.9	11.5
Short-run costs	$ 751	$ 773	$ 841	$1231	$ 767	$ 902	$ 895	$1580
Long-run costs (steady-state)								
Wage increases[b]	$ 481	$ 495	$ 559	$ 804	$ 495	$ 580	$ 606	$1036
Seniority costs	1573	1573	1573	1573	1573	1573	1573	1573
Retirement Costs	1726	1726	1726	1726	1726	1726	1726	1726
Less training saving	−1655	−1655	−1655	−1655	−1655	−1655	−1655	−1655
Total costs	$2125	$2139	$2203	$2448	$2139	$2229	$2250	$2680

[a]Combat effectiveness of a 2.65-million draft-induced force. Details in Appendixes 6-A and 6-D, especially in Table 6-18.
[b]Excludes consideration of tax increases that return to the Treasury.

Now, holding population and other economic variables constant, the combination of diminished accessions and increased retention rates creates a new steady-state personnel flow through the system. An older and more experienced force results in the long run. Personnel costs rise with this increased seniority, as do retirement costs. Conversely, the dramatically reduced accessions of voluntarism imply large savings in training and support manpower that are realizable without reducing personnel in operating forces. The figures in the lower portion of Table 6-5 show the cost impact of these elements. In all cases, the force has the fighting ability of a 2.65-million draft-induced force, and the first-term reenlistment rate of enlisted men is assumed to average 36%. Long-run cost increments range between $2,125 million and $2,680 million, with the bulk due to retirement and seniority costs.[33] Reduced training and ancillary activities in the volunteer force save $1,655 million, as described in Appendix 6-C.

Costs increase if larger forces or lower retention rates are assumed. In the long run, a volunteer force with a combat size equal to a draft-induced force of 3 million men would cost $3 billion more than its draft-induced alternative.[34] Imagining the worst possible case in Table 6-5 (the last column), long-run costs increase by $4.6 billion if the reenlistment rate is only 30 rather than 36%.[35]

Summary

The added budget cost of a volunteer military is probably between $2.1 and $2.5 billion. The largest cost increases are caused by higher retention rates which, in turn, cause higher seniority and retirement costs that become manifest only in the long run. Initial wage increases for entrants are $0.5 to $0.8 billion in the long run, and $0.75 to $1.2 billion during the transition to voluntarism, if the draft is used to phase in voluntarism. These surprisingly small estimates are primarily due to population growth and the structure of the military compensation system. If these projections prove optimistic, then enlistment bonuses differentiated among and within the services should inexpensively eliminate any recruiting deficit. The penumbra of uncertainty about the cost estimate may be easily dispelled by simply raising first-term military wages and observing enlistment response during a transition period of decreasing draft calls.

Appendix 6 - A

Manpower Requirements

This appendix develops the sequence of calculations for determining the annual accessions into a volunteer force. The sequence requires a new years-of-service profile to account for different retention rates. Comparing the old and new years-of-service profiles is also necessary for calculating the increased budget costs accruing from a profile shift from a younger, higher-turnover force to one somewhat older with less personnel turnover. An older force entails two cost increases: higher longevity pay to maintain civilian wage comparability, and higher retirement costs. Three cost benefits accrue from an older force: reduced annual accessions, reduced training costs, and higher labor productivity. Increased productivity is not measured in this study and is not used to offset my incremental budget costs. Such improvements do have great potential for reducing personnel requirements, but translating higher productivity into reduced manpower requirements is a major study in itself.

The first step in projecting demand is to determine force levels, which must be broken down into service, officer, and enlisted categories. The standard force for the volunteer military cost studies has been set at 2.65 million men. Its composition is shown in Table 6-6. These components are found by taking the 1964-1965 average for each service and proportionally reducing their total from 2.6805 to 2.65 million men.[36] Next, the service totals are separated into officer and enlisted strength.[37]

The second major step is calculated from the Decrement Tables developed by the DoD Actuarial Consultant. These tables show the years-of-service profile after perturbations are removed, such as those caused by large numbers of veterans, particularly officers, remaining after wartime periods. The mean officer input from 1960 to 1965 was 37,000;[38] yet, excluding the World War II and Korean "hump," the required input would have been 43,500 officers, an increase of 17.6%. The active-duty enlisted input would have been 498,600 rather than the 1960-1965 average of 482,700.[39] These requirements are based on a theoretically corrected decrement table, thereby excluding wartime per-

Table 6-6
Force Level Components

Group	Navy	Air Force	Marine Corps	Total Non-Army	Army	Total DoD
Officer	75,800	133,700	16,900	226,400	110,000	336,400
Enlisted	583,600	712,600	170,900	1,467,100	846,500	2,313,600
Total	659,400	846,300	187,800	1,693,500	956,500	2,650,000

turbations and slightly increasing the required number of annual accessions as compared with projections based on historical averages. Table 6-7 shows the expected years-of-service profile for voluntary enlistees compared with that for the draft-induced force.

Table 6-7 requires three calculations: estimating the new retention rates for a volunteer military; determining the new inflow of annual accessions; and making allowances for having to train fewer men.

No scientific method exists for estimating the new retention rates for a volunteer military. The most reliable estimate would come from longitudinal surveys based on the reenlistment rates of men who claim, at the time of entry, that they would have enlisted in the absence of a draft. (The critical assumption of this method is that the new and the old true volunteer populations are identical.) Since these data do not exist, I use Oi's assumption that draft-induced volunteers have the same reenlistment propensities as draftees.[40]

Table 6-8 shows the retention rate for draftees and first-term volunteers, as well as the percentage of draft-motivated volunteers. These parameters are then applied to the formula

(1) $$DM(9.2) + (1 - DM)(x) = (1)(FT),$$

where DM = fraction of draft-motivated volunteers
FT = first-term retention rates
x = true volunteer's reenlistment rate.

This calculation yields the Table 6-9 estimate of retention rates for a volunteer force.

Given the retention rate estimate, the second step in calculating Table 6-7 is to determine the new inflow of annual accessions. This calculation is based on a reprint of several columns of the DoD Decrement Tables (shown in Table 6-10) that give average man-years for each year of completed service from an initial one-million-man input. Since no change in institutional practices is postulated,[41] we can multiply years 3 to 30 for the Army and years 4 to 30 for the other services by the retention rate increase for each service, giving an expanded number of average man-years for careerists. This figure is added to the unchanged number of average man-years for first-termers, for a total average man-years based on an initial input of one million men. Dividing this number into actual service strength yields the required accession number. The formula is thus

(2) $$A\left[\sum_{i=0}^{2\,or\,3} M_i + RRI \sum_{i=3\,or\,4}^{30} M_i\right] = SS,$$

Table 6-7
Enlisted Men: Years-of-Service Profile for a 2.65-Million-Man Effective Force (In thousands)

Years of Service	Draft-Induced[a]	Volunteer[b] Army	Volunteer[b] Non-Army	DoD
Entry	498.6	112.1	200.8	312.9
1	478.5	107.8	191.5	299.3
2	441.6	100.3	176.2	276.5
3	292.4	94.2	165.9	260.1
4	192.0	41.4	139.7	181.0
5	84.5	41.4	68.4	106.0
6	73.4	33.9	59.0	93.0
7	68.8	30.4	56.5	87.0
8	62.9	28.0	51.8	79.7
9	55.8	25.2	45.7	70.9
10	50.9	23.4	41.5	64.8
11	47.9	21.9	39.0	61.0
12	45.9	20.9	37.5	58.4
13	44.4	20.2	36.3	56.5
14	43.4	19.9	35.3	55.2
15	42.5	19.6	34.5	54.1
16	41.8	19.4	33.9	53.3
17	41.3	19.2	33.4	52.6
18	40.8	19.0	33.0	52.0
19	40.4	18.9	32.6	51.5
20	37.8	18.7	29.7	48.5
21	23.9	12.3	18.4	30.7
22	16.4	8.7	12.4	21.1
23	11.8	6.1	9.1	15.2
24	8.9	4.4	7.0	11.4
25	7.1	3.4	5.7	9.1
26	5.9	2.7	4.8	7.5
27	4.9	2.2	4.0	6.2
28	4.0	1.9	3.3	5.1
29	3.3	1.5	2.7	4.2
30	2.7	1.2	2.2	3.4
Total Avg. Man Years	2315.8	765.0	1411.0	2176.1
Corrected for Rounding Errors	2313.6	765.2	1411.5	2176.0

[a]1965 Multiple Decrement Table for the Department of Defense, Office of the Actuarial Consultant, DoD.

[b]Training reductions of 9.6% for Army and 3.8% for non-Army.

Table 6-8
Draft-Motivated Volunteers and First-Term Retention Rates (In percent)

Group	Army	Navy	Marine Corps	Air Force
Draft-motivated volunteers[a]	43.2	32.6	30.4	42.9
First-term retention rate[b]	23.5	24.1	17.4	32.5
Draftee retention rate[b]	9.2	–	–	–

[a]Altman and Fechter, op. cit., p. 23.
[b]*Selected Manpower Statistics,* FY 1958-1965, p. 51.

Table 6-9
Estimated Retention Rates for a Volunteer Force (In percent)

Service	True Volunteer Retention Rate	Increase in Retention Rate[a]
Army	34.3	46.2
Non-Army	38.0	39.0
Navy	31.2	29.8
Marine Corps	20.9	20.5
Air Force	50.1	53.8

[a][(true volunteer rate ÷ first-term rate of a draft-induced force)] − 1 x 100.

where A = annual accessions ÷ 1,000,000
       M_i = average man years for each year completed service as given by Decrement Table (Table 6-10)
   RRI = retention rate increase
   SS = service strength in average man years (Table 6-6).

Table 6-7 entries *without* training reductions may now be found by dividing the product of M_i and A into SS.

The third calculation concerns the beneficial overall impact of having to train fewer men: less training means a smaller training establishment and less overhead in general to support any given number of operating or output forces. This impact is iterative. If operating forces are held constant and the number of accessions is cut, then the training forces are proportionately reduced, which implies a cut in the supporting and transient/patient categories, as well as a further reduction in the training forces. The reduction process can be described as a simultaneous equation (see p. 193, "The Effect of Training Savings on Force Size") which can be approximated by the geometric series:

(3) $$FR = \frac{ar}{1 - r},$$

Table 6-10
Enlisted Men: 1965 Multiple Decrement Tables[a] (In thousands)

Years of Service	DoD	Regular Army	Navy	Regular Marine Corps	Air Force
1	959.8	961.4	951.7	954.9	955.2
2	885.7	894.6	873.6	888.5	877.9
3	586.5	840.4	826.7	838.2	822.1
4	385.2	252.4	701.4	710.6	685.8
5	169.4	234.3	209.7	198.8	285.1
6	147.2	207.1	198.3	171.6	232.0
7	137.9	185.7	193.1	155.3	221.9
8	126.1	170.6	182.4	141.3	199.1
9	111.8	153.8	172.2	121.0	167.6
10	102.1	142.5	154.7	106.2	154.1
11	96.1	133.8	144.9	97.3	146.5
12	92.0	127.4	138.6	92.1	141.4
13	89.1	123.3	134.0	89.1	137.0
14	87.1	121.3	130.3	87.2	133.5
15	85.3	119.7	127.1	85.6	130.3
16	83.9	118.5	124.6	84.1	127.9
17	82.8	117.2	122.5	82.8	126.4
18	81.9	116.1	121.1	81.8	124.9
19	81.1	115.2	119.8	81.0	123.4
20	75.9	114.2	98.6	70.9	121.8
21	47.9	75.0	59.9	53.4	73.9
22	32.8	53.0	34.7	41.3	53.0
23	23.7	37.2	23.3	33.1	40.1
24	17.9	26.9	16.7	26.8	31.6
25	14.3	20.7	12.6	23.0	26.1
26	11.8	16.6	9.6	20.2	22.2
27	9.7	13.6	7.3	17.8	18.8
28	8.0	11.0	5.6	15.6	15.7
29	6.6	9.0	4.3	13.6	13.1
30	5.4	7.3	3.2	11.9	10.6
Total Avg. Man Years	4641.0	5519.8	5902.5	5395.4	6218.9

Source: Office of the Actuarial Consultant, DoD.

[a]Average man years based on a one-million-man entry.

where a = the reduced accessions of a volunteer force (Table 6-12),

   FR = force reduction from reduced accessions,

and

(4) $$r = T + T(S/2 + P),$$

where the initials stand for the force heading of Table 6-11.

Inserting the parameters of Tables 6-11 and 6-12 into Eqs. (3) and (4) yields the following force reductions:

Army	.096
Non-Army	.038
DoD	.059

Table 6-11
Mean Allocation of Military Personnel by Program Category: 1958-1962
(In percent)

Services	(O) Operating Forces	(S) Supporting Forces	(T) Training Forces	(P) Transients & Patients
Army	64.6	16.6	16.6	2.1
Non-Army[a]	63.1	15.5	17.4	4.0
Navy	60.1	16.0	16.8	7.0
Marine Corps	63.2	10.2	19.6	7.0
Air Force	65.8	16.7	17.3	0.2

Source: *Allocation of Military Personnel by Program Category,* 1950-1959 and 1960-1962, Statistical Service Center, Office of Secretary of Defense, 17 December 1960 and 5 December 1962.

[a]Weighted average by accessions.

Table 6-12
Volunteer and Draft-Induced Accessions (In thousands)

Group	(1) Volunteer Force[a]	(2) Draft-Induced Force[b]	(3) Accessions Reduction[d]
Army	124.0	217.1[c]	0.429
Non-Army	208.7	247.6	0.157
Navy	87.6	98.7	
Marine Corps	29.4	34.3[c]	
Air Force	91.7	114.6	
DoD[e]	332.7	498.6	0.333

[a]From Eq. (2).

[b]Numbers do not sum to DoD Decrement total because the theoretically correct Army and Marine Corps components cannot be computed from the Decrement Tables.

[c]Based on actual 1958-1965 experience rather than Decrement Tables.

[d]Army and non-Army estimates are low because Army and Marine Corps accessions are based on lower historical data rather than the higher Decrement data. This leads to a smaller training saving and a slightly higher accession requirement.

[e]Enlisted costs are entirely based on Army and non-Army estimates. In this study only relatively small incremental officer costs have been based on DoD aggregates.

Table 6-7 entries which *include* training reductions can now be calculated by

(5)
$$m_i = (1 - FR) (A)M_i, i = 0, \ldots 2 \text{ or } 3,$$
$$m_j = (1 - FR) (A) (RRI)M_j, j = 3 \text{ or } 4, \ldots 30,$$

Equation (5), with the non-career/career break occurring at the third-year point, yields the Army column of Table 6-7 directly. The non-Army column is weighted by the volunteer force accessions given in Table 6-12. Finally, we list below the annual accessions required in $[(A)(1 - FR)]$ to support the average man-years in Table 6-7.

Army	112,100
Non-Army	200,800
DoD	312,900

The Effect of Training Savings on Force Size

Assuming (1) linearity; (2) operating forces held constant in size; and (3) that only half the supporting forces respond to iterative reductions in the training, supporting, and transient/patient categories, the exact formula for training savings is

(6)
$$A = A_0 \left(\frac{\overline{O} + S + T + P}{F_0} \right) = a_0(\overline{O} + S + T + P),$$

(7)
$$T = a_1 A,$$

(8)
$$S = a_2 T + \beta_2 P + \gamma_2 \overline{O} + \delta_2(S - \overline{S}_0) + \overline{S}_0,$$

(9)
$$P = a_3 T + \beta_3 P + \gamma_3 \overline{O} + \delta_3 S,$$

where $\overline{O}$ = number in operating category, to be held constant
T = number in training category
S = number in supporting category
P = number in patient and transient category
S_0 = minimal support base (i.e., the initial $1/2$ that is invariant)
A_0 = "raw" accessions/year required in a volunteer force before training reduction (Table 6-12)
A = "true" accessions/year
F_0 = initial enlisted strengths (Table 6-6).

Rearranging equations (6) to (9) into the generalized matrix form gives

(10) $\qquad$ A $\qquad -a_0 S - a_0 T \qquad - a_0 P = a_0 \overline{O}$,

(11) $\quad a_1 A \qquad\qquad - T \qquad\qquad = 0,$

(12) $\qquad (\delta_2 - 1)S + a_2 T \qquad + \beta_2 P = {}_-\gamma_2 \overline{O} + \delta_2 \overline{S}_0 - \overline{S}_0$,

(13) $\qquad\qquad \delta_3 S + a_3 T + (\beta_3 -1)P = -\delta_3 \overline{O}$.

The coefficients for these equations can be found in Table 6-11. These coefficients imply that for every 100 Army men, 16.6 are needed in supporting forces, etc. Therefore,

(14) $a_2 = \beta_2 = \gamma_2 = \delta_2$ which equals $S/2$ or .083 for the Army,

(15) $a_3 = \beta_3 = \gamma_3 = \delta_3$ which equals P or .021 for the Army.

The constants can be computed from the force levels of Table 6-6, the volunteer accessions from Table 6-12, and the proportion of operating and supporting forces from Table 6-11. For the Army, these give

(16) $\qquad\qquad \overline{O} = .646(846,500) = 546,839,$

(17) $\qquad\qquad A_0 = 124,000; a_0 = \dfrac{A_0}{846,500} = .1465,$

(18) $\qquad\qquad S_0 = .083(846,500) = 70,260,$

(19) $\qquad\qquad a_1 = \dfrac{.166(846,500)}{217,100} = .647.$

Substituting values (14) through (19) into Eqs. (10) through (13) yields the solution

$$A = 111,769$$
$$S = 127,751$$
$$T = 72,314$$
$$P = 16,021$$
$$S + T + P = 216,086$$
$$\overline{O} = 546,839$$
$$\text{Force strength} = 762,925$$
$$\text{Force reduction} = 1 - \frac{762,925}{846,500} = 1 - .901 = .099$$

The percentage category relationships for the Army follow:

Category	Volunteer	Draft-induced
Operating Forces	71.7	64.6
Supporting Forces	16.7	16.6
Training Forces	9.5	16.6
Transients/Patients	2.1	2.1

Thus operating forces have increased in percentage terms at the expense of training forces. Support forces are also slightly higher due to the overhead assumption.

The approximation indicated by Eqs. (3) and (4) for the geometric progression yields the series

$$(20) \qquad \frac{\Delta F}{F_O} = ar + ar \left[(1 - a)r \right] + ar \left[(1-a)r \right]^2 + \dots$$

$$(21) \qquad = \frac{ar}{1 - (1 - a)r}$$

$$(22) \qquad = \frac{ar}{1 - r + ar} .$$

However, Eq. (22) underestimates the true force reduction because its r term excludes the interaction between the supporting and transient/patient categories. By dropping the ar term in the denominator, we get the closer approximation:

$$(23) \qquad \frac{\Delta F}{F_O} = \frac{ar}{1 - r} .$$

In the case of the Army, Eq. (23) yielded a force reduction of .096 rather than the true estimate of .099. The advantage of Eq. (23) is its simplicity. Equation (23) also gives a slight underestimate. This means a slight overestimate of total costs because of lower training savings and a slightly higher accession estimate of 112,100 instead of 111,800.

Other Studies

How do these annual accession requirements of 112,100 Army and 200,800 non-Army, a DoD total of 312,900, compare with other studies? Altman and Fechter cite at length the 1964-65 DoD study, which set the tone of the public policy discussion with its mean cost estimates of $5.4 to $8.3 billion (but with high standard deviations).[42] They estimate that to maintain a 2.65-million-man active force, 500,000 entrants would be required at the overall rate of 5.5% unemployment, and 512,000 at 4% unemployment. The accession inflow required for the pre-Vietnam draft-induced Decrement Table is 498,600 (their Table 7), or 500,000, rounded off. The DoD cost estimate therefore really is an initial transitional cost, rather than a long-term steady-state cost. Furthermore their estimates do not consider the transitioning to voluntarism with the draft or a phasedown from the high Vietnam levels. Draft assistance is desirable not only as a hedge against the estimates and to reduce transitional costs, but also to prevent long-run distortions in the military pay structure.

Oi corrects for the DoD transition costs and estimates an accession requirement of 333,500.[43] This agrees with my estimate in Table 6-12 of 332,700 before training reductions. Oi excludes training-force reductions, but states they would be "at least 3 percent and still retain the same number of men in an 'effective' status."[44] I estimated these reductions as 9.6 and 3.8% for Army and non-Army respectively. With this correction, the required annual accessions to support a 2.65-million-man effective force are 312,900. The gross total thus corresponds to Oi's calculations.

The major and crucial difference is the Army estimate. Oi estimates Army accessions at 144,600.[45] My comparable estimate is 124,000, which drops to 112,100 after the 9.6% training correction. Since the Army is the service that drives voluntarism's cost estimates, this 29% difference in accession requirements is extremely important; particularly if non-Army enlistees receive the Army wage, as Oi presupposes.

Oi implies that Army accessions will be 144,600 of 333,500, or 43.4% of volunteer military accessions. His own figures show that Army enlisted accessions averaged 45.5% during the 1960-1965 period. Yet replacing draftees with longer-term, higher-retention-propensity volunteers suggests that the Army's share of accessions will now correspond more closely to its 36.3% share of total manpower (Table 6-6). Reconstructing his calculations from the appendix to the longer, unpublished version of his *Army Economic Review* article, Oi apparently inadvertently used the Multiple Decrement Table for *all* DoD personnel, rather than only Army personnel. Substituting the 1965 Multiple Decrement Table for *Regular Army enlisted* personnel into his own Table 2.5 to get a lower turnover rate, using his true volunteer retention rate of 33.0%, and his Army force strength of 857,000 (versus my 846,500), Oi's corrected accession requirement is 123,840. This corresponds to my estimate of 124,000 before the 9.6% training correction.

Appendix 6 -B

Perceived Present Value of Officer Pay

In 1968, a second lieutenant with under two years of service received the following:

Basic pay	$4,118
Quarters allowance	1,321
Subsistence	575
Tax Advantage	333
	$6,347

He perceived only 76% of this amount ($4,824).[46] After 18 months, he became a first lieutenant, and his second-year perceived pay was $5,365. His perceived third-year pay climbs to $6,049. Assuming a three-year tour, his subjectively discounted three-year perceived pay is:

$$\text{PPV} = \$4824 + \frac{\$5365}{(1+.10)} + \frac{\$6049}{(1+.10)^2} = \$14,700.[47]$$

Assuming a pay increase of 10%, this figure would increase to $16,170 for 1970.

The 1970 average DoD "Total Income" of first-term officers is assumed to be ($6,347 + $6,850 + $7,550)(1 + 10%)/3 = $7,600.

Appendix 6-C

The Incremental Longevity, Retirement, and Training Costs of a Volunteer Force (at 1970 Pay Rates)

Substituting true volunteers for draftees and draft-induced volunteers implies a force with longer enlistments and higher retention rates, and consequently less turnover. Such a force would be more productive as well as more costly. These costs are of three types: (1) higher pay for personnel with more years of service, (2) more retirees, and (3) a negative cost (saving) due to reduced training. All are future costs and would not immediately affect voluntarism's budget costs. Higher pay due to increased seniority and reduced training requirements would not be felt until two years after voluntarism began; although the full impact would not be felt until 30 years later, it would be substantial by the eighth year. Increased retirement costs would not make themselves felt until 20 years later, because military retirement is currently an unfunded system and funds are disbursed on a past-services basis.

In this study both the incremental short-run transition and long-run steady-state budget costs of voluntarism are shown, with the emphasis, of course, on the latter. The present pay profile is assumed to be the same under voluntarism except for the increased costs of first-term enlistees. That is, I assume that the lifetime pay profile of the average enlisted man will not fall because of a slower promotion pattern under voluntarism. This assumption facilitates comparisons and ensures that voluntarism will not lower career wages.

Seniority (or Longevity) Costs

Voluntarism's incremental costs due to higher retention rates can be calculated with this formula:

$$(24) \qquad \Delta C = (1.233)(1.204) \sum_{i=0}^{30} B_i (N_i^V - N_i^{DI}) \quad,$$

where i = completed years of service

B_i = base pay by years of service, Table 6-13

N_i = number of personnel in their i^{th} year of service in the volunteer (V) and draft-induced systems (DI), Table 6-13

1.233 = an adjustment factor representing compensation as functionally related to basic pay, Table 5-2

1.204 = an adjustment factor representing basic pay raises of 6.9 and 12.6% since 30 June 1968.

The manpower frequencies and wage costs summarized in Table 6-13 are sensitive to both force levels and assumed retention rates.[48] Table 5-3 shows the various percentage relationships among items of military compensation. In fact, many items have a constant absolute per capita cost rather than a constant percentage markup above base pay. Only the quarters allowance is closely related to basic pay, so the 1.233 cost blowup factor in (24) is taken from the quarters line (line 4), column 3, Table 5-2.

Table 6-13 shows basic pay costs of $8,004,196,000 and $7,101,165,000 for the volunteer and draft-induced systems. Correcting for rounding errors to a 2.31-million enlisted force, these basic pay costs become $8,006,597,000 and $7,094,676,000, respectively. Multiplying this difference by $(1.223)(1.204)$ yields a differential of +$1,342,800,000.

Retirement Costs

The second major long-run cost in going to a volunteer system stems from increased retirement. Incremental retirement cost computations are complex and cannot be derived entirely from DoD sources, which underestimate the economic accrual costs of retirement.

Incremental retirement costs can be computed as follows:

$$(25) \qquad \Delta RC = (.365)(1.204) \, F \sum_{i=0}^{30} B_i N_i P_i,$$

where i = completed years of service

P_i = probability that person in ith year of service will stay until retirement, Table 6-15

N_i = number in the draft-induced system with i years of service, Table 6-13

B = basic pay, Table 6-13

F = Government cost as percentage of basic pay, Table 6-14

1.365 = the relative increase in retirees (volunteer versus draft-induced system) before the training reduction:

$$\text{in Table 6-13} \quad (N_{20}^V/N_{20}^{DI}) = 1.365 \, .$$

1.204 = increase in basic pay since 1968.

The complex calculation is F. This requires computing retirement costs as a function of basic pay for individuals who retire with certainty from military service. The next step is to weigh these costs by the rank and years of service of those retiring, as in Table 6-13. The weighted factor F (derived as a weighted

Table 6-13

Basic Pay and Number of Personnel, by Years of Service (In thousands)

(1) Years of Completed Service	(2) Average Annual Basic Pay (Actual Dollars)[a]	Volunteer Force		Draft-Induced Force	
		(3) Number of Personnel[b]	(4) Cost	(5) Number of Personnel	(6) Cost
0	$1440	318	$ 458,281	479	$ 689,066
1	1973	294	580,240	442	871,235
2	2762	277	764,118	292	807,675
3	3009	191	574,638	192	577,866
4	3401	114	386,262	84	287,228
5	3515	99	347,616	73	258,029
6	3797	92	350,923	69	261,127
7	3864	85	327,497	63	242,883
8	4106	75	309,609	56	228,918
9	4210	69	290,187	51	214,331
10	4393	65	284,825	48	210,473
11	4424	62	274,576	46	202,960
12	4655	60	279,682	44	206,770
13	4691	56	275,531	43	203,608
14	4904	58	282,323	43	208,518
15	4970	57	281,665	42	207,945
16	5127	56	286,861	41	211,730
17	5291	55	292,836	41	216,106
18	5423	55	297,050	40	219,154
19	5582	52	288,098	38	211,106
20	5776	33	189,043	24	137,914
21	5947	23	133,879	16	97,257
22	6264	16	101,627	12	74,097
23	6384	12	77,783	10	56,945
24	6508	10	63,010	7	46,311
25	6668	8	53,031	6	39,094
26	7504	7	49,354	5	36,439
27	7627	5	41,132	4	30,432
28	7758	4	34,539	3	25,586
29	7758	4	27,983	3	20,760
30+	7324	0	0	0	0
Total	$2841[c]	2313	$8,004,196	2316	$7,101,565
Corrected for Rounding Errors		2314	$8,006,597	2314	$7,094,676

[a]*Average Annual Basic Pay for Military Personnel (Enlisted) on Active Duty 30 June 1968 by Length of Service for Pay Purposes,* 1968 pay scale, Office of Assistant Secretary of Defense, Manpower, Actuarial Consultant, 16 December 1968.

[b]Before training reductions. Costing was based on non-rounded numbers.

[c]Weighted average.

Table 6-14
Retirement Cost Factors

(1) Rank	(2) Average Years of Service Completed	(3) Percent of FYs 1963 and 1964 Retirees[a]	(4) Basic Pay Factor[b]
E9	25	3.1	.915
E8	24	8.1	.901
E7	21	32.6	.895
E6	20	27.7	.907
E1-5	20	28.4	.847

[a]*Number of Retirements from Active Duty by Active Duty Pay Grade and Service,* fiscal years 1963 and 1964, Office of Assistant Secretary of Defense, Manpower, 12 April 1965.
[b]Table 5-9.

average of column 4, Table 6-14) is .886 of basic pay. Thus the government's cost for an enlisted careerist averages 88.6% of his basic pay during each year of service.

Table 6-15 shows

$$\sum_{i=0}^{30+} B_i N_i P_i = \$3,887.8 \text{ million}.$$

Multiplying this by .886 yields a retirement cost of $3443.7 million for the pre-Vietnam draft-induced system. The corresponding DoD accrual cost estimate is only 23% of its base payroll of $7094.7 million, or $1.6318 million.[49] Thus DoD underestimates its enlisted accrual costs by 52.6%.

Multiplying $3443.8 million by (.365)(1.204) in formula (25) yields an increased retirement cost of $1512.2 million. If we were to use the DoD accrual method (as others have), our incremental retirement costs would be only $716.7 million and, correspondingly, our overall cost estimate of voluntarism would be $0.8 billion lower.

Training Costs

A volunteer military has less personnel turnover because it substitutes true volunteers with higher reenlistment propensities for draftees and draft-induced volunteers. Lower personnel turnover, in turn, means fewer annual accessions to maintain force size. Also, fewer training personnel are needed to instruct the diminished flow of new recruits, so a secondary reduction in force size is

Table 6-15
Retirement Cost and Probability of Retiring

(1) Years of Completed Service	(2) Draft-Induced Cost[a] (In $ Thousand)	(3) Probability Factor[b]	(4) Columns 2 X 3 (In $ Thousand)
0	$ 689,066	.091	$ 62,705
1	871,235	.098	85,381
2	807,675	.146	117,921
3	577,866	.221	127,708
4	287,228	.497	142,752
5	258,029	.568	146,561
6	261,127	.604	157,721
7	242,883	.658	159,817
8	228,918	.740	169,399
9	214,331	.808	173,180
10	210,473	.856	180,165
11	202,960	.892	181,040
12	206,770	.918	189,815
13	203,608	.937	190,781
14	208,518	.953	198,718
15	207,945	.965	200,667
16	211,730	.973	206,013
17	216,106	.980	211,783
18	219,154	.985	215,867
19	211,106	.989	208,783
20	137,914	1.000	137,914
21	97,257	1.000	56,945
22	74,097	1.000	97,257
23	56,945	1.000	74,097
24	46,311	1.000	46,311
25	39,094	1.000	39,094
26	36,439	1.000	36,439
27	30,432	1.000	30,432
28	25,586	1.000	25,586
29	20,760	1.000	20,760
30	0	0	0
Total	$7,101,565		$3,891,613
Corrected Total	$7,094,676		$3,887,838

[a]Table 6-13.

[b]*Percentage of Military Personnel (Enlisted) on Active Duty 30 June 1965 Expected to Continue on Active Duty Until Retirement by Length of Service*, Office of Assistant Secretary of Defense, Manpower, Actuarial Consultant, 2 August 1966.

possible. Table 6-16 gives the reduction in accessions and in overall forces made possible by voluntarism.

The obvious and more accurate method to cost the training saving is via the classified Five Year Programs Document; the unclassified method adopted here fully costs only military manpower savings. This gives an underestimate of savings because civilian manpower, procurement, and construction to support training are necessarily excluded.

The formula for military manpower savings is

$$(26) \qquad TS = (1.204)(2.159) \sum_{i=0}^{30} B_i \Delta n ,$$

where i = completed years of service

B = basic pay as of 30 June 1968, Table 6-13

Δn = manpower difference permitted by force size reduction, Table 6-17

1.204 = pay raise since 30 June 1968[50]

2.159 = cost of all compensation elements as a percentage of basic pay, exclusive of the non-budget tax advantage, Table 5-2, column 3.

Table 6-17 shows

$$\sum_{i=0}^{30} B_i \Delta n = \$475.2 \text{ million.}$$

Multiplied by (1.204)(2.159), this yields a training saving estimate of $1235.2 million.

Officers

Officer retirement and seniority costs are calculated using formulas (24) and (25). Using (25), we obtain retirement cost increases of $214 million. Seniority

Table 6-16
Enlisted Men: Accessions and Force Reductions from Voluntarism (In thousands)

Service	Type of Force		Total Accessions Reduction	Force Size Reduction
	Volunteer	Draft-Induced[a]		
Army	112.1	217.1	.484	.096
Non-Army	200.8	247.6	.189	.038
DoD	312.9	498.6	.372	.062

[a]Based on actual 1958-1965 experience rather than Decrement Tables. Numbers do not sum to DoD decrement total because the theoretically correct Army and Marine Corps components cannot be computed from the Decrement Tables.

Table 6-17
DoD Training Saving in Enlisted Men (In thousands)

Years of Service	Avg. Man Years *Before* Training Reduction	Cost	Avg. Man Years *After* 5.9% Training Reduction	Cost
Entry	333		313	
1	318	$ 458,281	299	$ 430,933
2	394	580,240	276	545,525
3	277	764,118	260	718,424
4	191	574,638	181	544,849
5	114	386,262	107	363,223
6	99	347,616	93	326,772
7	92	350,923	87	330,191
8	85	327,497	80	308,135
9	75	309,609	71	291,218
10	69	290,187	65	272,867
11	65	284,825	61	267,832
12	62	274,576	58	258,233
13	60	279,682	57	263,031
14	59	275,531	55	259,074
15	58	282,323	54	265,434
16	57	281,665	53	264,787
17	56	286,861	53	269,655
18	55	292,836	52	275,264
19	55	297,050	51	279,209
20	52	288,098	48	270,459
21	33	189,043	31	177,317
22	23	133,879	21	125,482
23	16	101,627	15	95,319
24	12	77,783	11	73,020
25	10	63,010	9	59,203
26	8	53,031	7	49,849
27	7	49,354	6	46,405
28	5	41,132	5	38,692
29	4	34,539	4	32,498
30	4	27,983	3	26,331
Total Avg. Man-Years	2313	$8,004,196	2176	$7,529,241
Corrected for Rounding Errors	2314	$8,006,597	2177	$7,531,424

costs are $230 million from (24). However, a saving of $420 million results from a 5.9% reduction in the officer force (equal to the reduction of the enlisted force) permitted by smaller training activity (Eq. 26).

Comparative Costs

How do these incremental longevity, retirement, and training costs of +$1.5, +$1.7, and −$1.6 billion compare with the three most publicized estimates of the costs of voluntarism? The DoD study by Fechter and Altman excludes longevity costs completely; this can be justified because their estimates are only the short-run costs of a system unassisted by the draft during the changeover.[51] They show retirement costs of $200 to $2040 million, depending on the range of their total budgetary estimates from $3.7 to $16.7 billion. While their retirement costs appear similar to my estimates, theirs are actually underestimated by their own method; by granting careerists pay increases of from 15 to 90%, they correspondingly raise the cost of each individual retirement benefit. As for training savings, which are excluded in their estimated increases, Fechter and Altman state they "would grow to rather substantial sums and by 1976 would range between $370 and $750 million."[52]

Oi's article explicitly includes greater seniority costs. They are much less than mine because of the pay raises in the interim period, and because mine include the quarters allowance as well as basic pay. As for retirement costs, Oi excludes them when he says: "the budgetary costs of moving to an all-volunteer force would be even higher if one considered the transitional period and additional retirement benefits."[53] Oi does not quantify the training savings, either, though he says that "the voluntary force strength would be reduced by at least 3 percent."[54] Fisher's study considers none of the cost elements mentioned above.

Appendix 6-D

Cost and Sensitivity Analysis

Table 6-18 summarizes the costs for eight alternative cases, which contain different assumptions about wage variables, youth unemployment, and the elasticity of supply. The calculations for the first case (column 1) are discussed in detail to illustrate the methodology. Costs for the cases presented range from $2.1 to $2.7 billion, and are fairly insensitive to a marginal change in one assumption.[55]

Steps in the Cost Estimate

The following alternatives are considered to test the cost system for sensitivity:

1. The pay variable: perceived present value (PPV) or DoD "total income"?
2. The youth unemployment rate (U/P): 14.9 or 11.5%?
3. The effective force level: 2.65 or 3.0 million men?
4. The elasticity of supply (ES): unity or one-half?
5. The true volunteer rate: correctly surveyed or 16% overstated?
6. The average DoD first-term reenlistment rate (r): 30 or 36%?
7. The cost changes: long-run or short-run?

For these seven points a plausible assumption set follows:

a. Pay = PPV.
b. U/P = 14.9%.
c. Force = 2.49 million in 1970-1971, which, because of the 5.9% force drawdown permitted by reduced training loads, has the same effective combat manpower as a draft-induced force of 2.65 million.
d. ES = 1.
e. The true volunteer rate is correctly surveyed: in peacetime 62% of enlisted men and 59% of officers are true volunteers.[56]

A, d, and f were explained in the main text. The remaining assumptions, b, c, and e, are somewhat related. The deescalation of the Vietnam War in 1970, combined with tight money, causes a mild recession and a rise in the youth unemployment rate from 13.8% (January 1970, and it is rising) to 14.9%, the 1960-1965 average. If the war lasts longer and voluntarism is introduced later, the cost estimates can be lower (assuming 1970 wages hold) because the manpower pool continually increases through the 1970s. With "peace," the

Table 6-18
Cost Calculations

| | Perceived Present Value of Wages | | | | DoD Wage Definition | | | |
| | 1.0 ES | | 0.5 ES | | 1.0 ES | | 0.5 ES | |
Measure	(1) U/P 14.9%	(2) U/P 11.5%	(3) U/P 14.9%	(4) U/P 11.5%	(5) U/P 14.9%	(6) U/P 11.5%	(7) U/P 14.9%	(8) U/P 11.5%
I. Pay rationalization of the enlisted men inflow (in $ million): C_1 (14.9% PPV increase)	$445	$445	$445	$445	$445	$445	$445	$445
II. Army cost increases over (I)								
A. Enlisted men								
1. Army enlisted men required inflow (table 6-3)	124,000	124,000	124,000	124,000	124,000	124,000	124,000	124,000
2. Requirements after 9.6% training saving	112,100	112,100	112,100	112,100	112,100	112,100	112,100	112,100
3. Less 20% permissible category IV proportion	22,400	22,400	22,400	22,400	22,400	22,400	22,400	22,400
4. Category I-III requirements: (2)-(3)	89,700	89,700	89,700	89,700	89,700	89,700	89,700	89,700
5. Category I-III supply at no change in relative pay	84,800[a]	72,800[b]	84,800[a]	72,800[b]	84,800[a]	72,800[a]	84,800[a]	72,800[b]
6. Percentage deficit in category I-III [(4)/(5)-1] 100%	5.7	23.3	5.7	23.3	5.7	23.3	5.7	23.3
7. Percentage ΔW required	5.7	23.3	11.4	46.6	5.7	23.3	11.4	46.6
8. Less 14.9% pay rationalization (under I), and 7% relative enlisted men pay gain since 1963	21.9	21.9	21.9	21.9	17.7[c]	17.7	17.7	17.7
9. Required % PPV increase for Army enlisted men	0	1.4	0	24.7	0	5.6	0	28.9

10. Dollar value to be paid with PPV = $8800; DOD = $13,600	0	$123	0	$2174	0	$762	0	$3930
a. Bonus paid per man	0	$123	0	$2000	0	$762	0	$2000
b. Enlistment bonus (in $ million) ($2000 limit) cost for 112,100 enlistees	0	$14	0	$224	0	$85	0	$224
c. Remaining PPV to be paid	0	0	0	$174	0	0	0	$1930
d. Amount to be absorbed in profile under 2 years' service (maximum is $940 or $846 when paid in 2 equal installments of $470, as $1456 has already been filled in (I))	0	0	0	$174	0	0	0	$940
e. Cost of under 2 years' profile absorption (in $ million) (table 6-7) (for Army enlistees under 2 years' service)	0		0	$21	0		0	$103
f. Remaining amount to be spliced into first-term profile	0		0	0	0		0	$990
g. Cost of splicing (in $ million)	0		0	0	0		0	$103
h. Wage inversion	0	0	0	0	0	0	0	0
i. Cost of wage inversion (in $ million)	0	0	0	0	0	0	0	0
11. Total Army increase over (I) (in $ million): b + e + g + i	0	$14	0	$245	0	$85	0	$430
B. Officers								
12. Officer requirements	10,800	10,800	10,800	10,800	10,800	10,800	10,800	10,800
13. Supply of officers	9000	9000	9000	9000	9000	9000	9000	9000
14. Deficit: (12)-(13)	1800	1800	1800	1800	1800	1800	1800	1800
15. Percentage deficit: (14/13)	20.0	20.0	20.0	20.0	20.0	20.0	20.0	20.0
16. Percentage ΔPPV required	14^d	14^d	29^e	29^e	14	14	29	29

Table 6-18 (cont.)

| Measure | Perceived Present Value of Wages | | | | DoD Wage Definition | | | |
| | 1.0 ES | | 0.5 ES | | 1.0 ES | | 0.5 ES | |
	(1) U/P 14.9%	(2) U/P 11.5%	(3) U/P 14.9%	(4) U/P 11.5%	(5) U/P 14.9%	(6) U/P 11.5%	(7) U/P 14.9%	(8) U/P 11.5%
17. Less 7.2% relative pay gain for officers since 1963	7.2	7.2	7.2	7.2	7.2	7.2	7.2	7.2
18. Required percentage ΔPPV: (16)-(17)	6.8	6.8	21.8	21.8	6.8	6.8	21.8	21.8
19. Dollar value of bonus with PPV of 2d 1t = $16,170; DOD = $7600 x 3 years (Appendix B)	$1100	$1100	$3525	$3525	$1550	$1550	$4970	$4970
20. Multiply (19) by 10,800 officers inflow = officer bonus cost (in $ million)	$12	$12	$38	$38	$17	$17	$54	$54
III. Non-Army Cost increases								
A. Enlisted men								
21. Non-Army enlisted men required inflow	208,700	208,700	208,700	208,700	208,700	208,700	208,700	208,700
22. Requirements after 3.8% training saving	200,800	200,800	200,800	200,800	200,800	200,800	200,800	280,800
23. Less 10% permissible category IV proportion	20,100	20,100	20,100	20,100	20,100	20,100	20,100	20,100
24. Category I-III requirements: (22)-(23)	180,700	180,700	180,700	180,700	180,700	180,700	180,700	180,700
25. Category I-III supply at no change in relative pay	189,900	162,900	189,900	162,900	189,900	162,900	189,900	162,900
26. Percentage deficit in category I-III: [(24)/(25)-1] 100%	0.0	10.9	0.0	10.9	0.0	10.9	0.0	10.9

27. Less 14.9% PPV (or 10.7% DOD) pay rationalization (under I) and 7.0% relative enlisted men pay gain since 1963	21.9	21.9	21.9	21.9	17.7	17.7	17.7	17.7
28. Required bonus to Non-Army enlisted men	0	0	0	0	0	0	0	0
29. Cost (in $ million)	0	0	0	0	0	0	0	0
B. Officers								
30. Officer requirements	21,500	21,500	21,500	21,500	21,500	21,500	21,500	21,500
31. Supply of officers (DOD-Army)	18,000	18,000	18,000	18,000	18,000	18,000	18,000	18,000
32. Deficit: (30)-(31)	3500	3500	3500	3500	3500	3500	3500	3500
33. Percentage deficit	19.5	19.5	19.5	19.5	19.5	19.5	19.5	19.5
34. Percentage ΔPPV required	14	14	29	29	14	14	29	29
35. Less 7.2% relative pay gain for officers since 1963	7.2	7.2	7.2	7.2	7.2	7.2	7.2	7.2
36. Required percentage ΔPPV: (34)-(35)	6.8	6.8	21.8	21.8	6.8	6.8	21.8	21.8
37. Dollar value of bonus with PPV of 2d 1t = $16,170; DOD = $7600 x 3 years	$1100	$1100	$3525	$3525	$1550	$1550	$4970	$4970
38. Multiply (37) by 21,500 officer inflow = officer bonus cost (in $ million)	$24	$24	$76	$76	$33	$33	$107	$107
IV. Short-run transitional cost increase for volunteers[f]								
39. Accession wage increase (in $ million) 1.59 [(I) + (11) + (29)] + 1.16 [(20) + (38)]	$751	$773	$841	$1231	$767	$902	$895	$1580
V. Long-run cost increase (all in $ million)								
40. Accession wage increase = (I)+(11)+(20)+(29)+(38)	$ 481	$ 495	$ 559	$ 804	$ 495	$ 580	$ 606	$1036
41. Enlisted men seniority cost	1343	1343	1343	1343	1343	1343	1343	1343
42. Officer seniority cost	230	230	230	230	230	230	230	230
43. Long-run wage increase: (40)+(41)+(42)	$2054	$2068	$2132	$2377	$2068	$2153	$2179	$2609

Table 6-18 (cont.)

| | Perceived Present Value of Wages | | | | DoD Wage Definition | | | |
| | 1.0 ES | | 0.5 ES | | 1.0 ES | | 0.5 ES | |
Measure	(1) U/P 14.9%	(2) U/P 11.5%	(3) U/P 14.9%	(4) U/P 11.5%	(5) U/P 14.9%	(6) U/P 11.5%	(7) U/P 14.9%	(8) U/P 11.5%
44. Retirement costs								
a. Enlisted men	1512	1512	1512	1512	1512	1512	1512	1512
b. Officers	214	214	214	214	214	214	214	214
45. Training savings								
a. Enlisted men	1235	1235	1235	1235	1235	1235	1235	1235
b. Officers	420	420	420	420	420	420	420	420
46. Long-run total cost increase: (43)+(44)−(45)	$2125	$2139	$2203	$2448	$2139	$2229	$2250	$2680

[a]Altman and Fechter, op. cit., p. 25, Table 5. They give 106,000, but 20% of this is category IV, so only 84,800 are categories I-III.

[b]Ibid. They give 91,000, but 20% of this is category IV, so only 72,800 are categories I-III.

[c]The 14.9% PPV increase is only a 10.7% DoD wage increase.

[d]ES = 37/26 = 1.42, Altman and Fechter.

[e]ES = .71, a halving of the Altman and Fechter estimate.

[f]Short-run transition costs during 1970-71, either with a draft or a Vietnam phasedown, are approximately 59% greater than the steady-state accession wage increase, corresponding to the 59% larger inflows (498.6 versus 312.9 in Table 6-7) required to maintain force levels temporarily until the higher reenlistment rates and longer tours of volunteers are realized.

force level is assumed reduced to the 1960-1965 effectiveness level of 2.49 million enlisted men and officers. The true volunteer rate of 1964[57] is then assumed to apply.[58]

Accession Costs

The immediate post-Vietnam cost impact of a volunteer force is not great, as reflected in the accession wage increases summarized in Table 6-18. As mentioned earlier, I concentrated on the case presented in column 1. The pay of enlisted men (especially Army recruits) and officers is raised, but fewer are required. Although it is cheaper to give all military wage increases as bonuses, it seems desirable to flatten the pay profile of all enlisted men (Figure 5-6) by increasing the first-term pay to the federal minimum wage of $1.65 per hour.[59] The extremely low first- and second-year "total income" salaries of $2,440 and $2,857, which would exist in 1970 if present standards were maintained, could be raised to $3,168 and $3,585 in 1970 by meeting the minimum wage level (i.e., there would be equal increases of $728 each year). At the assumed discount of 25%, the present value of these increases is $1,310, which raises the 1970 PPV_m (=$8,800) by 14.9%, to $10,110. Because relative military wages have climbed 7% since 1963, this amounts to a 21.9% relative wage increase over the 1963 data base. The $728 increase costs $445 million, when multiplied by the 312,900 annual required inflow of new enlisted men and the 299,300 flow for the second year.[60] This cost appears in line 1 of Table 6-18.

To avoid recruiting deficits, additional wage increases are given when necessary for Army enlisted men (line II-A, Table 6-18), Army officers (II-B), non-Army enlisted men (III-A), and non-Army officers (III-B).[61] The wage increases that are given in bonuses to raise PPV by an equal amount are small, so no wage inversion occurs.[62] Steady-state accession wage increases are then $481 million, the sum of the wage increases on lines I+11+20+29+38.

The initial transitional costs for a volunteer force are accession wage increases. These costs can be limited to slightly more than 159% of steady-state accession wage increases by using the draft to phase in voluntarism. The initial accession wage increase would then be designed to attract slightly more than the steady state inflow while the deficit is temporarily drafted but paid the volunteer premium. If this procedure is not followed, military pay scales will be too high for the number of required entrants when, after two years, demand begins to fall sharply because of shifts in the length of service composition.

Steady-State Costs

Long-run costs must consider three factors: increased seniority costs caused by shifts in the length-of-service composition of the officer and enlisted men forces due to increased retention; increased retirement payments; and training savings. All three are derived in Appendix C and summarized in Section V of Table 6-18. In the long run, officer and enlisted men seniority costs increase by $230 and $1,343 million, respectively (lines 42 and 41).

Total retirement costs (line 44) increase by $1,726 million because of a higher first-term reenlistment rate. This impact will not be felt for 20 years, however, when the true volunteers begin to retire. Total training savings are $1,655 million (lines 45a and b).

My total long-run cost of $2,125 million is much lower than that of most previous studies due to training-force savings (from the reduced inflow necessary to stock the volunteer force), the use of the present value of perceived pay, and enlistment bonuses. These elements also prevent wage inversion. The recent Presidential Commission also estimates long-run costs of $2.3 billion but, as noted in Appendix 6-E, they exclude retirement costs and do not consider the full impact of seniority costs.

Since Army manpower deficits are the most serious, efforts are needed to increase the supply and retention of Army personnel. This may be accomplished through reenlistment bonuses or through improvements in the quality of Army life, especially if wage discrimination among the services is not permitted. Alternatively, the Army's demand for manpower could be reduced by shifting some of its functions to the other services.

Sensitivity of the Estimates

A glance across lines (39) and (46) of Table 6-18 indicates that neither short-run nor long-run cost increases vary by more than $1 billion for changes in our assumptions about the youth unemployment rate, the elasticity of supply, or the correct wage variable. The worst case (column 8) has short-run costs of $1,580 million and long-run costs of only $2,680 million. The worst case is unlikely because youth unemployment has been high in the past; it was 13.8% and rising in January 1970, for example. Higher minimum wage laws tend to reduce the number of unskilled youth demanded at the very time more are entering the labor market.

Bonuses are limited to $2,000 for enlisted men and $4,000 for officers in this study. If in some future scenarios the required wage increase were greater for Army enlisted men, then successive pay increments (discounted where necessary) could be spliced into the wage profile of Figure 5-6, and would involve the expenses shown on lines (10d) to (10h) of Table 6-18. Splicing, combined with enlistment bonuses, prevents a uniform upward shift in the pay of all military personnel and would be an economical way to keep cost increases under control.

Halving the supply elasticities from $ES = 1$ to $ES = 0.5$ with a given recruitment deficit has the same cost effect as doubling the deficit (in percentage terms), given that ES = 1. Wage increases required to close the deficit are the same in both cases. As an example, assume that post-Vietnam aversion to war reduces the volunteer rate by 16%. For calculations, this is equivalent to a 16% overstatement of the true volunteer rate in the 1964 DoD survey. Table 6-18 indicates that such a supply variation would not seriously increase cost; one merely moves from one case to another one, identical in all respects except that ES is smaller. At constant low unemployment, costs increase $309 million in moving from column 2 to 4 (line 40) in Table 6-18, for example.

Greater use of mental category IV people will ease any moves to a force level higher than 2.49 million. The Air Force is now receiving 20% category IVs, over twice its past average, and the other services are doing likewise. Also, lines (24) to (28) of Table 6-18 indicate an excess supply of non-Army enlisted men at the pay package I propose. Men probably queue up to enlist, so inflows may be increased rapidly up to a certain point. Of course, large buildups could be handled by the existing draft machinery.

Alternative Scenario: Lower Retention Rates

Given the force size, inflow requirements are a function of the first-term reenlistment rate of volunteers. These rates were previously derived in Eq. (1) (and displayed in Table 6-9, Appendix 6-A) by assuming that the reenlistment rate of the draft-motivated (DM) enlistees equalled that of draftees (9.2%):

$$DM(9.2) + (1 - DM)(x) = (1)(FT).$$

But we assume that the draft-induced enlistee, by the very fact of his enlistment, is less adverse to military life than the draftee.

Assume that the reenlistment rate for DM enlistees is some weighted average of the reenlistment rates of draftees and volunteers. With the former rate of 9.2% and the latter equal to X%, assume that the DM rate lies halfway between the two. Thus in Eq. (1) the 9.2% DM rate becomes $1/2(9.2 + X)$, and (1) becomes

$$(78) \qquad DM[1/2(9.2 + X)] + (1 - DM)X = (1)FT.$$

Using the DM fractions of Table 6-8, Appendix 6-A, the new volunteer rates (X) become those shown in Table 6-19.

The DoD rate (a weighted average of the rates in Table 6-19) is now 30%. Of

Table 6-19

Alternative First-Term Retention Rates for a Volunteer Force (In percent)

Service	True Volunteer Retention Rate	Increase in Retention Rate[a]
Army	28	18
Navy	27	12
Marine Corps	18	4
Air Force	38	15

[a][(true volunteer rate ÷ first-term rate of a draft-induced force)] − 1 x 100.

course, these retention rates are smaller than the corresponding rates in Table 6-9, Appendix 6-A. The percentage increase in first-term retention rates shown in Table 6-19, when compared with the draft-induced rates, implies corresponding increases in the manpower frequencies of Table 6-10, Appendix 6-A. Each term in the Army is increased 18% for years 3 to 30, the Air Force by 15% for years 4 to 30, and so on. With the new retention rates of Table 6-19 and the force sizes postulated in Table 6-6, Appendix 6-A, the enlisted inflow requirements of Table 6-20 can be derived.

Table 6-20

Required Inflow of Enlisted Men, with Lower Retention Rates (In thousands)

Service	Number of Enlistees
Army	140.4
Navy	94.0
Marine Corps	31.2
Air Force	107.1
Non-Army	232.3
DoD Total	372.7

Comparing these numbers with the inflows required to support a draft-induced force in Table 6-12, Column 2, Appendix 6-A, we find the following flow reductions:

Army	35.3%
Navy	4.8%
Marine Corps	9.0%
Air Force	6.5%
Non-Army	6.2%
DoD	25.3%

These decreases imply corresponding savings in training and other support personnel:

Army	7.1%
Navy	1.1%
Marine Corps	3.1%
Air Force	1.5%

Applying such secondary-force reductions to Table 6-20 gives the new accessions required to maintain a 2.65-million-man effective force level, shown in Table 6-21.

Allowing 20% of the Army enlistments and 10% of the non-Army enlistments to be category IV personnel, we obtain the required category I-III accessions. Compared with DoD projections of category I-III volunteers (Table 6-3) we have the figures shown in Table 6-22.

The wage increase necessary to eliminate these deficits is not great, especially if one accepts the theory and empirical estimate of ES = 1.5. Conversely, with the most costly set of assumptions,[63] the procedure of Table 6-18 generates a steady-state accession wage increase of only $3122 million, as is seen in Table 6-23.

Appendixes 6-A and 6-C detail steps for calculating the long-run cost increase. Table 6-20 indicates that an inflow of 372,700 is needed with the 30% retention rate, but normal first-year losses cause the first year to average 358,555 men. The new force profile appears in Table 6-24. Now compare the column 2 total of

Table 6-21
Net Required Accessions of Enlisted Men (In thousands)

Service	Number of Enlistees
Army	130.4
Navy	93.0
Marine Corps	30.2
Air Force	105.5
Non-Army	228.7
DoD Total	359.1

Table 6-22
Recruiting Deficits for Category I-III Enlistees (In thousands)

		Supply		Percent Deficit	
Group	Demand	U/P=14.9%	U/P=11.5%	U/P=14.9%	U/P=11.5%
Army	104.3	84.8	72.8	23(6)[a]	43(23)
Non-Army	205.8	189.9	162.9	8(0)	26(11)

[a]The corresponding recruiting deficits generated by the original, more optimistic retention rates (Table 6-18, II-6) are in parentheses.

Table 6-23
Cost of Long-Run Wage Increase (In $ million)

Line of Table 6-18	Item	Costs
I	Pay rationalization	$ 445
II-A-II	Total Army increase	1600
II-B-20	Army officers	65
III-A-29	Non-Army (enlisted)	940
III-B-38	Non-Army (officers)	72
Total		$3122

Table 6-24 with the Column 4 total of Table 6-13, in Appendix 6-C, and put these into Eq. (24) to derive a seniority cost increase of $860 million.

Retirement cost increments are calculated from Eq. 2 of Appendix 6-A, using the information of Tables 6-13 and 6-24. This increment is $1,376 million for enlisted men. Training savings come from Eq. (3) of Appendix 6-A. The manpower reduction is 3.7% (Table 6-20 versus Table 6-21). This saves $285 million in base pay (Table 6-24), but Eq. (3) inflates this to a $740-million training saving.

Assuming that officer-cost increments are unchanged, total long-run costs are thus only $4,642 million for the most pessimistic case illustrated in Table 6-25.[64] If the supply elasticity were about 1.5, however, as argued in Appendix D of Canby-Klotz, the wage increases of Table 6-25 would fall to about $1,000 million and total costs would be only $2,600 million.

A Three-Million-Man Force

What would the long-run cost increment be if world tensions indicated a 3.0-million volunteer force? This level is 14% greater than the 2.65 million previously assumed. Steady inflows and the manpower frequencies at each seniority level would be increased by 14% (Appendix 6-A), so that retirement and seniority costs would also rise by 14%, as would training savings. Take column 1 of Table 6-18 as an illustrative case. With ES = 1.0, U/P = 14.9% and using the PPV definition of wages, these three major cost elements (lines 41, 42, 44, 45) now sum to $1.88 billion. The long-run wage increase (line 40) must be derived and added to this sum to obtain long-run total costs.

Assume that the total force increase of 14% corresponds to an Army expansion of 20% and a non-Army growth of only 11% for both officers and enlisted men.[65] Army requirements for categories I-III enlisted men are now 197,600 (line II-4 of Table 6-18), and a 26% manpower deficit arises. But line 8 indicates that only a 4% pay increase is necessary in addition to the pay rationalization of line I. Working through Table 6-18, we obtain wage increases (line 40) of $1.13 billion. Since seniority and retirement elements, minus

Table 6-24
Basic Pay and Number of Personnel for Volunteer Force, by Years of Service[a]

Years of Service	(1) Avg. Annual Basic Pay	(2) Number in Force (In thousands)	(3) Cost (In $ thousand)
Entry	$1440	358.6	$ 516,319.2
1	1973	331.3	653,722.0
2	2762	311.7	860,887.8
3	3009	215.2	647,410.4
4	3401	101.0	343,412.6
5	3515	87.9	309,052.9
6	3797	82.2	311,995.7
7	3864	75.4	291,167.9
8	4106	67.0	275,262.1
9	4210	61.3	257,997.2
10	4393	57.6	253,230.1
11	4424	55.2	244,116.3
12	4655	53.4	248,656.1
13	4691	52.2	244,964.0
14	4904	51.2	251,006.3
15	4970	50.4	250,423.4
16	5127	49.7	255,042.6
17	5291	49.2	260,354.2
18	5423	48.7	264,094.7
19	5582	45.9	256,141.2
20	5776	29.1	168,070.0
21	5947	20.0	119,029.2
22	6264	14.4	90,351.9
23	6384	10.8	69,151.5
24	6508	8.6	56,020.9
25	6668	7.1	47,149.4
26	7504	5.8	43,875.9
27	7627	4.8	36,563.8
28	7758	4.0	30,706.2
29	7758	3.2	24,879.9
30	7324	0.0	0.0
Total[b]		2,312.9	$7,681,055.5

[a]30% retention rate assumed.

[b]Items may not add to totals because of rounding.

training-saving, are $1.88 billion, we obtain a cost increment of $3.01 billion to establish a volunteer force with the same number of men in combat units as a 3-million-man draft-induced force.

In a real sense, the cost of a 3-million-man volunteer force seems politically

Table 6-25
Long-Run Cost Increase: Worst Case[a] (In $ million)

Factor	Cost
Wage increase	$3122
Seniority cost	
Enlisted men	860
Officers	230
Retirement Cost	
Enlisted men	1376
Officers	214
Subtotal	$5802
Less training saving	
Enlisted men	740
Officers	420
Subtotal	$1160
Total	$4642

[a]Assuming ES=0.5, U/P=11.5%, R=.30, Wage=DoD "total income."

irrelevant. A world in which defense needs are this great would probably be considerably different from the relatively tranquil world of the 1957-1964 period. Supply and cost may dramatically increase or decrease depending on the popularity of the particular conflict. Military supply curves may be quite unstable and/or inelastic in a world in which the United States engages in limited conflicts. Thus a considerable element of uncertainty is involved in the $3-billion cost increment for a 3-million-man force. A high-tension world would probably find the United States constantly preparing for a police action or actively engaged in one. In either case, the government would most probably reinstitute the draft lottery to build up and maintain a large military force. It is plausible to assume that it would shift from a volunteer system back to the current mixed volunteer-draft system as required-force levels rose toward 3 million.

Appendix 6 - E

Cost Estimates of the Presidential Commission on an All-Volunteer Armed Force

The President's Commission on an All-Volunteer Force estimates that $3.1 billion (excluding reserves and tax returns) is the incremental budget cost of a volunteer force of 2.5 million men in 1971.[66] This estimate refers to the short-run cost; my comparable short-run estimate is $0.75 to $1.2 billion for a slightly larger force of 2.65 million.

Table 6-26 compares the long-run and short-run items considered in this study and in the Commission report. It indicates that the Commission does not, for example, recommend enlistment bonuses or differential pay for the Army. Also, the base from which wage increases are calculated is the DoD's "total income" rather than the perceived present-value used here. However, the major difference in short-run costs is my use of the draft during the transition period. Whereas the Commission advocates a premium wage to attract the large number of accessions required before longer enlistment tours and higher reenlistment rates lower accession requirements, I would advocate paying the estimated wage for a steady-state volunteer military and drafting the residue for several years until longer tours and high reenlistment rates take their effect and reduce accession requirements.

Note further that (1) the Commission's cost-sensitivity calculations are tied only to variations in force size, and (2) its long-run calculations do not consider

Table 6-26
Comparison of Cost Studies

Items	Presidential Commission	Canby
Short-Run Costs		
1. Volunteer Projections from Surveys and Population Growth	Yes	Yes
2. Higher Volunteer Reenlistment Rates	Yes	Yes
3. Training Savings	Yes	Yes
4. Large Army Recruiting Deficit	Yes	No
5. Theory of Supply	Yes	No[c]
6. Econometric Supply Curve	Yes	No[c]
7. Enlistment Bonuses	No	Yes
8. Army Receives Differential Treatment	No	Yes
9. Pay Base is Perceived Present Value Concept	No	Yes
10. Miscellaneous Costs and Savings	Yes[a]	No

Table 6-26 (cont.)

Items	Presidential Commission	Canby
Short-Run Costs		
11. Cost Sensitivity Analysis		
a. Force Size	Yes	Yes
b. Supply Elasticity	No	Yes
c. Unemployment Rate	No	Yes
d. Pay Base (PPV or Total Income)	No	Yes
e. Reenlistment Rate	No	Yes
f. Attitude Shift	No	Yes
Long-Run Steady-State Costs		
12. Retirement Costs	No	Yes
13. Seniority Costs	No[b]	Yes
14. Training Savings	Yes	Yes
15. Cost Sensitivity Analysis	No	Yes

[a]About $0.5 billion, including increases for proficiency and reserve pay and the fraction of wage increases repaid to the Treasury in taxes.
[b]Only eight-year transition costs are computed until 1977-79.
[c]Included in Canby-Klotz.

retirement costs or the full weight of seniority costs. Thus, their steady-state costs of $2.3 billion (excluding the reserves and the savings from increased Treasury tax returns) are in reality much higher than my estimate of $2.1 to $2.5 billion.

Appendix 6- F

Cost Implications of Alternative Enlistment and
Retention Policies

A major constraint on my volunteer budget cost estimate and on other published estimates has been the acceptance of existing institutional manpower practices. This can be termed the "muddling-through" version of voluntarism, which attempts to reduce the impact of voluntarism on the military by leaving other practices unchanged. Muddling-through is a high-cost version of voluntarism. Removing the institutionally imposed manpower constraints can only reduce costs.

Two broad alternatives to the present policy are possible: (1) to relax many existing constraints while still operating within institutional preferences; and (2) to challenge existing manpower concepts. The second would require a complete restructuring of service incentive, compensation, and promotion policies. This appendix explores the first alternative—modifying only existing enlistment and retention policies.

The draft itself has caused certain practices that may be undesirable in a volunteer era. As long as the services depend on draftees and draft-induced volunteers, tours of duty will be relatively short. Thus, the services emphasize high trainability through an extensive formal schooling system, which minimizes training time and gains a reasonable payoff period for its human capital investment. This contributes to such practices as enticing high-caliber youths into expensive training programs, even though as a group such individuals have low reenlistment rates. If the draft were eliminated, the relatively short enlistments should also be eliminated.

While it is true that longer enlistments imply higher pay because of seniority and the disutility of longer enlistment contracts,[67] higher pay does not necessarily imply higher *total costs*. Major elements in total costs are productivity, training, and retirement. Though military productivity has remained elusive, longer payoff periods after training imply longer on-the-job experience and higher productivity. And longer payoff periods reduce training costs. Military retirement is also expensive, averaging 89% of basic pay for the individual retiree. The Army and Marine Corps have valid reasons for maintaining a relatively youthful force for their ground combat arms (as do the Air Force and Navy in their pilot corps). Thus, the services need to lengthen their payoff periods but not to the extent that too many men are attracted to retirement or that combat branches become overaged.

The policy guidelines are therefore (1) an increase in initial enlistments from their current 3 and 4 years to 6 to 10 years and (2) a curtailment of reenlistments. Figure 6-2 compares the years-of-service profiles of three enlist-

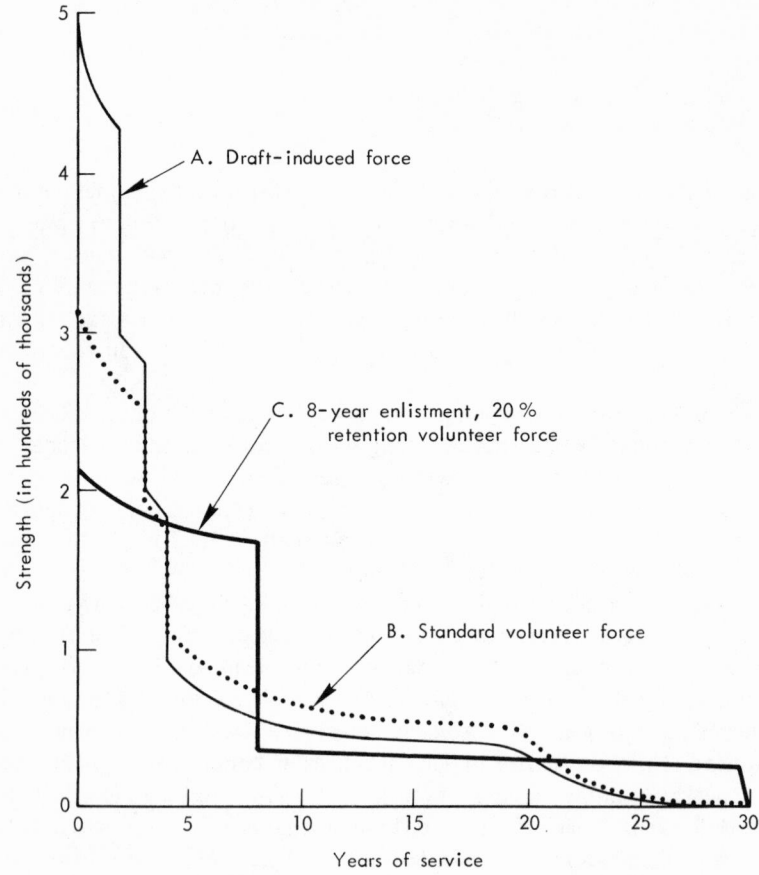

Figure 6-2. Enlisted Strength Profile for Three Force Alternatives.

ment systems: A, the current draft-induced force; B, the standard muddling-through version of voluntarism; and C, an 8-year enlistment system with retentions limited to 20% at the 8-year point. The salient feature of the graph is the shift from A, with low-experience and low-productivity individuals, to C, with longer-term and more productive individuals. The standard volunteer system largely accomplishes this shift by substituting long-term personnel for individuals with less than 3 years of completed service.[68] The 8-year enlistment system substitutes 4- to 8-year men for those with less than 4 or more than 8 years of completed service. A system like C would suit all the services better than either the draft-induced or standard volunteer force. It approaches the optimal force profile for the Army and Marine Corps; however, for the Air Force

Table 6-27
Incremental Cost of Three Enlisted Force Alternatives (In $ billion)

Measure	Standard	8 Years	
		20% Retention	10% Retention
Accession costs	+0.45	?	?
Longevity costs	+ 1.34	+ 2.00	+ 1.12
Retirement costs	+ 1.51	− 1.44	− 2.55
Training savings	− 1.24	− 2.04	− 1.59
Reenlistment bonuses	unchanged	− 0.33	− 0.33
System cost	2.06	?− 1.81	?− 3.35

and Navy even fewer first-termers and more careerists would be desirable if longer service could be transformed into higher productivity and lower manning levels.

Table 6-27 shows the incremental cost of three different force alternatives, using the draft-induced force as the base. Longevity, retirement, and training costs can be computed from the methodology outlined in Appendixes 6-A and 6-C. A longer enlistment also eliminates a reenlistment bonus. The question marks represent the unknown personnel cost needed to induce enlistees into a longer tour.[69] While unknown, this cost would probably not be much greater than the $500 million for accessions to the standard force. The reason is the sharp drop in accessions from 313,000 for the standard force to 215,000 and 258,000 for the 8-year, 20% and 10% retention systems, respectively. With smaller accession requirements, a smaller premium is necessary to attract enough volunteers. Part of the incremental premium necessary to offset a longer enlistment tour will therefore derive from the original $500-million premium of the standard volunteer force and the discontinuance of reenlistment bonuses.

The major shift in costs is due to reduced retirements. The result is that, even though accession costs are unknown, total system costs would be substantially reduced and a youthful force would be maintained. Moreover, productivity would be increased. Longevity costs are a rough proxy for productivity: in the case of 20% retention, productivity is almost certainly increased; with 10% retention, productivity approximates that of the standard volunteer force. In all three volunteer systems, productivity is higher than in the draft-induced force.

7

Postwar Manpower Procurement in Perspective: Military Manpower Policy in Disequilibrium

Military necessity (including the protection of the economic base for mobilization) and budget cost were the principal criteria of procurement policy after World War II. Other criteria, such as equity, were secondary. Underlying manpower decisions was a "cultural lag"; the future was viewed from the perspective of the past. In consequence, Universal Military Training and industrial mobilization—two structures no longer appropriate to contemporary military technology—were officially advocated. UMT was an early casualty, but the underlying rationale of industrial mobilization remained, and eventually eroded Selective Service's political acceptability.

Policy Choices

Decision makers after World War II faced manpower policy choices regarding the size of the standing forces and reserves and type of recruitment. Military necessity ruled out the traditional small army and small reinforcing reserves policy of the past. The choices thus narrowed to: a small military with massive reserves (UMT), or large standing forces-in-being.[1]

The Air Force and its Congressional supporters argued that past experience was no longer valid in an age of nuclear weapons and that the military requirement was now moderately large forces-in-being (meaning, of course, air power). Though the fact was not recognized at the time, UMT was no longer appropriate for ground warfare either. Nevertheless, the Administration, backed by the Army and Navy, advocated UMT and the traditional force balance.[2] UMT became a center of political controversy as well, with each side offering familiar assertions such as the dangerous values imparted by compulsory military training on one side[3] and the alleged social values associated with UMT on the other.[4] Somewhat ironically, as noted by Huntington, it was

opposing civilian groups generally unconcerned with strategy and hostile to military needs that helped prevent the country from adopting a popular policy, backed by the Army, which would have been ill-suited to the military needs of the nation.[5]

The second decision before policy makers was recruitment. During periods of high military demand, the military had traditionally opposed voluntarism and held voluntarism responsible for many of mobilization difficulties. A second difficulty was voluntarism's inability to meet the military's moderate demands during the 1946-1948 volunteer period. After the reenactment of the draft in 1948, recruitment again increased and a draft holiday existed from January 1949 until the Korean War began in June 1950. The failure of voluntarism to meet demand was given as sufficient reason for a draft. There seems to have been no awareness that the temporarily exhausted manpower pool would have strained any procurement system. For instance, in May 1946, General Hershey reported that only 36,000 men were left in the 1-A pool of eligibles aged 18-29, while the Army's forthcoming requirement in June was for 50,000.[6] Given a drained pool, the letdown following a major war, and no attempt to offer competitive entry wages, this experience was not conclusive proof against voluntarism. Equally plausible is the contention that the draft holiday (following the reinstitution of the draft) showed that voluntarism was a feasible alternative, particularly since at the same time enlistment tours were lengthened, acceptance standards raised, married men excluded, and draft pressure was minimal.

After Korea, voluntarism was no longer feasible except at a high budget cost. Korea again temporarily drafted the available manpower, but, more important, the military's post-Korean demand increased by 70% from pre-Korean levels while supply remained unchanged (the number of men coming of military age actually declined by 10.8% between World War II and Korea).

Selective Service in Operation

Thus, because of cold-war pressures, conscription became the accepted practice, though apparently it was always viewed as an expedient until the return of normal times and voluntarism.[7] Throughout the postwar period Congressional *intent* was to equalize the burdens of military service. But equality came to be interpreted as *equal obligation*, which was used to justify such inequalities of practice as student deferment (i.e., students retain the obligation but never fulfil the burdens of service). President Truman's Advisory Committee Report on UMT explicitly made this distinction and strongly recommended closing the loophole.[8] General Hershey, on numerous occasions before Korea, maintained that the only viable and acceptable draft must be based on equal service and democratically call up people from all walks of life.[9] Chairman Vinson of the House Armed Services Committee claimed:

The strength of Selective Service is its *uniformity*. It applies to everybody equally and alike. As long as we keep that as the fundamental basis, we are on sound ground.[10] [Emphasis added.]

Few Congressmen, at least in public, agreed with Senator Russell's frank statement:

There is discrimination in all fields of living and until human institutions achieve perfection and there is nothing in human history to cause us to believe they ever will, we will have some. . . . Some people will be compelled to contribute more to their country than others in military service, taxation, and other fields.[11]

Because the draft was considered a politically sensitive issue, Congress and the Executive permitted Selective Service and the military to exercise their own judgment in selecting military manpower without adequate Congressional and Executive review. In the absence of such supervision, and without constraints forcing the military and the SSS to consider goals other than their own, manpower policies were designed to suit the administrative conveniences of the SSS and the services. A constant-sized military and a growing 18-year-old age cohort after 1957 encouraged the services to raise acceptance standards to ease their immediate training and disciplinary problems. Concurrently, SS arrogated to itself the function of channeling the nation's youth. Beginning with its 1957 annual report, the SSS described itself as a "storekeeper of manpower" with the function not only of procuring manpower for the Armed Forces but also that of channeling it into essential civilian activities.[12] The result was a class-correlated squeeze in which the better-educated upper classes were increasingly exempted from military service, and the lower classes, who often found the military attractive, were increasingly excluded. In short, in the name of national security, an abundance of cheap and available manpower induced questionable social practices with regard to the procurement and utilization of manpower.

The draft, by permitting low entry wages, also had the advantage of appearing cheap. For the Army, with its large numbers of easily trained personnel, the draft was undoubtedly a major boon during the particularly tight budget years of the Eisenhower New Look. For the Air Force and Navy, which depend on more highly trained technicians, the draft may have been deleterious. Their narrow recruitment policy—allocating technical training to the best qualified—attracted a disproportionate number of draft-induced volunteers with low reenlistment propensities. The draft was thus instrumental in causing high turnover in the technical occupations. Not only did the military lose its "private" investment, but society lost investment in human capital, since most ex-servicemen did not use their service-learned skills in the civilian sector.[13]

High turnover, accompanied by low retention rates, was the obvious symptom of an unhealthy manpower system. Its meaning, however, was ambiguous. Economists viewed it as a technical sign of inadequate pay levels and inefficiency.[14] Reflecting economic theory, the 1957 Cordiner Committee found that

the basic problem was modernization of compensation practices which were clearly out of step with the times and inadequate for national defense.[15]

But by focusing on the symptom of low retention rates (rationalized as a manifestation of low careerist pay, particularly for the most senior personnel), the Cordiner Committee ignored the empirical reality of a poorly designed, inefficient pay structure and actually accentuated a compensation policy that was the cause of much of the difficulty.[16]

Political scientists, though they often advocated inappropriate solutions, correctly saw high turnover as indicative of an outmoded nation-in-arms strategy, and thus a symptom of disequilibrium among significant elements of military policy caused by "inherited [mobilization] policies, ideas, and practices conflicting with new demands of deterrence."[17] Conscription and induced voluntarism conflicted with the increasing technological complexity of the postwar military. The pre-French Revolutionary professional soldier was needed again. Professor Huntington's more elegant analysis was that

a strategy of deterrence could best be served by reliance upon career soldiers rather than citizen soldiers. . . . By 1960 the United States had developed a strategy of deterrence, but in many important ways it still lacked the appropriate military structure to support that strategy. In each specific area of structural policy, strategic needs and values came into direct conflict with other values and established patterns of behavior. Disequilibrium still existed among the significant elements of military policy. If deterrence remained the strategy, however, presumably the structural elements of policy would eventually be brought into line with its needs.[18]

The present traumatic search for an alternative to Selective Service can thus be viewed as a structural response to changed needs.

The Ledger

This study has focused on reestablishing an equilibrium between the strategic and structural components of military policy and between military structure and domestic goals, as related to manpower procurement. The strengths and weaknesses of SS in the 1960s should be noted. First, the system did provide the desired manpower. Second, up to the emergence of the postwar baby crop in the early 1960s, budget cost to the federal government was minimized. (However, a constant-sized military and a growing population was rapidly eroding this advantage.) Third, large drafted and draft-induced standing military forces had not provided any noticeable threat to democracy.

Against this positive side of the ledger, a negative account was accumulating. The draft was not minimizing *economic* or *social*[19] costs. It had introduced a hidden tax which masked the system's real cost, induced inefficient military practices, and distorted manpower allocation throughout the economy.

Selection was also becoming increasingly arbitrary, inequitable, and class-correlated. As the military's relative demand dropped due to rapid age-cohort growth after 1960, Selective Service, in order to maintain its "oldest first" selection criterion, gradually broadened its deferment and exemption policies as the military progressively tightened its mental acceptance standards. The burden of military service fell increasingly upon the high-school graduate, who either did not desire or could not afford college, while excluding underprivileged groups who often saw the military as an avenue of advancement. Third, despite these increasingly arbitrary deferment and acceptance standards, selection by "oldest first" caused an upward age creep among draftees, adding to the uncertainty and the burden on those selected. Moreover, by replacing a high-unemployment-propensity potential enlistee with a low-employment-propensity older draftee, twisting occurred in the labor force which caused higher unemployment among youths.[20] Fourth, the wage discrepancy between the increasingly smaller percentage of the age cohort drafted (or coerced to enlist) and his civilian counterpart continually grew as military pay raises were denied first-term servicemen on the grounds of obligations of citizenship and the alleged value of the training received. Fifth, military personnel policies remained premised on an expansionable cadre concept; high turnover among short-term personnel as well as careerists was believed desirable to build a trained wartime manpower pool and to ensure a youthful, vigorous career force.

Sixth, the SSS proved to be administratively rigid. It rejected more efficient processing procedures for fear of undermining its local basis. It did not sense the changing political winds of concern for social equity and centralization to alleviate local discrepancies and abuses.[21] It was unable to perceive that increasing national integration and labor mobility reduced the importance of local considerations. And, perhaps most important, the SSS still viewed war in terms of an obsolete mobilization strategy. In short, the SSS became increasingly anachronistic with respect to the political culture as well as to the needs of military technology.

Notes

Notes

Chapter 1
An Evaluative Framework for Military Manpower Recruitment

1. For a development of this conceptual framework, called "The Dimensions of Military Policy," see Samuel P. Huntington, *The Common Defense*, Chapter I.

2. In Huntington's conceptual framework, these disequilibria are, respectively, between (1) foreign policy and the strategic component of military policy, (2) the strategic and structural components of military policy, and (3) the structural component of military policy and domestic policy.

3. National Advisory Commission on Selective Service, *In Pursuit of Equity*, p. 66.

4. As, for example, the old English bias against standing armies. Ibid., p. 12.

5. A Harvard Study Group, "On the Draft," *The Public Interest*, No. 9, Fall 1967, p. 94.

6. They are dealt with only briefly in this study. The criterion of technical workability excludes national service as administratively infeasible. Universal military service, while administratively simple, has little military value, and the civic values imparted can only be justified by individual value judgments.

Chapter 2
Criteria Analysis and Evaluation of Procurement Alternatives

1. Alan Fechter at the Institute for Defense Analyses has found a strong positive correlation between Army enlistments and casualties. In my own sample survey of the Los Angeles Armed Forces Examination and Entrance Station in January-February 1969, I found that the *number* of non-draft-induced enlistees (as projected from percentage rates) had grown approximately by population growth for the Air Force and Navy since the 1964 DoD sample surveys [*Review of the Administration and Operation of the Selective Service System (RAOSSS)*, HCAS, Hearings 89-2, Washington, D.C., June 1966, pp. 10044-10045] but increased sharply for the Army and Marine Corps.

2. Grant this single premise, the case for *selective* conscription collapses.

3. The skilled segment includes electronics, other technical machinery and repair, and crafts. The remaining occupational areas are: ground combat, clerical, and services.

4. For a detailed discussion of deferment policy, see Chapter 3.

5. As stated, a demand curve is unnecessary. As a first approximation, the

military has an inelastic demand curve derived from a linear production function composed of a few alternative processes. In the short run, change is deterred by existing equipment, rigid organizational "building block" units, tactical procedures, traditional behavior modes, and the uncertainty associated with departing from proven practices. Even in the long run, the military's production processes and factor proportions change slowly. Many factors account for this. Perhaps the basic reason is lack of effective pressures for continual reappraisal and questioning of existing procedures—a difficult task in any bureaucratic organization. Secondary causes are the fragmented authority to institute changes and the military's unfamiliarity with (and abhorrence of) economic logic. As a result, manning requirements usually do not respond to small changes in relative prices and other factors; rather, change hinges on more climatic events.

The one area where labor cost could play a major role is in the design and introduction of new equipment, particularly of expensive weapons systems. Typically, the labor cost of operation and maintenance has been neglected in the design of and choice among competing systems. Many reasons account for this: its inherent complexity; the engineer's bias for goldplating; Congressional constraints on numbers of end items (which encourage the services to buy oversophisticated items); and DoD's ignorance of its own budgetary labor costs for an occupied billet (much less economic and budgetary costs to other agencies such as Veterans Administration). As of mid-1967, several of the services did not know their occupational training costs; none knew their capital and land costs; and none had systematically estimated the cost of a billet. Thus, there have been proposals for the "matching of personnel and training to the design as it progresses through development and production, . . . but no inputs of data to form the basis of design and trade-off analyses so that the design is influenced by the manpower factors." (John Poindexter, *Manpower Considerations in Development*, OSD(SA), unpublished study, Fall 1967.)

6. A more subtle approach is to raise and lower official and unofficial qualification standards according to supply at given wage rates. This was standard practice in the Air Force and Navy before Vietnam. The Army followed another policy, of setting the highest enlistment standards, accepting all who qualified, and drafting the deficit. The policy objective was to ensure the army its "fair share" of manpower quality.

7. Voluntarism's peacetime budgetary costs are greater than the draft's only if the premises and constraints of the present military manpower system are left unexamined and unchanged. Yet the thrust of all published cost estimates and the Nixon Administration's volunteer military program is to leave the system unchanged except for substituting volunteers for draftees.

8. The direct economic gain is $\sum_{i=1}^{n} O_D - O_V$ where $O_D - O_V$ stands for the economic gain (opportunity cost) of substituting a volunteer for a draftee or

draft-induced volunteer. Other economic gains came from a reduced training base, higher productivity, and, it is to be hoped, more rationalized allocation procedures.

9. Voluntarism's budget costs are always greater than its social and economic opportunity costs. The mechanisms of voluntarism are such that intramarginal rent cannot be avoided, whereas social and economic costs are calculated on a discriminating monopsonist basis.

10. The tone of the public discussion was set by the 1965 DoD draft study estimate of from $4 to $17 billion. The errors in the DoD and other published budgetary estimates, including the more recent Presidential Commission on An All-Volunteer Force estimate, are specified in Chapter 6.

11. This is strictly true only if volunteering is a function of economic opportunity costs. Draft systems are generally well within the curve. However, a highly discriminating selective system and a universal system by age cohorts (youngest first) can approach the locus.

12. The military opposes such reduction in labor quality for its *ceteris paribus* adverse effect on discipline, training, and operations.

13. For a discussion of organizational identification and loyalties hindering marginal changes and innovative activity, see Herbert A. Simon's chapter on "Loyalties and Organizational Identification," *Administrative Behavior*, pp. 198-219.

14. Many other cited examples of poor labor utilization allegedly induced by conscription's cheap labor and easy manpower access would also remain. For instance, H. von Thunen castigated conscription for inducing the military to sacrifice "in a battle a hundred human beings in the prime of their lives without a thought to save one gun." The reason being "the purchase of a cannon causes an outlay of public funds, whereas human beings are to be had for nothing by means of a mere conscription device." (Quoted by Theodore W. Schultz, "Investment in Human Capital," in Peter M. Gutmann (ed.), *Economic Growth*, Prentice Hall, Englewood Cliffs, 1964, New Jersey, p. 127.) This is an oversimplification, for all types of behavior motives are involved, many of which are less than rational. Moreover, von Thunen neglected to mention that short-run constraints may cause valuations sharply different from production cost.

Another example is conscription's being blamed for inducing the military to use its labor trivially. This too overlooks the fact that many units must be organized and manned for wartime peak loading and have little to do in peacetime, just as firemen have little to do except during fires (and preparing for them). For the combat units, moreover, too much training can be unproductive and induce poor behavior patterns. To consume idle time, many trivial military tasks were explicitly introduced by Frederick the Great during the period of expensive professional armies. In peacetime, the marginal cost of these apparently meaningless activities is zero. What is objectionable is that the military hierarchy has often allowed manning authorizations to balloon *pari passu* with increases in legitimate workloads, rather than replacing the trivia with useful work.

15. For examples of military operations designed to meet tight political and economic constraints, see Moshe Dayan, *Diary of the Sinai Campaign*, Harper & Row, New York, 1966.

16. Secondary considerations are reducing the size and social isolation of an allegedly dangerous professional military.

17. Dr. Harold Wool, former DoD Director of Procurement Policy (Manpower), notes that the shift from contract to in-house performance of military logistical functions occurred in World War I because of

... the apparently unlimited availability of military manpower through the draft in contrast to the more uncertain civilian labor recruitment outlook in a competitive wartime labor market ... [the draft] made available to the army a broad occupational cross-section of the nation's manpower resources and without the complications inherent in hiring of either domestic or overseas civilian labor.

("The Military Specialist," unpublished dissertation, The American University, 1967, p. 38.)

Another aspect of this availability was the concurrent discontinuance of the accepted practice of permitting skilled personnel lateral entry into the military with rank commensurate with their skills.

18. Factor-saving in the Joan Robinson sense. (*The Rate of Interest and Other Essays*, Macmillan, London, 1952, pp. 42 and 50.)

19. An exception is that voluntarism is not efficient during popular wars, when powerful nonmonetary motives exist. During nation-in-arms conflicts of the recent past, direct labor allocation has sometimes been necessary, as in Britain in 1916, to prevent highly skilled manpower from enlisting.

20. Its special disadvantage is the possibility of speculative holdbacks in enlistments.

21. Associated with citizenship is a Greek nation-in-arms notion of public service which expresses itself as a direct personal burden whose weight cannot be reduced substantially by the economic and social influence of the obligee. This is quite distinct from the essentially militarily unthreatened European monarchial system which encouraged the burgher to maintain the community's defense with his purse rather than his sword. (David C. Rapoport, "A Comparative Theory of Military and Political Types," in Samuel P. Huntington (ed.), *Changing Patterns of Military Politics*, The Free Press of Glencoe, New York, 1962.) America thus reflects a dual inheritance. The burgher inheritance is more appropriate in peacetime; the Greek concept, in wartime.

22. As explained in Appendix 2-A, this is not really a risk-to-life argument because careerists (as opposed to noncareerists) have a low-risk incidence.

23. Short enlistment tours, of course, can be functionally equivalent to opting-out at critical moments. Short enlistments coming due nearly simultaneously after a military expansion began was perhaps the primary cause of manpower deficiency before the Civil War Enabling Act of 1863.

24. For a development of this important argument, see Appendix 2-A.

25. Conscription to avoid decadence is of course undermined by student/occupational deferments. Nor can this inconsistency be avoided by claiming that deferments only postpone military service. Postponement is obviously advantageous to individuals in time of war. In peacetime postponement is equitable but economically inefficient because the supply of draft-induced college graduates exceeds the military's peacetime demand for officers. Finally, to the extent that postponement can be pyramided into exemption, it produces a personal advantage for the student deferred. The logic of deferment is discussed in Chapter 3.

26. For a rigorous proof of this and other themes, see Steven L. Canby, *Military Manpower Procurement: A Policy Analysis*, unpublished Ph.D. dissertation, Harvard University, 1971, pp. 28-30.

27. By Webster's definition, taxes are a forced contribution of wealth to meet the public needs of a government. Forced labor is as much a tax as a pecuniary payment.

28. The proof is as follows:

Let c = military compensation and e = equal probability of random selection.

Assume:

(1) 2 groups, rich (r) exemptees and poor (p) selectees

(2) Burdens (B) are equal to foregone income opportunities (y) and taxes

(3) Taxes = $t(y)$, where $0 \leqslant t'(y) \leqslant 1$

(4) $y > c$, the coercion condition

For selective service the respective burdens are $B_r = t(y)$ and $B_p = y - c + t(c)$. Differentiating $\dfrac{dB_r}{dy} = t'(y)$ and $\dfrac{dB_p}{dy} = 1$. Since $t'(y) < 1$, the rich are paying a distinctly smaller tax rate than the poor's 100%. Because of tax avoidance, the upper poor may also be paying higher *average* rates than the richest of the privileged (i.e., $\dfrac{B_p}{y} > \dfrac{B_r}{y}$).

For a random system, the burden is $B = e[y - c + t(c)]$. Differentiating, $\dfrac{dB}{dy} = e$. The tax rate is therefore constant regardless of income. Proportionately the rich bear a larger relative share (R) as $R = \dfrac{B}{y} = \dfrac{e[y - c + t(c)]}{y}$ and $\dfrac{dR}{dy} = \dfrac{e}{y^2}[c - t(c)] > 0$. The relative burden therefore increases with income opportunities.

29. Empirically, black reenlistments have been more than double white rates. Though only imperfectly perceived, military compensation for careerists consid-

erably exceeds mean earnings for civilians of comparable age and education. Relative ratios are particularly large for black careerists.

30. For further details, see Appendix 2-B.

31. Contrary to the allegations of many antimilitary liberals, professionals are less prone to such incidents than conscripts because greater experience and training teaches more ways to handle adverse situations. However, the key distinction is the difference in officers. Professional officers tend to be educated (however narrowly) and possess a developed code of ethics; the combat arms of nonprofessional armies often have large numbers of junior officers who have risen from the enlisted ranks. While many liberals naïvely view this as egalitarian and therefore desirable, two costs are attached. One is a lowering of officer quality. A second is a narrowing of the "firebreak" (some would say aristocratic distinction) between officers and men; this leads to officers sharing the emotions of their men, and, consequently, less detached and more emotional decisions.

For an excellent analysis of the American problem, see *The Economist*, "The Only Innocents," November 29, 1969, pp. 15-16.

32. National Advisory Commission on Selective Service, *In Pursuit of Equity*, p. 12.

33. U.S. Congress, House, Committee on Armed Services, *Civilian Advisory Panel on Military Procurement*, p. 18.

34. See Introduction.

35. The many reasons for this are explained in Chapter 6. The total additional costs of voluntarism are of the order of $2.1 to $2.5 billion. The cost difference is due to a shift in the composition of the force to a more productive, older, force with higher personnel costs.

36. See Appendix 5-E.

37. U.S. Congress, House, Armed Services Committee, *Hearings, UMT, & S Act Extension*, 1955, 84C-1.

38. In principle, all unfairness can be removed by compensation; in practice, administrative convenience, concealed preferences, and the equity requirement of equal pay for equal work prevent perfect "transfer" wages.

39. A given equitable wage can be distributed in the form of nonfully perceived fringe and postservice benefits. Strong political, economic, and paternalistic arguments can be made for such a policy in wartime. First, it would discourage wartime voluntarism. If peacetime voluntarism draws heavily from the lower classes, wartime inductions would then be more heavily weighted with the upper classes, thus producing a more representative military when equal distribution is most socially desirable and important. Second, deferred pays are cyclically stabilizing when consumption is postponed from an inflationary (wartime) to a potentially recessionary (postwar) period. Third, young soldiers and sailors are notorious spendthrifts. By deferring some pay, individual funds will be reserved for postservice benefits, partially obviating the need for additional public expenditure. Fourth, reducing available free cash by deferred

and nonmonetary compensation can also be individually advantageous because of the inelastic supply of many desired commodities around military posts at home and abroad. This reduces demand, permitting the same commodities to be bought at a lower price, thus reducing (1) economic rents and windfalls, (2) the American dollar outflow, and (3) the inflationary disruption of local economies, particularly in low-wage, underdeveloped countries such as Vietnam.

40. Of course, the economic definition of fairness may not coincide with ethical definitions.

41. A.C. Pigou, *The Economics of Welfare*, 4th ed., London, Macmillan, pp. 813-814.

42. Ibid., p. 550.

43. "First 12 Months Compensation—No Dependent," *DoD Congressional Briefing Book*, April 3, 1965.

44. Steven Canby and Jack Carlson, "Cost Estimates of Fair Pay Based on the 1965 and 1967 Federal Minimum Wage and 30 June 1964 Force Strengths, with Implications for a Volunteer Military," unpublished memo, Harvard Seminar on Selective Service, May 1967.

45. See S.L. Canby, *Military Manpower* (dissertation), pp. 17-31.

46. Gary S. Becker, *Human Capital*, National Bureau of Economic Research, New York, 1964, p. 17. Draft inducement actually means that volunteers and draftees have borne a large and hidden share of the military's total training costs. For a critique of the Becker model's applicability to military compensation, see Appendix 5-A.

47. Ibid., pp. 20-21.

48. Dwight D. Eisenhower, "This Country Needs Universal Military Training," *Reader's Digest*, Volume 89, September 1966, pp. 49-55.

49. Harry Gilman, "Military Manpower Utilization" in *Defense Management*, S. Enke (ed.), Prentice-Hall, Englewood Cliffs, N.J., 1967, p. 254.

50. Lester C. Thurow, "Impact of Service in the Armed Forces on Non-White Incomes," unpublished memo, Harvard Seminar on Selective Service, April 12, 1967.

51. An academic curiosity is the functioning of the Hicks-Kaldor compensatory criterion. By this criterion, reducing pay inequity (i.e., the draft's hidden tax) for draftees is preferable to the concomitant increase in rejectee inequity. This is because draftees can always, in principle, compensate rejectees for their equity loss. The reverse is not true because psychic income increases to rejectees through less desirable recruit wages cannot be translated into compensatory payments.

52. From various data compiled from the Office of the Surgeon General, Department of the Army.

53. "Rejection Rates at Pre-Induction Examinations, by Cause, 1952-65," *RAOSSS*, p. 10031.

54. Based on annual 1951-1967 time-series data from the *Statistical Abstract of the U.S.*

55. Jacking of acceptance standards began in 1956, tightened considerably during the 1958 recession, and peaked in 1963-65. Secretary McNamara tried to reverse this process in 1964 with his STEP proposal, which ran aground on the shoals of military-Congressional opposition. His later Project 100,000 was similarly motivated, but also conveniently provided manpower for Vietnam.

Standards were lowered during the Vietnam period. With the reduced manpower demand from the Vietnam phase-out and the shift to voluntarism, standards have again been increased to their pre-Vietnam levels.

56. National Advisory Commission on Selective Service, op. cit., pp. 66-67.

57. 1964 survey data indicate that (1) employment difficulty and draft uncertainty experienced by men increased with age and education, (2) almost half of employers restricted hiring of draft-liable college graduates, and (3) considerable uncertainty and employment difficulties. *RAOSSS*, pp. 10008-individuals; even men in exempted categories experienced lower but still considerable uncertainty and employment difficulties. *RAOSS*, pp. 10008-10010.

58. "Reference Material from the Department of Defense Study of the Draft," *RAOSSS*, p. 10014.

59. Ibid., p. 10015.

60. This is the real reason why Selective Service has opposed electronic data-processing. Many critics have failed to realize that EDP would not remove the ailment but only speed up the notification process. For a brief summary of the SSS position on EDP, see: House Committee on Armed Services, op. cit., p. 20.

61. Variation in individual preference as to induction timing suggests permitting draftees some choice of induction dates in peacetime. Scope for choice is possible under either random or selective conscription. How much uncertainty would accompany such a scheme depends on the age of selection. Uncertainty could be minimized by actual *selection* at an early age, with *induction* postponed for several years according to choice. However, SSS procedures would be unworkable without arbitrary exemptions at such an early age. For this reason, "early selection, choice of induction dates" implies a lottery with limited latitude, such as: selection at 18, final induction by 22, and individual opting between 18-22. The cost would be a limited amount of war speculation by the already selected, and a slight increase in uncertainty during the cohort period of exposure. In wartime, of course, one would want to cancel extant options. For further details, see Appendix 3-A.

62. National Advisory Commission on Selective Service, op. cit., p. 160.

63. Kingman Brewster, president of Yale University, complained that the SSS "seems heedless of the differences in both need and capability, which have been brought about by change in population and military technique. . . . The result has been to encourage a cynical avoidance of service, a corruption of the aims of education and a tarnishing of the national spirit." Quoted in *RAOSSS*, p. 9728.

64. Higher turnover also induces greater labor mobility from low-wage, labor-surplus areas to higher wage areas.

65. This is distinguished from the continental tradition, where the standing army was approved as an instrument of a strong royal authority. These differing conceptions owe to differences in institutional evolution. In England the medieval king's feudal function (involving reciprocal obligation) predominated, and it was thought appropriate that his power be circumscribed. This "populist" notion, a carry-over from Germanic tribal heritage, eventually extended from the barons to include the new commercial classes. On the continent, the king's theocratic function, inherited from Rome, predominated because the greater geographic vulnerability of continental states made defense paramount. Also, the new commercial classes saw reciprocal obligation as perpetuating the old corporate society with its special privileges for the nobility and its rules hampering commercial development. Thus, on the continent, the army was favorably regarded as a royal tool for reducing customary privilege, whereas in England it became an instrument in the struggle between the king and Parliament. See Walter Ullman, *Principles of Government and Politics in the Middle Ages*, New York, Barnes & Noble, 1961, and Guido de Ruggiero, *The History of European Liberalism*, Boston, Beacon Press, 1959.

66. The Brazilian army skims the best; Peru formally uses a lottery, but deferments effectively place the burden on the lower classes.

67. Though advocates of national service would strenuously object, this could also be interpreted as a form of national service with unequal sacrifice as determined by the SSS.

68. Quoted in Merriam H. Trytten, *Student Deferment in Selective Service*, Minneapolis, University of Minnesota Press, 1952, p. 131.

69. *RAOSSS*, p. 9799.

70. Selective Service System, *Selective Service Orientation Kit* memo on "channeling," GPO, Washington, 1965, pp. 3-4.

71. A classic manifestation of this principle, both in this country and in England, has been some form of locally organized armed citizens. Fulfilling this role in the United States today is the National Guard, whose chain of command runs through the state government.

72. The literature of militarism and political tyranny almost always identifies a nation's army, not its navy or air force, as the coup instrument. The navy's exclusion is partly historical and partly because it is usually too remote from political power centers (and improperly armed and trained) to be a serious domestic threat. The major exceptions are the navy's role in prewar Japan and the sailors' role in the Russian Revolution. The air force's position is similar to the navy's: its weapons, particularly those of advanced technology, are too destructive to be used discriminatingly against one's own population. The air force also cannot operate independently from the army because its ground bases are vulnerable to attack.

73. Samuel P. Huntington, *The Soldier and the State*, Cambridge, Mass., Harvard University Press, 1957, pp. 222-270.

74. In smaller countries, the colonels may be the dangerous group because only a few units of regimental size are required to stage a coup, and the personal control and charisma of a commander dissipates rapidly above this level. In larger countries, a coup requires the collusion and complicity of a large number of officers. Individual idiosyncrasies, which are often decisive in the smaller countries, are correspondingly less important than the consensus of the dominating military hierarchy.

75. The current exceptions to this are the protégé and "old boy" networks. These informal networks are prevalent only among general/flag officers.

76. For an excellent exposition of this thesis, see Alfred Stepan, *The Military in Politics: Changing Patterns in Brazil*, Princeton, N.J., Princeton University Press, 1971.

77. If the services would allocate their best talent by special assignments instead of dispersing them through standardized career patterns, the military would be more attractive to high opportunity-cost talent and fewer would be needed.

78. Because the services can always obtain officers by promoting noncollege men, eliminating or reducing ROTC on college campuses because of concern that ROTC promotes unjust wars is counter-productive; rather, this reaction lowers officer quality and narrows social representation within the officer corps.

79. Huntington, *The Soldier and the State*, p. 463 and pp. 59-79.

80. A case in point is MacArthur's crossing the 38th Parallel. (Richard E. Neustadt, *Presidential Power*, New American Library, 1964, pp. 119-140.)

81. A classic example is the Cuban missile crisis. The Navy has a standard repertoire for blockades keyed to the enemy's air umbrella. The Navy therefore initially placed its destroyers at such a distance from Cuba that Soviet decision makers had little time to react before an embarrassing fait accompli. The Navy's internal mechanisms were therefore inconsistent with the raison d'être for the blockade. Had not a strong Secretary of Defense (1) personally supervised the blockade and (2) recognized the inconsistency, events could have been much different. The Navy, of course, resented the intrusion.

82. For an account of this deficiency in American Government, see Don Price, *Government and Science*, New York University Press, 1954; and Senate Committee on Government Operations, *Specialists and Generalists*, 1968, Subcommittee on National Security and International Operations.

83. For an account of the adverse consequences during World War II and Korea, see Huntington, pp. 315-337, and Neustadt, op. cit., pp. 120-140.

84. It is said that paying fair wages will attract too many from the lower classes, thereby reducing the number of randomly selected draftees; however, this does not necessarily follow. First, even if wages are not raised, those naturally attracted will continue to enlist, largely in the relatively safe "overhead" portion of the military. Second, since pay for equity and pay for supply are not identical, voluntarism could be discouraged by greater deferred and

income-in-kind compensations. Third, a number of special rules could be adopted to discourage voluntarism; a precedent already exists in the enlistment suspensions during both world wars. To deter the better educated from opting into the military's safer "havens," enlistment contracts could be temporarily lengthened to reduce the attractiveness to draft-induced volunteers.

85. The classic example is Thucydides' account of the Peloponnesian War. David Rapoport also notes that universal, nation-in-arms states have been historically the most aggressive and have tended towards "total war" and demands for "unconditional surrender." On the other hand, the volunteer monarchial system was among the least aggressive because the kings had difficulty providing "coin" to pay volunteers. (Samuel P. Huntington (ed.), *Changing Patterns of Military Politics*, Glencoe, N.Y., Free Press, 1962, pp. 75, 92, and 95.) To generalize, the causal nexus in both cases is not institutional, but the ideological commitments of the populace.

86. A reserve callup is another. However a reserve callup does not necessarily imply wide class participation; this would depend on the original selection scheme. Individual inequity is also involved if the recalled reservists are ex-servicemen serving the remainder of their obligated tours. A callup then resembles an extension of the enlistment contract. The advantages of having to use the reserves before the draft are that military commitments would necessarily be less open and that greater stress would have to be placed on the reserves' efficiency. However, greater efficiency would require more stringent federal supervision, which might reduce the reserves' role as a counterweight to central authority.

87. Vietnam and the Dominican Republic can be used to support the allegation that a selective system promotes foreign adventures. Selective service possesses neither the budgetary dampers of voluntarism nor the wide participation of the lottery.

88. If the "salami slices" of increased pressure are too thin, a minor opponent finds physical and psychological adjustment possible by incremental belt-tightening; yet if the slices are too thick, outside groups may feel as though they must aid the beleaguered enemy.

89. In addition, the disadvantaged government may also be too constrained to take short-term risks for the sake of long-term benefits.

90. Though the popular mind today associates the dangers of a "standing army" with voluntarism and professionalism, national conscription was formerly feared for the authority given the federal government to tap the source of military power without the pluralistic diffusion of state intermediaries.

91. *Hearings*, HMAC, 65-1, "Selective Service Act, 1917," p. 5.

92. *RAOSSS*, p. 9621.

93. SSS budget justification for fiscal 1967. Quoted in National Advisory Commission on Selective Service, op. cit., p. 20.

94. *RAOSSS*, p. 10067. Of course, ultimate responsibility rests with the

Congress for providing (in Sec. 6(h)) that "No person within any such category shall be deferred except upon the basis of his individual status." This in turn was a superficial reaction to the equity criticism of blanket occupational deferments in World War I.

95. For a summary of this trap, see George H. Sabine, *A History of Political Thought*, New York, Holt, 1961, pp. 63-66. The crucial point is that there is an ineradicable moral distinction between subjection to the law and subjection to the will of another human being, even though that other be a wise and benevolent despot. The difference is that the first is compatible with a sense of freedom and dignity while the second is not. Derived from this distinction is the principle that governments derive their just powers from the consent of the governed.

96. National Advisory Commission on Selective Service, op. cit., pp. 20 and 32. The Marshall Commission missed the theoretical essence of personalization and attacked the SSS's administrative procedures on its own grounds when it said that "the 'neighborly' character of local boards seems to exist more in theory than in fact" and currently only in rural areas. On p. 41 the Commission did come to the "uncomfortable realization that a case-by-case basis without binding guidelines had led to some of the worst and most widespread unevenness. . . . Thus the inequity of according special privilege to students has been compounded by the administrative inequities which student deferment policy invites."

97. Leach, J.F., *Conscription in the United States*, Rutland, Vt., Tuttle, pp. 452-455.

98. Kreidberg and Henry, *History of Military Mobilization in the United States Army, 1775-1945*, Washington, D.C., Department of the Army, 1955, p. 105.

99. *RAOSSS*, p. 10073.

100. Locke, John, *Second Treatise on Civil Government*, New York, Barnes and Noble, 1966, paragraphs 137 and 142.

101. Ibid., paragraph 160.

102. Ibid., paragraph 161.

103. Some tradition also exists for minimizing legal technicalities. Jeremy Bentham, for instance, advocated legal simplification, informal pleading, and "every man his own lawyer." *(Fragment on Government.)* Professor Pigou also argues that technicalities and lawyers should not be admitted before (arbitration) boards (op. cit., p. 422).

104. An organizational plan for a hypothetical national service is contained in Appendix A, "A Profile for National Service," in Donald J. Eberly (ed.), *National Service*, New York, Russell Sage Foundation, 1968, pp. 513-546. Pages 51-60 contain a brief but excellent critique of national service by Eli Ginzberg entitled "Manpower Dimensions of National Service."

105. Bernard D. Karpinos, *The Mental Qualification of American Youths for*

Military Service and Its Relationship to Educational Attainments, Medical Statistics Agency, Department of the Army, 1966, p. 2.

106. Quotas and credits can also adversely affect Congressional decision making due to the Southern hold on committee chairmanships. With such low qualification rates, quotas relieve the relative burden on the Southern labor force. Given the South's low wages, credits also reduce the draft's effect on the higher-quality residue. A volunteer military would have an opposite wage equalization impact by increasing Southern but reducing Northern incidence of military service. In 1965, average weekly earnings of production workers varied from $74.98 in Mississippi to $143.79 in Michigan. U.S. Bureau of the Census, *1966 Statistical Abstract*, #335, p. 240.

107. Listed as footnote 1, p. 249.

108. His fundamental complaint against the lottery was "the inordinate lack of general understanding displayed by its proponents concerning the *fundamental principles and philosophy upon which the Selective Service System is founded and under which it operates*." (Emphasis added.) "A Study Made by the Selective Service System Concerning the Feasibility of a Lottery System," *RAOSSS*, p. 10090.

109. A standby draft to pick up small recruiting deficits is ex-post inequitable to the selected, permits the military to raise acceptance standards at no budget cost, and undermines the discontinuity damper on decision makers of a sequential system.

110. DoD enlisted skill/grade model, OSD, 1965.

111. G.W. Beebe and M.E. DeBakey, *Battle Casualties*, Springfield, Ill., Charles C. Thomas, p. 42. Lest one feel these data are outdated, current Army planning factors indicate that 80% of battle losses within an infantry division will occur in rifle platoons, which are 20% of the division. FM-101-10-1, *Staff Officers Field Manual: Organization, Technical and Logistical Data*, January 1966, pp. 2-4.

112. The legal minimum for draftees is the tenth percentile; however, this has been effectively shifted upward by imposing additional screening tests (see pp. 35-36).

113. Other factors contributing to a higher black draftee rate are fewer student/occupational deferments and blacks' low participation in reserve units due to overt and inadvertent discrimination, the latter caused by the reserves' policy of accepting the best qualified among potential volunteers. For instance, black participation in the Army National Guard varied from 1.2 to 1.4% from 1965 to 1968; for the Air Guard, from 0.7 to 0.8%.

114. Figure 2-4 shows that 77.4 and 28% of whites and blacks, respectively, are mentally qualified. The medical rejection rate is 15.2% and 5.9% for whites and blacks, respectively. This leads to the ratio:

$$\frac{.774(1-.152)(.88)}{.28\ (1-.059)(.12)} = 18.3$$

115. These calculations are based on Figure 2-4 and the population statistics in Tables 5 and 62, pp. 8 and 53 of the *1966 Statistical Abstract.*

116. A black army is quite possible; but this would mean excluding blacks from the more highly skilled specialities of the other services.

117. The formula is: $\dfrac{ES\,(.88)}{2ES\,(.12)} = \dfrac{W}{60,000 - W}$.

118. First-term reenlistment rates for all services in 1964 were 21.6 and 46.6% for whites and blacks respectively. National Advisory Commission on Selective Service, op. cit., p. 161.

119. The Gates Commission estimate was 12.8 to 16.0%. *Presidential Commission on an All-Volunteer Force*, p. 149. The difference in estimates is due to the retention rate parameter. Though theoretically yielding identical solutions, my use of relative reenlistment rates yields a higher estimate than their use of blacks as a percent of first-term reenlistments. The divergence is caused by considerably fewer blacks being qualified for reenlistment. Thus under existing practices, the Gates estimate is the more accurate; under revised procedures, mine is more accurate.

120. United States Bureau of the Census, *Characteristics of the Population* Vol. 1 (Tables 101 and 102), 1960; *Historical Statistics*, Series H., p. 395-406.

121. Based on Figure 2-4 and Table 2-5, the military allocates its technical specialties to enlistees on the basis of the best qualified, which are generally Mental Categories I and II men. In FY 1960-65, Categories I and II men were 37.4% of all accessions and were as high as 46% for Air Force enlistees. *RAOSSS*, pp. 10021-2.

122. In 1966, while 9.5% of the overall and 10.6% of the Vietnam military were black, 16.3% of the battle deaths were black. Similarly, while 13.9% of Army enlisted strength was black, 22.4% of enlisted battle deaths were black (versus 20.6% inclusive of officers). After the buildup, black participation in Vietnam dropped to 9.8% in December 1967; as of June 1969 black deaths were 13.0% of the DoD total. OASD Office of the Assistant Secretary of Defense (Manpower and Reserve Affairs) (M&RA).

123. *RAOSSS*, p. 10039.

124. For details, see S.L. Canby, op. cit.

125. The report of the *Presidential Commission on an All-Volunteer Force*, Washington, D.C., GPO, February 1970, p. 126.

126. Ibid., pp. 99-100.

127. National Advisory Commission on Selective Service, *In Pursuit of Equity*, pp. 162-163.

128. For example, *Life's* article, "Bald Case in Point: pro football's magical immunity; the draft; with case histories," December 9, 1966.

129. "Selected Characteristics of Enlistees into Reserve Forces (REP) and Active Forces, March 1967–June 1969," OASD (M&RA) PP & GR, 17 September 1969.

130. "Military Service Status of Men Aged 26-29 Years, by Color," National Advisory Commission on Selective Service, op. cit., p. 159. The same data source as the footnote above shows that blacks compose only 1.5% of 1969 Army Reserve enlistees.

Chapter 3
Deferment Policy: Logic and Issues

1. Prior to the replacement of the "oldest first" selection technique with the lottery in 1970, the induction sequence, as revised in 1965, was:

(1) Delinquents who have attained the age of 19 in the order of their dates of birth with the oldest being selected first.

(2) Volunteers who have not attained the age of 26 years in the sequence in which they have volunteered for induction.

(3) Nonvolunteers who have attained the age of 19 years and have not attained the age of 26 years and who (a) do not have a wife with whom they maintain a bona fide family relationship in their homes, in the order of their dates of birth with the oldest being selected first, or (b) have a wife whom they married after August 26, 1965, and with whom they maintain a bona fide family relationship in their homes, in the order of their dates of birth with the oldest being selected first.

(4) Nonvolunteers who have attained the age of 19 years and have not attained the age of 26 years and who have a wife whom they married on or before August 26, 1965, and with whom they maintain a bona fide family relationship in their homes, in the order of their dates of birth with the oldest being selected first.

(5) Nonvolunteers who have attained the age of 26 years in the order of their dates of birth with the youngest being selected first.

(6) Nonvolunteers who have attained the age of 18 years and 6 months and who have not attained the age of 19 years in the order of their dates of birth with the oldest selected first.

2. Selective Service System. *Selective Service Orientation Kit* memo on "Channeling," GPO, Washington, 1965, p. 4.

3. Director of Selective Service, *Annual Report*, GPO, Washington, 1966, p. 15.

4. For an elaboration of these points and their caveats, see Clark Kerr, "An Effective and Democratic Organization of the Economy," in *Goals for Americans*, Prentice-Hall, 1960; for a detailed exposition of the working of the market mechanism, see T. Scitovsky, *Welfare and Competition* (1951), pp. 29-188, and A.P. Lerner, *The Economics of Control* (1944).

5. A sophisticated rationalization for channeling is that because human capital accumulation is undesirable during full mobilization, stocks must be

accumulated at other times; hence, channelization. Further, free markets cannot be assumed to remedy the situation. During full mobilization fixed stocks of skills may have positive shadow prices. So long as the occurrence of mobilization has some nonzero probability, the return to those who acquire "critical" skills should be greater than their current marginal productivity by the discounted (for both time and probability of mobilization) present value of the difference between the shadow price of the skill during mobilization and current marginal productivity. Since the skill is "critical" to the nation and not necessarily to the firm, the problem can be viewed as an externality. Offering inducements in the form of service avoidance (channelization) is a substitute for wages higher than current marginal products.

This argument implies labor force inefficiency in peacetime; yet the major argument for student deferment was efficient use of resources for a long-term struggle against communism. A second problem is that the term "critical" is an operationally difficult one. The Trytten committees (see pp. 85-86) did not specify specific skills because of the difficulty of predicting which would be critical in the future. For instance, physicists have long been alleged to be critical; yet if an excess supply exists even in wartime, they can hardly be termed critical. Furthermore, many weapons systems have become so sophisticated and have such long lead times that the usefulness of "crashing" scientific talent into weapons development during full mobilization will often be limited. Third, while full mobilization may imply positive shadow prices, their *expected* value approaches zero, and may even be negative because of the exceedingly low probability of World War I and II mobilizations, the difficulty of identifying critical skills, and the opportunity loss implied by overinvesting in skills unnecessary for a peacetime economy. Fourth, the possibilities of other externalities inducing a greater supply in the absence of any guidance from wartime demand can degenerate into additional education simply to avoid service.

6. National Advisory Commission, on Selective Service, *In Pursuit of Equity*, p. 41.

7. A Harvard Study Group, "On the Draft," *The Public Interest* (No. 9), Fall 1967, p. 95.

8. In World War II, the services relied extensively on accelerated courses for military personnel on university campuses and deferred a limited number of students, mainly in the healing arts.

9. *RAOSSS*, pp. 9648-9649.

10. M.H. Trytten, *Student Deferment in Selective Service*, University of Minnesota Press, Minneapolis, 1952, pp. 82-83.

11. Ibid., p. 4.

12. Gary Becker estimates an 8-to-11% social rate of return for all college entrants (10 to 13% for white male graduates) as opposed to an 8-to-12%

before-tax rate of return on all business capital. Becker estimates the payoff period for white male graduates to be between 10 and 15 years. *Human Capital*, NBER, pp. 112 and 120. Since a wartime society has a short-time horizon and a large social discount rate, the Becker analysis implies that only a few critical fields justify the opportunity costs of deferment during full mobilization.

13. These figures were computed by adjusting Theodore Schultz's estimated college costs of $3,305 in 1956, including a 59% non-GNP-registered opportunity cost, to 1965, and multiplying by 1965's university population. *The Economic Value of Education*, Columbia University Press, New York, 1964, pp. 29 and 34. *1966 Statistical Abstract*, No. 15 and No. 191, pp. 111 and 135.

By including females and physically unqualified males, these estimates implicitly include a "work-or-fight" assumption whereby deferees are required to work in war-related industries in order to maintain their deferments from military service.

14. D.M. Blank and G.J. Stigler, *The Demand and Supply of Scientific Personnel*, NBER, New York, p. 5.

15. These are nonadditive and are adjusted to include law and medical/dental doctorate degrees. The percentages are for 1966 graduates and a 21-25 year male population base of 6.539 million; *1968 Statistical Abstract*, No. 199, p. 135, and *1966 Statistical Abstract*, No. 5, p. 8.

The U.S. Office of Education estimates that baccalaureate degree production will increase by 75% in the decade 1965 to 1975. In 1978 American colleges and universities will produce almost a million bachelor's degrees each year. (*Projections of Educational Statistics to 1977-78*, 1968 ed., GPO, 1969, p. 31.)

The growth in production of advanced degrees is even more spectacular. In 1968 two and a half times as many Ph.D.'s were produced as in 1958. Production is expected to continue to increase, with 1978's production almost doubling 1968's. 1978 doctoral production, estimated to be in excess of 40,000, will be more than five times the production of 1958.

Allan Carter, Chancellor of New York University, in his article, "The Economics of Higher Education" states that the supply of Ph.D.'s will exceed the demand for them by the mid-1970s, and that the surplus will widen as a result of stable or slightly reduced demands, but continued growth in production. Less than half of those who seek academic positions in 1980 will be needed. Of course, these conclusions should not be interpreted to suggest that there will be large numbers of unemployed Ph.D.'s; rather, they will be employed in occupations not currently able to attract them. (In Neil W. Chamberlain (ed.), *Contemporary Economic Issues*, Richard D. Irwin, Inc., Homewood, Illinois, 1969, pp. 145-184.)

16. Trytten, op. cit., p. 42.

17. Blank and Stigler, op. cit., pp. 31-32, 103-106. For a lucid exposition of the causes of "shortage" misunderstandings, see Rashi Fein, *The Doctor Shortage*, The Brookings Institution, Washington, D.C., 1967, pp. 6-21.

18. One apparent objection to educational interruption is inefficient manpower use. The efficiency of SD involves three distinctions: (1) selectivity is economically more efficient than randomness; (2) SD coupled with pyramiding is more efficient than SD alone; (3) the efficiency of SD without pyramiding is a function of the military's college-absorptive capacity.

Deferment for graduate students (as opposed to undergraduates) does create a significant externality favoring more education. While some have asserted this is a good in itself, the externality may introduce economic inefficiency unless other imperfections are offset. In addition, since this externality works on manpower *supply* to overcome a potential future shortage, there is less market guidance and hence less assurance that the enlarged skill reservoir is as relevant to economic and mobilization requirements than an enlargement due to the greater *demand* for specific skills created by draft interruptions. Finally, the deferment externality has the undesirable attribute of causing the individual's educational decisions to be partially based on considerations of service avoidance.

19. The median male age at first marriage was 24.3 years in 1940 and has varied from 22.6 to 23.1 from 1950 to 1968. *1969 Statistical Abstract*, p. 60.

20. See pp. 35-36.

21. As modified in 1967, the Act now reads: "However, no person who has received a student deferment shall thereafter be granted another deferment, except for extreme hardship to dependents (under regulations governing hardship deferments) or for graduate study, occupation, or employment necessary to the national health, safety, or interest." This reduces the possibility of pyramiding through dependency (i.e., unequal burden), but sustains the possibility of pyramiding through activity considered in the national interest (i.e., unequal value).

The Executive Order of 23 April 1970 eliminated all future occupational and dependency deferments (except extreme hardship).

22. For instance, many educators, scientists, engineers, and their professional organizations have, according to the SSS, convinced large segments of the public that dedicated civilian service in their fields "constitutes the ultimate in their expression of patriotism." *Selective Service Orientation Kit*, memo on "Channeling," p. 3.

23. All eligible Swiss males have military assignments. Those unable to meet military acceptance standards or those abroad pay, until age 35, special property and income taxes, the latter amounting to approximately two weeks' wages.

24. National Advisory Commission, op. cit., p. 27.

25. S. Altman and A. Fechter, "The Supply of Military Personnel in the Absence of a Draft," *American Economic Review*, Vol. 57, No. 2, May 1967, p. 25.

26. *RAOSSS*, p. 10039.

27. National Advisory Commission, op. cit., p. 43.

28. *1966 Statistical Abstract*, pp. 111 and 137.

29. National Advisory Commission, op. cit., p. 39.

30. The exception is General Hershey, who terms student deferments without occupational deferments an "impossible situation." *RAOSSS*, p. 10061.

31. The percentage of first-tour physicians, dentists, lawyers, and other professionals who were draft-motivated was 57.8 versus 41.3 for the overall average. *RAOSSS*, p. 10039.

32. Some have mistakenly argued that the military's demand for MDs is so high that a lottery without SDs would mean two periods of military service for some MDs. The confusion is caused by failure to realize that (1) the military's percentage of the MD output is steadily decreasing because medical schools are now expanding, and (2) draftees are only about a fifth of annual accessions. The calculation, in round numbers, is: 2 million males reach draft age annually, of which 40% fail the military's acceptance standards, and the active duty military requirement is 1/2 million, of which 100,000 are draftees, then the probability of qualified men being drafted is one-eighth, or 12%. If the military required 40% of medical school graduates, the total MD participation rate would be 52%, versus 25% for the total population, and 42% for those qualified for service.

Thus, double service is precluded, but double jeopardy is *not* in the absence of SD. Since the military requires 40% of the MD output regardless of the procurement system, the relevant policy focus is upon the incremental 12%. The policy issue is how much society is willing to pay in terms of other goals to eliminate this additional incidence of service on MDs.

33. High military participation rates can also be viewed as the price the medical profession pays to restrict supply into the profession.

34. Milton Friedman and Simon Kuznets, *Income from Independent Professional Practice*, New York, National Bureau of Economic Research, 1954, pp. 8-21.

35. As disaggregated from Figure 3-1, the 1900-1905 average output of MDs and dentists was 5,452 and 2,280 respectively; in 1964, 7,342 and 3,196. From 1900 to 1964, while population climbed 152%, real per capita income 208%, and bachelor degrees 1,730%, medical and dental school output edged up only 34% and 40%, respectively. The stock of doctors has decreased from 157 in 1900 to 136 per hundred thousand in 1964. The United States in recent years has also imported 18% of its new licentiates from poorer countries. Until 1950, the medical output was actually less than it was 50 years earlier. For the immediate future, Fein estimates that demand for medical services will grow 1.8 times faster than population; this is slightly greater than the supply growth and hence widens rather than narrows past shortages. Fein, op. cit., pp. 60, 85, 135, and 144; *Historical Statistics*, Series B 180-194, F1-5, A17-21; *1966 Statistical Abstract*, p. 138.

36. Fein, for instance, maintains that private medicine could profitably imitate many of the Medical Corps's procedures. Ibid., p. 117.

37. Given the current draft and below-cohort parity wages for entrants, any ration price is readily labeled as regressive. This charge could be neutralized by a sliding-scale price or, preferably, by a major restructuring of the pay system.

38. A cross-section regression by occupational area of FY-64 Navy reenlistment rates and dependency gave an R^2 of 0.838 (see footnote 62, p. 262).

39. Particularly if the probability of eventual service for an ROTC commitment is less than one.

40. For example, in Version A, if in Year 1 the age cohort is 2 million males, the minimum qualification is the 10th percentile, peacetime inducements have already attracted 400,000 lower class (LC) enlisted men and 40,000 upper class (UC) officers, and the universities produce 400,000 B.A.'s and 90,000 advanced degrees, then any wartime expansion must come from the cohort residue composed of 400,000 LCs (1,000,000 − 400,000 enlistees − 200,000 in the 0-9 percentile) and 1,560,000 UCs (1,000,000 of this year's UCs + 400,000 of this year's college graduates + 200,000 from cancelling all graduate deferments − 40,000 officers). Thus in Year 1, assuming the population is evenly divided between LCs and UCs, UCs have a 3.8 times higher draft rate (79% versus 21%).

41. Proportionate burden-sharing also depends on the social class distribution within the military and the expansionary ground combat arms. Prior to Vietnam, 28% of the Army and 39% of the Marine enlisted strength were in this category, for a total of 303,600 EM (out of 2,273,300). Such a small base is easy to flood with UC youth in a composite system, as indicated below. The important conclusion is that although LCs will have considerably more men in the total military (stock), UCs will have more men in the ground combat arms and hence higher casualty rates, thus tending to equalize social class burdens. But in systems that completely abolish SD or permit wartime deferment, UC burdens are lighter except for very large expansion. The relative participation in high casualty rate ground combat arms can thus be shown as:[a]

	With Composite Student Deferment			Without Student Deferment		
	LC	UC	LC/UC	LC	UC	LC/UC
Peacetime Stock	300 E	30 O	10.0	300 E	30.0	10.0
Doubling Increment[b]	63 E	237 E	1.2	111 E	189 E	1.65
		30 O			30 O	
Tripling Increment[b]	126 E	474 E	.75	222 E	378 E	1.11
		60 O			60 O	

[a]Absolute numbers in thousand. E stands for enlisted men; O, for officers.
[b]Accessions required to double (triple) ground combat strength.

Chapter 4
Costing Military Manpower

1. Manifestations of this theme are large reserves, "up-or-out" promotion policies, early retirement, large staffs relative to command positions, and rapid

rotational assignments for officers to provide potential generals rather than specialists.

2. This section is based on a computational model for aggregating military specialties into apprentice, journeyman, and supervisory groupings. S.L. Canby, "Costs of Military Personnel by Duty Billet," OSD(SA), September 1967.

3. Defined as total service less time spent training, service accession, and termination processing, and the leave accumulated therein. The expected total number of years' service can be found by a system of average number of years in each grade (by occupational area) weighted by rank distribution. For instance, the expected years' service for an E4 is the average for each grade E4 to E9 weighted by the rank distribution of E4 to E9. This process is repeated and the weights changed for each grade above E4.

Chapter 5
Budget Costs and the Military Compensation System

1. Additional savings could be obtained if existing personnel policies were changed to conform with voluntarism, rather than trying to minimize voluntarism's impact on policies designed for nation-in-arms conflicts. An example of the savings from different enlistment and retention policies is shown in Appendix 6-F.

2. The Hubbell Report (Office of the Secretary of Defense, *Modernizing Military Pay*, Washington, D.C., 11 November 1967), which is the analytical basis of current DoD proposals for pay reform, focuses on only the second factor, which it terms "visibility." Moreover it recommends visibility and pay increases for careerists only. The report contends that noncareerists are already adequately compensated; it justifies this allegation through a "residual" income concept which is both specious and inconsistent, since miscellaneous in-kind benefits are termed income for noncareerists but not for careerists. For a more extensive critique, see Appendix 5-E.

3. SCAS, 84-1, *Career Incentive Act of 1955*, 1955, p. 21.

4. For an account of these learning curves, see Gorman C. Smith, *Differential Pay for Military Technicians*, unpublished Ph.D. dissertation, New York, Columbia University, 1964.

5. This is another example of myopic and adverse interaction between the Congress and the military. In 1922, Congress refused to give the military a pay raise after the World War I inflationary period and suggested a reallocation among married and unmarried personnel. Although the basic principle of compensation has always been on responsibility borne as manifested by rank, many anomalies did not begin to creep in until 1922, when Congress replaced economic criteria with the criteria of "compensation that would allow the officer to maintain himself and his family with *reasonable decency under the various conditions of service* and *at minimum cost to the government.*" (Emphasis added.) Unfortunately, the latter was narrowly defined and excluded

side effects. Of course, to the extent that bachelors are discriminated against, the military becomes more attractive to large-family men who are budgetarily more expensive and a political liability in that overseas deployment causes highly visible "little Americas."

6. These items are Quarters, Dependents' Indemnity Insurance, Medical, Commissary & Exchange, and Mortgage Insurance. Another 1.4% is accounted for by Family Separation, Dislocation, and Overseas Station Allowance.

7. Governments, of course, often intervene by taxing families less. In this country, the rationale has been based on a needs philosophy; in Europe, and in particular France, the rationale was to encourage population growth for military reasons.

8. U.S. Department of Defense, Office of Assistant Secretary of Defense, Manpower, *Number and Percentage of Entrants Without Prior Military Service that Will Remain on Active Duty Until Retirement for a Total Force Similar to That on 30 June 1965*, 5 May 1966.

9. U.S. Department of Defense, *Estimated Marital Dependency Status of Military Personnel on Active Duty*, as of 31 March 1964, 25 November 1964.

10. In the case of quarters, it may even be undesired and compulsory.

11. Office of the Secretary of Defense, op. cit., Vol. I, p. 45.

12. Department of Defense, Office of the Assistant Secretary of Defense, Manpower, *Average Annual Basic Pay of Military Personnel on Active Duty, 30 June 1966, by Years of Active Service*, 14 February 1967.

13. Residual pay involves comparing available free spending power of military personnel and civilians after subtracting for the military's in-kind and special pricing benefits, such as the Post Exchanges. For an example of its use, see the critique of the Hubbell Report in Appendix 5-E.

14. Neglect of this concept can lead to major cost overestimates and incorrect decisions. In the 1964-65 *Department of Defense Study of the Draft*, it was one of the major causes of a multi-billion-dollar overestimate which biased public policy against voluntarism and led many to believe that voluntarism was infeasible.

15. Most studies of a volunteer military have used a double log transformation for estimating the wage elasticity. In this case the true relationship, in simplified form, is

(1) $v = aw_p{}^b$ where, b = wage elasticity, w_p = perceived wage. However the observed relationship is

(2) $v = aw_m{}^b$ where, the observed military wage $w_m = \gamma w_p$ and $\gamma \geqslant 1$.

The double log transformation yields

(3) $\log v = \log a \, \gamma^b + b \log w_p$.

Least squares applied to (3) gives an unbiased estimate of the elasticity coefficient "b" and, of course, an unbiased but incorrect estimate of the intercept term of (1)—which can be important if (3) is also used to estimate supply levels.

For the linear form, the true relationship is

(4) $v = A + bw_p$

The observed relationship is

(5) $v = \alpha + B\, w_m$

Least squares applied to (5) yields correct estimates for the intercept and an unbiased estimate of B. But B is an incorrect estimate of b, as

(6) $\hat{B} = W'_m\ W_m)^{-1} W'_m\ V = \dfrac{b}{\gamma}$

However, the *true* and *observed* elasticity estimates are identical, as

(7) $ES_T = \dfrac{b\,w_p}{v}$ and $ES_O = \dfrac{bw_m}{\gamma v} = \dfrac{bw_p}{v}$.

Ergo while proportionate errors in the wage variable cause no statistical difficulties, cost estimates using w_m will overestimate costs by γ, assuming linearity.

16. In S. Enke (ed.), *Defense Management*, Englewood Cliffs, N.J., Prentice-Hall, 1966, p. 259.

17. For example, a dollar discounted at 25% for 15 years is equivalent to 3.57 cents.

18. Consistent with a retirement dollar's low efficacy is retirement being a strong motivating factor after the 8th year of service because (1) time-preference rates diminish with age, (2) fewer years exist to discount, and (3) benefit size progressively increases with rank and years of service.

19. In principle, pay increases have been across the board since 1965. However, the services still prefer the older policy and the Hubbell proposals dusted off the old argument of residual pay to justify pay reform and increases only for careerists.

20. U.S. Bureau of the Census, *Present Value of Estimated Lifetime Earnings*, Technical Paper 16, GPO, 1967, pp. 9-10, and *Economic Report of the President*, 1969, Tables B-30 and B-31.

21. *Number of Retirements from Active Duty by Retired Pay Grade and Service*, FY 1963, 1964. *Number of Retirements from Active Duty by Years of Service and Type of Retirement*, FY 1963, 1964, OASD (M) 12 April 1965. In this study a careerist is defined as a person who remains or *intends* to remain in the military for a period of at least 20 years. For pay calculation purposes, the difference between a careerist and a noncareerist is the receipt of the retirement accrual. At different career points the probability of remaining in service is:

Completed Years of Service	Officers	EM
0	17.9%	9.1%
4	45.4	49.7
8	68.1	74.0
12	90.4	91.8
16	95.9	97.3

Source: *Percentage of Military Personnel on Active Duty 30 June 1965, Expected to Continue on Active Duty Until Retirement, by Length of Service, 1965 Multiple Active Decrement Tables for DoD Officers and Enlisted Men.*

22. *Estimated Educational Level of Military Personnel on Active Duty as of 31 December 1965, Selected Manpower Statistics*, pp. 36-37. These percentages are climbing over time. In 1956 the respective percentages were 55.5% for officers and 55.2% for enlisted men. Younger men have a higher average level of formal schooling due to increasing opportunity and the services' recruiting emphasis on formal schooling.

23. As a briefing officer in 1958 succinctly put it: "Obviously, when taking 96% of all applicants, we have no quality selection." *Hearings on Military Pay*, SCAS, 85-2, 1958, p. 203. Also in *Hearing on Military Pay Increases*, SCAS, 88-1, 1963, p. 11. The Cordiner Committee also found that over 78% of the officers seeking retention fell below the 50%-median point efficiency index of the career group. *Report of the Defense Advisory Committee on Professional and Technical Compensation*, May 1957, Washington, D.C., p. 87.

These manpower quality factors carry a double meaning. One is that careerists even in 1957 were overpaid. The other, and the important one for policy, is that perceived pay prior to the raises beginning in 1963 were insufficient to attract and retain higher-quality personnel.

24. Except for the relative quality of enlisted accessions in which the military services look very good, data for comparisons of NCOs and officers in general are virtually nonexistent.

25. U.S. Bureau of the Census, op. cit., p. 5.

26. "Moonlighting," *DoD Congressional Briefing Book*, April 1965; and *Special Labor Force Report No. 18*, BLS, October 1961.

27. In February 1965, 21% of enlisted men's wives (stateside) were employed; the March 1965 comparable civilian percentage was 34.7%. "Employment of Dependents," and Table 10, *Handbook of Labor Statistics*, Washington, D.C., U.S. Bureau of Labor Statistics, 1968.

28. For a detailed discussion, see footnote 54, p. 260.

29. These cost figures exclude the additional 8.5% of military salary that I have termed non-compensatory benefits, under heading II in Table 5-2.

30. "Comparison of Military and Job Corps Compensation," *DoD Congressional Briefing Book*, Washington, D.C., April 1965. The relevance of 1964,

besides data availability, is that it was the year of the DoD all-volunteer cost study which overestimated voluntarism's incremental cost by a factor of 4 because of its neglect of such institutional considerations as compensation structure.

31. The inclusion of the low-visibility fringe benefits would flatten this profile, since these benefits do not progress as rapidly as basic pay.

32. The 1967 Hubbell Report on *Modernizing Military Pay* was the first quadrennial review.

33. The retention problem existed before World War II, but the military's small size masked its seriousness. (Harold Wool, "The Military Specialist," Ph.D. thesis, The American University, Washington, D.C., 1964-65, p. 53.)

34. Mathematically, to remove a constraint, assuming *given* prices, leads to an "equal to or greater than" position.

35. This phenomenon is not unknown in the market economy. It is expressed in Schumpeter's dictum that dynamic innovations or "creative destruction" dominate the importance of the marginal conditions of static efficiency. Joseph A. Schumpeter, *Capitalism, Socialism and Democracy*, 2nd ed., Harper, New York, 1947, Chapter VII.

36. A lucid exposition of this model is Alain Enthoven's *The Mathematics of Military Pay*, The Rand Corporation, P-1100, 7 June 1957.

37. The infantryman is still believed to be only a modern counterpart to the World War I "over-the-trench" doughboy. Mechanized warfare has somewhat upgraded the marginal product of the infantryman, particularly that of junior leaders. Guerrilla warfare, however, requires a highly trained infantryman with an ability to sense the nuances of a situation. This involves a slow learning curve except in wartime's survival-of-the-fittest conditions. Thus, had the U.S. had a highly trained infantry rather than a low-skilled, high-turnover infantry more suitable to World War II, events in Vietnam might have turned out differently. For instance, General Westmoreland has implied that one determinant of his "attrition" and "search-and-destroy" tactics in Vietnam was his feeling that the American infantryman was unsuited to British-style counterinsurgency tactics, namely long-range, small-unit patrolling.

38. The manpower quality volunteering for a specialty may be partially adjusting by being inversely related to the specialty's disutilities, but full adjustment is constrained by a common wage. Arbitrary assignments within the military are another constraining factor.

39. This argument is often phrased in terms of morale. For the Hubbell group's phrasing of this argument, see Vol. I, pp. 101-103. Up to 1920, however, skill differentials were an integral part of the pay scales; even after the 1920 restructuring for simplification, specialist differentials on a reduced scale were retained. Wool, op. cit., pp. 22 and 51-52.

40. The entertainment submarket is the other prominent example; even its enforcement is by the civil rather than the criminal code.

41. Gary S. Becker, *Human Capital*, National Bureau of Economic Research, New York, 1964, p. 17.

42. Ibid., p. 22.

43. A.C. Pigou, *The Economics of Welfare*, St. Martin's Press, 4th ed., New York, 1962, p. 550.

44. The sole exception was the 1948 Hook Commission, which considered an all-volunteer context.

45. Reenlistment bonuses at any time other than at the critical initial reenlistment point are largely economic rent because the individual is already career-committed.

46. The draft motivation rates are 44.0, 33.2, and 29.2% for mental groups I & II, III, and IV respectively. (Department of Defense *Survey of Active Duty Personnel*, as of October 1964.)

47. For white airmen these percentages varied from 20.2% for those who would definitely have volunteered in the absence of a draft to 2.1% of those who would definitely not have volunteered. The same data show that those volunteering for economic reasons had the highest retention propensity (34%), while those volunteering for training had one of the smallest (7%). Data supplied by G. Brunner, The Rand Corporation.

48. Office of the Secretary of Defense, *Modernizing Military Pay*, Vol. II, p. 55.

49. Ibid., p. 52.

50. The peacetime exceptions are medical and dental personnel. In wartime, lawyers and enlisted Seabees have been excepted.

51. Comparability and its implied pay progression are independent of rank and promotion progression. Except for a "rank illusion" effect, nothing is gained by inflating rank standards. Yet the services' "up or out" policy is partly based on this illusion.

52. The better-known are the Hook (1948), Cordiner (1957), Randall (1962), and Hubbell (1967-69) groups.

53. For an argument based on a *Harvard Business Review* article (November and December 1955) that since wing commanders manage considerably more labor and capital resources than many outstanding young corporation presidents, wing commanders ought to be paid at least as much, see SCAS, *Hearings on Military Pay*, 89-2, 1958, pp. 462-464.

54. Details are shown in Appendix 5-C. This calculation is based on the 1950-68 average of 2.06% for the Consumer Price Index and an average interest rate of 3.63%, reflecting the government's cost of long-term financing. The annuity contribution is, of course, sensitive to these parameters. For example, if interest rates increase from 5 to 10%, the implicit contribution for a lieutenant colonel drops from 59 to 21% of basic pay. Such sensitivity raises the open question in the economic literature of what is the appropriate discount rate. (William J. Baumol, "On the Social Rate of Discount," *American Economic*

Review, September 1968, pp. 788-802). At one extreme, some economists have argued that since retirement is unfunded, zero is the appropriate rate. Other economists, using a rate of social return analysis to rank competing alternatives, argue that the correct rate is always 8 to 10%. In fact, two different and valid concepts are involved. For ranking alternatives and social costing, 8-10% is correct; but for determining the government's budget and accounting costs, given the government's borrowing in the financial markets, the projeected long-term bond rate is the relevant rate. Moreover, if social discounting is used, civil-service and civilian retirement costs fall proportionately (though much less absolutely), since the social costs of capital (as opposed to financial costs) are constant throughout the economy.

The government currently uses an interest rate of 3 1/2% and the 1937 annuity tables for the Civil Service and Social Security funds. The DoD Actuarial Consultant copies this practice. Most insurance companies base their charges for individual policies on 3 1/2% interest rates, 9% loading, and a 12% safety factor built into their mortality tables. The most attractive group plans use variable annual interest rates (4 3/4-6% for Spring 1968), 1/2% loading, and a 12% safety factor. My parametric method excludes loading and safety charges by charging no administrative costs, and using actual mortality tables, which causes an additional cost underestimation because military personnel are a medically select group.

55. The Hubbell Report implied that an explicit contribution of 6.5% out of military salary would make military and civilian retirement benefits comparable. This accounts for only the tip of the military retirement iceberg and is one reason why the Report "proved" that military careerists are underpaid compared with civilians. See Appendix 5-E.

56. See Appendix 5-D. The civil service retirement fund also runs a continual, if smaller, deficit for the same reason.

57. The reason that steady-state disbursements (for a given number of retirees) grow less rapidly than accrual costs is that wage increases have an immediate impact on the latter; the former receive only the CPI increase except for the current year's retiree group.

58. *Modernizing Military Pay*, op. cit., Vol. IV, p. 2-1.

59. Vesting means allowing earned retirement credits to accompany departing employees. While deferred retirement benefits are not a powerful inducement to enter a military career, they are an inducement to continue in a career, becoming increasingly attractive as retirement approaches, as evidenced from surveys of its attractiveness to senior personnel. Recruiting on the basis of early retirement also has its disadvantages: many individuals, particularly officers, are not attracted by the implication of a second career. On the other hand, many EM are attracted by the notion of an early retirement income supplement.

60. See Table 5-11.

61. For an excellent account of these causal factors, see Charles de Gaulle,

The Army of the Future, J.B. Lippincott Co., New York, 1941, pp. 157-179.

62. A cross-section regression of the reenlistment rates in FY 64 of the Navy's 8 occupational areas by dependency showed a $\hat{B}$ of 9.44 and an R^2 of .838. Dependency is also a proxy for more cash allowances and higher in-kind benefits.

63. For an example of vesting reducing government costs, exclusive of side effects, see Appendix 5-E.

64. Until World War II, careers of up to 45 years were considered appropriate. During World War II, this apparently caused two serious problems in the senior personnel ranks: insufficient physical stamina and mental inflexibility due to reliance on experiences which were often no longer relevant.

65. The 1966 "Expectation of Life and Mortality Rate, by Age, Color, and Sex," shows the following relationship:

	Expected Life (Male)	
Age	White	Nonwhite
39	32.5	28.7
40	31.6	28.0
42	29.8	26.4
50	23.1	20.8
60	15.9	14.9
65	12.9	12.4

Source: U.S. Bureau of the Census, *1968 Statistical Abstract*, No. 67, p. 54.

66. Laure M. Sharpe and Albert D. Biderman, "Out of Uniform," *Monthly Labor Review*, BLS, January-February 1967, p. 43. Corroborating studies are Carl H. Fischer, et al., *A Study of the Military Retired System and Certain Related Subjects*, Ann Arbor, University of Michigan, 1961, and Allen Joseph Lenz, *Military Retirement and Income Maximization: An Examination of Economic Incentives to Extended Military Service*, unpublished doctoral dissertation, Stanford University, May 1967.

67. Lenz, op. cit.

68. The calculations were programmed by Stephen Allison of the RAND Resource Analysis Department.

69. U.S. Department of Health, Education, and Welfare, Public Health Service, *United States Life Tables: 1959-61*, Volume 1, Number 1, December 1964, pp. 10-11.

70. Basic pay for officers is roughly 75% of their military salary (basic pay, quarters and subsistence allowances, and tax advantage). Therefore, the retirement percentage of military salary for a lieutenant colonel/commander with 23

years of service is about 60% (.80 times .75). Basic pay for enlisted men is roughly 68% of military salary.

71. Carl Fischer, et al., *A Study of the Military Retired System and Certain Related Subjects*, Ann Arbor, University of Michigan, 1961, p. 15.

72. The DoD Actuarial Consultant lists retirement costs as 23.0 and 23.76% of basic pay for enlisted men and officers respectively. *Cost of Military Retirement Benefits for Entrants without Prior Military Service Stated as a Percentage of Basic Pay*, OASD(M), 10 August 1967.

73. The official FY 68 accrual estimate for a larger force was $2,502.2 million.

74. Memorandum for the Secretary of Defense, Summary of the First Quadrennial Pay Study, *Modernizing Military Pay*, op. cit., p. xiv.

75. Ibid., p. 12.

76. Ibid., p. S-1.

77. Ibid., p. S-2.

78. Ibid., pp. S-10 and S-11.

79. Base pay for all ranks increased 40.5% during this period; quarters and subsistence allowances, however, remained constant. This caused an increase according to rank with senior personnel receiving a larger increase because basic pay is a larger percentage of their total salary. In addition, senior personnel nearing retirement received large retirement windfalls that civilian (other than civil service) do not receive. This is because retirement benefits increase in proportion with basic pay. Such windfalls are one reason why military retirement benefits are so expensive for the government.

80. Table C-30, "Average Gross Weekly Earnings in Selected Non-Agricultural Industries," 1971 *Economic Report of the President.*

Chapter 6
The Budget Cost of a Volunteer Military

1. This chapter is an adaption from a larger study written jointly with B.P. Klotz and published as *The Budget Cost of a Volunteer Military*, RM-6184-PR, The Rand Corporation, August 1970. The portion included here is the author's contribution.

2. The 1970 Presidential (Gates) Commission reported a $2.3-billion figure (excluding reserves and the savings from increased Treasury income tax returns). However, their estimate omits retirement costs and longevity costs accuring after eight years of service. The methodology in both studies is similar, particularly in the area of econometrics; the major difference is my emphasis on the institutional details of the military manpower system. *The Report of the Presidential Commission on an All-Volunteer Force*, Washington, D.C., G.P.O., February 1970.

An even greater difference exists between the estimates of transition costs (short-run costs). My estimate is an incremental $0.75 billion per year for the transition phase; the Commission estimate is $3.1 billion for a slightly smaller force (excluding reserves and tax returns). One reason for this difference is my assumption of a transition period of several years, when voluntarism would operate in conjunction with the draft; the Commission proposes an abrupt change to voluntarism.

3. Previous studies include S. Altman and A.C. Fechter, "The Supply of Military Personnel in the Absence of a Draft," *American Economic Review*, May 1967, pp. 19-31 (a synopsis of the 1965 DoD study); W. Oi., "The Economic Cost of the Draft," *American Economic Review*, May 1967, pp. 39-62; and A.C. Fisher, "The Cost of the Draft and the Cost of Ending the Draft," *American Economic Review*, June 1969, pp. 239-254. Central to these studies are econometric estimates of the supply curve of volunteers, described in Appendix F of Canby-Klotz.

4. Appendix 6-A describes the procedure for deriving these figures, which are presented in Table 6-7. These numbers are higher than the actual pre-Vietnam experience of 37,300 officers and 482,700 enlisted men that reflected the large number of World War II and Korea veterans still in the manpower pipeline.

5. U.S. Department of Defense, Secretary of Defense, Directorate for Statistical Services, *Selected Manpower Statistics*, 15 April 1969, p. 51.

6. Oi, op. cit., pp. 45-46.

7. See Appendix 6-A. The method assumes that (1) the 1965 DoD survey of enlisted men obtained an accurate estimate of true volunteers, and (2) the draftee retention rates equal those of draft-induced volunteers. The survey findings are consistent with other DoD studies. If (1) and (2) are false, retention rates may be less than 36%; but lower retention rates do not raise costs dramatically, as seen in Appendix 6-D.

8. Appendix 6-A, Table 6-7. Further reductions would stem from a greater use of civilians and women in noncombat tasks, tighter manpower utilization practices, and substitution of capital for labor. Also, the more experienced volunteer force should be more efficient and should require fewer men than indicated above.

9. Oi, op. cit., p. 50 (after correcting for a slightly smaller officer corps and attrition between entry and average initial year of service based on the 1965 Decrement Table for Officers).

10. Versus 3.8 and 5.9% for non-Army service and total DoD, respectively.

11. Minor buildups may be met by relaxed entrance standards. For example, 20% of 1969 Air Force enlistments were of mental category IV (below average) quality, as opposed to a previous average of less than 10%, due to changed DoD policy.

12. Altman and Fechter, op. cit., p. 25. Their Table 5 summarizes the DoD study in which they participated. It assumes accuracy of a 1964 survey of

enlistees to determine in 1970 those who would truly have volunteered without the draft and no change in antimilitary attitudes. The elasticity of DoD volunteers to changes in unemployment implied by the above figures is about 0.6.

13. Criticisms in Appendixes D and F of Canby-Klotz focus on the correct definition of variables in the econometric estimate of the volunteer supply equation; whether the equation contains enough important variables, such as the level of youth education and a Vietnam aversion factor; and whether the equation has the proper mathematical form.

14. For example, a simple category I-III projection would look like this:

Service	(1964 Enlistees)	True Volunteer X (Proportion)	1970-1964 X (Pop. Ratio)	= 1970 Volunteers
DoD	346,000	.60	1.28	266,000
Army	111,000	.56	1.28	79,000
Non-Army	234,000	.65	1.28	189,000

The 1970 volunteer projection is almost identical (and even closer if the same 18-19 age group is used) to the DoD projections shown in Table 6-3, Column 1, lines 4, 10, and 16. Enlistees for 1964 are taken from *Selected Manpower Statistics*, op. cit., after subtracting category IV proportions of 8, 5, and 10%. True volunteer proportions are from Altman and Fechter, op. cit., p. 23, also after a category IV correction. Population above refers to the 17-21 age group, the source of 90% of enlistments.

15. Fechter and Altman, op. cit., p. 27; Oi, op. cit., p. 48; op. cit., p. 180.

16. Fisher, op. cit., p. 249.

17. Appendix D of Canby-Klotz presents this methodology and a theoretical explanation of why the elasticity of supply quite probably lies in the 1.00 to 2.50 range in peacetime for across-the-board changes.

18. Only first-term wages instead of a lifetime income stream were considered, for three reasons: even a true volunteer has a 64% probability of leaving the service after four years (Table 6-1); military and civilian incomes are comparable after four years; and enlistees apparently have a subjective time preference rate of 28%. See R.L. Chaney, *Discounting by Military Personnel by Various Ages*, unpublished Defense Department study of military compensation, October 1962.

19. Figures 5-6 and 5-7.

20. Chaney, op. cit.

21. This is the normal use of total income; Oi used a similar definition and included clothing.

22. See Appendix 6-B, which uses a second lieutenant's salary and benefits as an example of how a young man views the total income package.

23. This discount was obtained by a RAND survey of entrants at the Los

Angeles AFEES. Survey data on careerists from the Hubbell pay study indicate an even larger discount. For details, see Tables 5-4 and 5-5.

24. Costs are not sensitive to the discount rate except for large "effective" recruiting deficits which result from a large deficit per se or small elasticities. A comparison of the estimates in Table 6-5 based on PPV_m and DoD total income shows very little variation from ES = 1. This is because a larger-than-market increase was arbitrarily given non-Army volunteers in order to obtain the standard of the 1970 federal minimum wage. For intermediate recruiting deficits (e.g., ES = .5, which doubles the "effective" deficit), accession costs are quite sensitive to discounting, but total costs are not. Only for very large recruiting deficits are total costs sensitive—largely because of the large economic rents to *careerists* needed to prevent wage inversion. The obvious effect of discounting is a smaller absolute increase due to its reducing DoD total income to the relevant perceived base; a leveraged effect is obtained because the smaller absolute increases postpone the points of wage inversion and reduce the number of men requiring wage increases.

The effect of discounting on cost is thus considerably more than a function of the discount rate. Discounting is one of many cost depressants (acting jointly and independently) whose omission from previous studies caused very large cost overestimates.

25. Ignoring for the moment the large and driving Army deficit, which is treated in detail in Appendix 6-D, "V" represents category I-III true volunteers.

26. Council of Economic Advisers, *Economic Report of the President*, 1968, and Department of Defense, Military Compensation Tables.

27. See Appendix 6-D, p. 213.

28. Outside of professional sports and entertainment, the military is apparently unique in its ability to sign employees to long-term contracts. It should, and does, take advantage of this to manipulate manpower supply through bonuses. An enlistment bonus, paid in full at entry, achieves a maximum economic impact on young men with high subjective discount rates. The bonus is the most cost-effective compensation tool, having these advantages: (1) it exploits the differential between individual time preferences and government borrowing costs; (2) it achieves wage flexibility without disturbing the necessarily more rigid pay structure; (3) it helps avoid pay inversion by paying "outside" the pay system; and (4) it facilitates pay discrimination among services (or among ability or skill groups).

Reenlistment bonuses, in widespread use today, are another way to reduce the total cost of a military system. An exit bonus can also be used to induce opting-out or to cushion forced egress at, say, the eight-year point and thus avoid large seniority and retirement pay. Soldiers could be paid a lump sum to leave the service. The military's unique advantage of a penal enforced contract and the bonus suggest that a basically six- to ten-year force with low retention thereafter may be optimal for the Army and Marines, whereas higher retention rates may be desirable for the more technical Air Force and Navy, which necessarily must invest more time in training their enlistees. See also Appendix 6-F.

29. See Appendix 6-D, p. 214.

30. Excluding perturbations caused by Korea and Vietnam.

31. It would also eliminate the sensitive task of having to progressively lower military wage rates as the inflow requirement dropped because of longer enlistment tours and higher reenlistment rates.

32. Alternatively, had a target wage been set early enough during the Vietnam phaseout, the transition could have been assisted and the draft reduced by exiting volunteers as force levels were reduced.

33. These elements, along with the training savings, are the same for all eight cases because reenlistment rates and force size are assumed constant.

34. See Appendix 6-D. This assumes ES = 1.0, unemployment (U/P) = 14.9%, and wages = PPV.

35. See Appendix 6-D, "A Lower Retention Rate."

36. *Selected Manpower Statistics*, "Average Military Strength (Man Years)," Directorate for Statistical Services, Office of Secretary of Defense, 1969, p. 21.

37. Ibid., "Active Duty Officer Personnel and Percent of Total Military Personnel 1923-1968," p. 24.

38. Ibid., "Summary of Enlisted Personnel Procurement FY 1951-1968," p. 44.

39. Oi. op. cit., pp. 39-62.

40. Ibid., p. 46. This assumption is arbitrary but not critical, as the reader will see in Appendix 6-D. Higher retention rates mean fewer required accessions and hence lower accession and training costs; but higher retention rates also imply higher seniority and retirement costs. Thus, as long as retention rates are sufficient to avoid large wage increases to entrants and wage inversion, costs are relatively insensitive to retention rates.

41. Such an assumption often forecloses otherwise viable options. In this particular case, reenlistment rates are based on only those eligible to reenlist. From 20 to 30% of first-term personnel are typically declared ineligible for reenlistment and are excluded from the statistics. This makes reenlistment data unreliable because (1) commanders have been known to classify eligibles as ineligible in order to enhance their own image, and (2) changes in acceptance standards cause a delayed effect on reenlistment eligibility rates.

From a volunteer military standpoint, a hard look at these institutional practices can lead to reduced annual accession requirements. Another institutional change to obtain higher retention rates would be better initial assignments of individuals to their preferred occupational areas. A major problem of economic analysis is that its aggregative statistical approach ignores these problems and therefore often biases the case against otherwise viable options.

42. Altman and Fechter, op. cit., pp. 19-31.

43. Oi, op. cit., p. 42.

44. Ibid., p. 50.

45. Ibid., p. 48.

46. Office of the Secretary of Defense, *Modernizing Military Pay*, 11 November 1967, p. 37 (Hubbell Report.)

47. Chaney indicates that the discount rate for officers is about 10%.

48. Table 6-13 supposes a force level of 2.65 million men (of whom 2.31 million are enlisted men), and reenlistment rates of 34.3 and 38.0% for Army and non-Army enlistees. It does not include the savings in training. See Appendix 6-D for the cost impact of alternative retention rates.

49. The DoD Actuarial Consultant lists retirement costs as 23 and 23.76% of basic pay for enlisted men and officers, respectively. Office of Assistant Secretary of Defense, Manpower, *Cost of Military Retirement Benefits for Entrants without Prior Military Service Stated as a Percentage of Basic Pay*, 10 August 1967.

50. This factor is overstated because all pay elements have not risen by this percentage; however, the total training savings estimate is still low due to the previously mentioned exclusions.

51. However, the authors themselves claim that their primary concern "was estimation of the long-run costs of eliminating the draft," Altman and Fechter, op. cit., p. 29, footnote 19.

52. Ibid., p. 30.

53. Oi, op. cit., p. 52.

54. Ibid., p. 50.

55. Fairly insensitive compared with the range generated by several other studies.

56. Altman and Fechter, op. cit., pp. 23-24.

57. Determined by the DoD survey of first-term enlisted men.

58. This may be reasonable despite the anti-military feeling that apparently sets in after a war. Aversion undoubtedly occurs, but the reaction may be merely a return to peacetime aversion levels. The wartime exhaustion of manpower pools should also cause enlistment declines, which could be confused with increasing aversion. As opposed to vocal subgroups during the initial stages of a war, evidently promilitary sentiment is engendered among the young, so any reaction may well be a fall from a high plateau to a more normal level. A lower true volunteer rate is considered later.

An unpublished DoD study indicates a V/E of 0.5, lower than the .62 proportion of 1964, but this merely reflects Vietnam's sharply higher military demands and the relatively fixed pool of true volunteers when military wage relatives are not increased.

59. The 1970 federal minimum wage is $1.65 per hour for a 40-hour, 48-work-week, year: $3,168.

60. Table 6-3, Column 5.

61. Note that the non-Army services experience no recruiting difficulties. Deficits are obtained from Table 6-2.

62. No senior soldiers are paid less than their juniors.

63. ES is 0.5 instead of 1.5, U/P is 11.5%, and the DoD wage definition is in effect.

64. Compare this with Table 6-18, lines 40-46, column 8. There, using identical assumptions except for higher reenlistment rates, the cost is $2,784 million.

65. The Army share typically rises in a general force expansion.

66. The President's Commission on an All-Volunteer Force, *The Report of the Presidential Commission on an All-Volunteer Force*, U.S. Government Printing Office, Washington, D.C., February 1970.

67. Long enlistment contracts themselves are opposed because they connote contractual labor. Such contracts also reduce labor mobility. However, longer contracts give the services an incentive for greater investments in human capital, not all of which need be specific to the military.

68. This substitution mainly affects the Marine Corps and Army—the services whose requirements drive the DoD manpower system. The Air Force and Navy already have 4-year enlistments and a draft-induced profile resembling their volunteer profile. Higher reenlistments for these two services will depress their projected first-term strength by 19% and raise their career force by 15%.

69. Included in this cost would be a gratuity for successful completion of the enlistment tour and the cost of commercially valuable training given to prepare servicemen for a remunerative civilian career beginning at approximately age 26.

Chapter 7
Postwar Manpower Procurement in Perspective: Military Manpower Policy in Disequilibrium

1. For a detailed account of these debates, see James Gerhardt, *Military Manpower Procurement Policies 1945-1967*, unpublished Ph.D. dissertation, Harvard University, 1967.

2. For a summary of the Administration's position, see John J. McCloy, "The Plan of the Armed Services for UMT." For an excellent critique, see O.G. Villard's "Universal Military Training and Military Preparedness," *The Annals of the American Academy of Political and Social Sciences*, Volume 241, September 1945, pp. 35-45.

3. Theodore Paullin (ed.), *Sourcebook on Peacetime Conscription*, American Friends Service Committee, Philadelphia, Pa., 1944, pp. 29-32.

4. Harry Truman, *Year of Decisions*, Doubleday, New York, 1958, p. 511.

5. Samuel P. Huntington, *The Common Defense*, Columbia University Press, 1961, p. 436.

6. *New York Times*, May 15, 1946, p. 1.

7. Gerhart, op. cit., p. 275.

8. *A Program for National Security*, 1947.

9. See, e.g., *The New York Times*, September 2, 1949, p. 9.

10. HCAS, *UMT, & S Act Extension, 1955*, Hearings, 84C-1, p. 39.

11. Senator Russell is technically correct. In the proper context, unequal service can be termed proportionate justice. Unequal taxation is often termed progressive and is designed to reduce inequality in "fields of living." However, Russell's meaning is the opposite of the normal interpretation of justice, for the poor are subsidizing the rich and the ratio of inequality is increasing rather than being narrowed.

      After SSS took on a channeling or allocative function for the nation's youth, particularly its college youth, General Hershey adopted a similar view. Hershey then wrote, "There is no equity in us. All we are doing is trying to go out in the name of the Government and grab for the Government what they can use best, and it isn't a matter of equity at all." HC on Appropriations, *Independent Offices Appropriations for 1955*, Hearings, 83C-2, p. 671.

12. *Annual Report*, 1957, pp. 61-62. For a detailed discussion see Chapter 3 on deferment policy.

13. *Modernizing Military Pay*, Report of the First Quadrennial Review of Military Compensation, Vol. II, DoD, 1 November 1967, pp. 45-55.

14. As J.R. Hicks noted, the greater the skills, the greater the advantage of "regularity." *Theory of Wages*, 2d ed., New York, Macmillan, 1963, p. 70.

15. Quoted in Huntington, *The Common Defense*, p. 436.

16. For details, see Chapter 5, on military compensation.

17. Ibid., p. 435.

18. Ibid., pp. 436-437.

19. The two are not synonymous unless the military's special job attributes net to zero.

20. This fact plus the lack of growth of the economy's largest employer of young men accounts for much of the unresolved argument in the economic literature between the structuralists and the Keynesians. For further details, see pp. 35-36.

21. For an outstanding institutional analysis of Selective Service—its adaptation to the American political culture and its failure to perceive changes in this culture—see Gary L. Wamsley, *Selective Service and a Changing America: A Study of Organizational-Environmental Relationships*, Charles E. Merrill, Columbus, Ohio, 1969.

Bibliography

Bibliography

Books

Aristotle, *Politics*, New York, Oxford Univ. Press, 1962.
———, *Rhetoric of Aristotle*, New York, Appleton, n.d.
Baumol, William J., *Welfare Economics and the Theory of the State*, Cambridge, Mass., Harvard Univ. Press, 1965.
Becker, Gary S., *Human Capital: A Theoretical and Empirical Analysis with Special Reference to Education*, National Bureau of Economic Research, New York, Columbia Univ. Press, 1964.
Beebe, Gilbert W. and Michael E. DeBakey, *Battle Casualties; Incidence, Mortality, and Logistic Considerations*, Springfield, Ill., Charles C. Thomas, 1952.
Bentham, Jeremy, *Fragment on Government*, New York, Barnes & Noble, 1967.
Berliner, Joseph, *Factory and Manager in the USSR*, Cambridge, Mass., Harvard Univ. Press, 1957.
Blank, David M. and G.J. Stigler, *The Demand and Supply of Scientific Personnel*, New York, National Bureau of Economic Research, 1957.
Bloch, Marc, *Feudal Society*, Chicago, Univ. of Chicago Press, 1968.
Blum, Albert A., *Drafted or Deferred: Practices Past and Present*, Ann Arbor, Univ. of Michigan Press, 1967.
Brown, E.H. Phelps, *The Economics of Labor*, New Haven, Yale Univ. Press, 1962.
Buchan, John, *History of the Great War*, Vol. 1, Boston, Houghton-Mifflin, 1922.
Challener, Richard D., *The French Theory of the Nation in Arms, 1866-1939*, New York, Columbia Univ. Press, 1955.
Chamberlain, Neil W., (ed.), *Contemporary Economic Issues*, Homewood, Ill., Irwin, 1969.
Chamberlain, Neil W., *Sourcebook on Labor*, revised and abridged with assistance of Richard Perlman, New York, McGraw-Hill, 1964.
Chapman, Bruce K., *The Wrong Man in Uniform; Our Unfair and Obsolete Draft—And How We Can Replace It*, New York, Trident Press, 1967.
Crowder, Enoch H., *Spirit of Selective Service*, New York, Century, 1920.
Cruttwell, Charles R.M.F., *History of the Great War, 1914-1918*, 2nd ed., Oxford, Clarendon Press, 1940.
Davis, James W. and Kenneth M. Dolbeare, *Little Groups of Neighbors*, Chicago, Markham Publishing Co., 1968.
Dayan, Moshe, *Diary of the Sinai Campaign*, New York, Harper & Row, 1966.
De Gaulle, Charles, *Army of the Future*, Philadelphia, Lippincott, 1941.
Derthick, Martha, *The National Guard in Politics*, Cambridge, Mass., Harvard Univ. Press, 1965.

Dunlop, John T. (ed.), *Theory of Wage Determination: Proceedings of a Conference Held by International Economic Association*, New York, St. Martin's Press, 1957.

Easton, David, *Political System: An Inquiry into the State of Political Science*, New York, Knopf, 1953.

Encyclopaedia Brittanica, Vol. 2, Chicago, Encyclopaedia Britannica, Inc., 1966.

Enke, S. (ed.), *Defense Management*, Englewood Cliffs, N.J., Prentice-Hall, 1966.

Evers, Alfred, *Selective Service: A Guide to the Draft*, Philadelphia, Lippincott, 1957.

Fay, Sidney Bradshaw, *Origins of the World War*, 2nd ed., New York, Macmillan, 1930.

Fein, Rashi, *The Doctor Shortage: An Economic Diagnosis*, Washington, D.C., Brookings Institution, 1967.

Fischer, Carl H., et al., *A Study of the Military Retired System and Certain Related Subjects*, Ann Arbor, Univ. of Michigan, 1961.

Fitzpatrick, Edward A., *Conscription and America*, Milwaukee, Richards Publishing, 1940.

——, *Universal Military Training*, New York, McGraw-Hill, 1945.

Foch, Ferdinand M., *Principles of War*, Boston, Chapman, 1948.

Folger, John K. and Charles B. Nam, *Education of the American Population*, Washington, D.C., Bureau of the Census, 1967.

Friedrich, Carl J. and Z.K. Brzezinski, *Totalitarian Dictatorship and Autocracy*, New York, Praeger, 1961.

Gordon, Robert A. (ed.), *Toward a Manpower Policy*, New York, Wiley, 1967.

Gutman, Peter A. (ed.), *Economic Growth*, Englewood Cliffs, N.J., Prentice-Hall, 1964.

Halpern, Morton H., *Limited War in the Nuclear Age*, New York, Wiley, 1963.

Hamilton, Alexander, *The Federalist Papers*, Vol. 26, New York, Modern Library, 1937.

Hartz, Louis, *Liberal Tradition in America*, New York, Harcourt, Brace, & World, 1955.

Hicks, John R., *Theory of Wages*, 2nd ed., New York, Macmillan, 1963.

Hitch, Charles J. and Roland N. McKean, *The Economics of Defense in the Nuclear Age*, Cambridge, Mass., Harvard Univ. Press, 1963.

Hoffman, Stanley, *Contemporary Theory in International Relations*, Englewood Cliffs, N.J., Prentice-Hall, 1969.

——, *State of War: Essays in the Theory and Practice of International Politics*, New York, Praeger, 1965.

Huidekoper, Frederick L., *The Military Unpreparedness of the United States; A History of American Land Forces from Colonial Times Until June 1, 1915*, New York, Macmillan, 1915.

Hume, David, "Of the Original Contract," in Ernest Barker (ed.), *Social Contract: Essays by Locke, Hume and Rousseau*, New York, Oxford Univ. Press, 1962.

Huntington, Samuel P. (ed.), *Changing Patterns of Military Politics*, Glencoe, Free Press, 1962.

———, *The Common Defense; Strategic Programs in National Politics*, New York, Columbia Univ. Press, 1961.

———, *The Soldier and the State: The Theory and Politics of Civil-Military Relations*, Cambridge, Mass., Harvard Univ. Press, 1957.

Janowitz, Morris (ed.), *The New Military*, New York, Russell Sage Foundation, 1964.

——— , *The Professional Soldier*, New York, The Free Press, 1960.

Janowitz, Morris and Roger Little, *Sociology and the Military Establishment*, revised ed., New York, Russell Sage Foundation, 1965.

Johnston, J., *Econometric Methods*, New York, McGraw-Hill, 1963.

Kendall, M., and Stuart, A.S., *The Advanced Theory of Statistics*, Vol. 2, New York, Griffin, 1961.

Kerr, Clark, *Goals for Americans*, Englewood Cliffs, N.J., Prentice-Hall, 1960.

Lang, Kurt, *Military Sociology: A Trend Report and Bibliography*, London, Basil Blackwell & Mott, 1965.

Leach, J.F., *Conscription in the United States: Historical Background*, Rutland, Vt., Charles E. Tuttle Publishing, 1952.

Lerner, Abba P., *Economics of Control*, New York, Macmillan, 1944.

Liddell-Hart, Basil H., *History of the World War, 1914-1918*, Boston, Little Brown, 1934.

Little, I.M.D., *A Critique of Welfare Economics*, 2nd ed., New York, Oxford Univ. Press, 1957.

Little, Roger W. (ed.), *Selective Service and American Society*, New York, Russell Sage Foundation, 1969.

Locke, John, *Second Treatise on Civil Government*, New York, Barnes & Noble, 1966.

McGuire, Martin, *Secrecy and the Arms Race*, Cambridge, Mass., Harvard Univ. Press, 1965.

Machiavelli, Niccolo, *Prince and the Discourses*, New York, Modern Library, 1940.

Mangum, Garth, L. (ed.), *The Manpower Revolution; Its Policy Consequences. Excerpts from Senate Hearings Before the Clark Subcommittee*, Garden City, N.Y., Doubleday, 1965.

Marshall, George C., et al., *The War Reports of General George C. Marshall, General H.H. Arnold, and Admiral Ernest J. King*, Philadelphia, Lippincott, 1947.

Millis, Walter, *Arms and Men: A Study in American Military History*, New York, New American Library of World Literature, 1958.

Millis, Walter (ed.), *American Military Thought*, Indianapolis, Bobbs-Merrill, 1966.

Musgrave, Richard A., *The Theory of Public Finance; A Study in Public Economy*, New York, McGraw-Hill, 1959.

Neustadt, Richard E., *Presidential Power*, New York, New American Library, 1964.

Oman, Charles W., *The Art of War in the Middle Ages*, New York, Cornell Univ. Press, 1960.

Palmer, Robert R., et al., *The Procurement and Training of Ground Combat Troops*, U.S. Army in World War II Series, Washington, D.C., Dept. of the Army, 1948.

Pigou, A.C., *The Economics of Welfare*, 4th ed., London, Macmillan, 1962.

Plato, *The Republic*, New York, Oxford Univ. Press, 1945.

Price, Don, *Government and Science*, New York, New York Univ. Press, 1954.

Robbins, Lionel C., *Politics and Economics; Papers in Political Economy*, New York, St. Martin's Press, 1963.

Robinson, Joan M., *Rate of Interest and Other Essays*, London, Macmillan, 1952.

Rossiter, Clinton L., *Constitutional Dictatorship; Crisis Government in the Modern Democracies*, New York, Harcourt, Brace & World, 1963.

Rousseau, Jean Jacques, *The Social Contract*, New York, Dutton, 1950.

Ruggiero, Guido de, *History of European Liberalism*, trans. by R.G. Collingwood, Boston, Beacon Press, 1959.

Sabine, George H., *A History of Political Thought*, New York, Holt, 1961.

Schelling, Thomas C., *Strategy and Conflict*, New York, Oxford Univ. Press, 1963.

Schultz, Theodore W., *Economic Value of Education*, New York, Columbia Univ. Press, 1964.

Schumpeter, Joseph A., *Capitalism, Socialism, and Democracy*, 2nd ed., New York, Harper, 1947.

Scitovsky, Tibor, *Welfare and Competition*, Homewood, Ill., Irwin, 1951.

Shanahan, William O., *Prussian Military Reforms, 1786-1813*, New York, Columbia Univ. Press, 1945.

Simon, Herbert A., *Administrative Behavior; a Study of Decision-Making Process in Administrative Organization*, 2nd ed., New York, Free Press, 1957.

Simon, Herbert and James G. March, *Organizations*, New York, Wiley, 1958.

Simon, Herbert, et al., *Public Administration*, New York, Knopf, 1950.

Smith, Adam, *The Wealth of Nations*, New York, Modern Library, 1961.

Stamps, T.D., and V.J. Esposito, *A Military History of World War II*, West Point, Dept. of Military Art and Engineering, 1950.

Tax, Sol (ed.), *The Draft*, Chicago, Univ. of Chicago Press, 1968.

Theil, Henri, *Economic Forecasts and Policy*, 2nd ed., Amsterdam, North-Holland, 1961.

Thucydides, *Peloponnesian War*, trans. by Thomas Hobbes, David Grene (ed.), 2 vols., Ann Arbor, Univ. of Michigan Press, 1969.

Trytten, Merriam H., *Student Deferment in Selective Service*, Minneapolis, Univ. of Minnesota Press, 1952.

Ullmann, Walter, *Principles of Government and Politics in the Middle Ages*, New York, Barnes & Noble, 1961.

Uniformed Services Almanac. 9th annual ed., Washington, D.C., Uniformed Services Almanac, 1967.

Vagts, Alfred, *A History of Militarism*, New York, Norton, 1937.

Walton, George, *Let's End the Draft Mess*, New York, David McKay, 1967.

Waltz, Kenneth, *Man, The State and War*, New York, Columbia Univ. Press, 1965.

Wamsley, Gary L., *Selective Service and a Changing America: A Study of Organizational Environmental Relationships*, Columbus, Ohio, Charles E. Merrill, 1969.

Wolfbein, Seymour L., *Employment, Unemployment, and Public Policy*, New York, Random House, 1965.

Wood, Leonard, *The Military Obligation of Citizenship*, Princeton, N.J., Princeton Univ. Press, 1915.

_____, *Our Military History*, Chicago, Reilly & Britton, 1916.

Government Publications

National Advisory Commission on Selective Service, *In Pursuit of Equity: Who Serves When Not All Serve?*, Washington, D.C., 1967.

Office of the President, *Economic Report of the President Transmitted to the Congress. Together with the Annual Report of the Council of Economic Advisers*, Washington, D.C., annual.

President's Commission on an All-Volunteer Force, *The Report of the Presidential Commission on an All-Volunteer Force*, Washington, D.C., U.S. Government Printing Office, February, 1970.

President's Task Force on Military Conservation, *One Third of a Nation: A Report on Young Men Found Unqualified for Military Service*, Washington, D.C., G.P.O., 1964.

Selective Service System, *Annual Report of the Director of Selective Service to the Congress of U.S. Pursuant to the Universal Military Training and Service Act as Amended*, Washington, D.C., 1956-.

_____, *The Classification Process*, Special Monograph No. 5, Vol. I, Washington, D.C., G.P.O., 1950.

_____, *Report of the Task Force on the Structure of Selective Service System*, Washington, D.C., G.P.O., October 16, 1967.

_____, *Selective Service Orientation Kit*, Washington, D.C., 1965.

_____, *U.S. Code, Selective Service Draft Act of 1917, 50 App., SS 201-204*, Washington, D.C., 1917.

U.S. Army, Fairchild, Byron and Jonathan Grossman, *The Army and Industrial Manpower*, U.S. Army in World War II Series, Washington, D.C., Department of the Army, 1959.

_____, Greenfield, Kent Robert, et al., *The Organization of Ground Combat Troops*, United States Army in World War II Series, Washington, D.C., Department of the Army, 1947.

Kreidberg, Marvin A. and M.G. Henry, *History of Military Mobilization in the United States Army, 1775-1945*, Washington, D.C., Department of the Army, 1955.

_____, Office of the Surgeon General (Medical Statistics Div.), Karpinos, Bernard D., *1-Y's for Mental Reasons*, Washington, D.C., 1967.

_____, Office of the Surgeon General (Medical Statistics Div.), Karpinos, Bernard D., *Qualifications of American Youth for Military Service*, Washington, D.C., 1962.

_____, Office of the Surgeon General, *Results of Surveys of Youths for Military Service*, Washington, D.C., September 1966.

_____, Office of the Surgeon General, *Results of the Examination of Youths for Military Service 1960, supplement to "Health of the Army,"* Washington, D.C., 1960.

_____, Office of the Surgeon General, *Supplement to the "Health of the Army,"* Washington, D.C., 1966, annual.

U.S. Army, *Staff Officers' Field Manual: Organization, Technical and Logistical Data*, Washington, D.C., January 1966.

_____, Service Forces (Special Services Division), *What A Soldier Thinks*, Washington, D.C., August 1943.

U.S. Army Infantry School, *Infantry Reference Data*, Washington, D.C., June 1966.

U.S. Bureau of the Census, *Historical Statistics of the U.S.–Colonial Times to 1957*, Washington, D.C., 1960.

_____, *Present Value of Estimated Lifetime Earnings*, Technical Paper No. 16, Washington, D.C., 1967.

_____, *Statistical Abstract of the United States*, Washington, D.C., annual.

U.S. Bureau of Labor Statistics, *Handbook of Labor Statistics*, Washington, D.C., 1968.

_____, *Private Pension Plan Benefits, Bulletin 1485*, Washington, D.C., June 1966.

_____, *Special Labor Force Report 18*, Washington, D.C., October 1961.

U.S. Congress, *American State Papers, Military Affairs 1832-1861*, Washington, D.C., Gales & Seaton, 1832-.

_____, House, Committee on Appropriations, *Hearings before a Subcommittee of the Committee on Appropriations*, 89th Cong., 2nd Sess., February 1, 1966, Washington, D.C., 1966.

_____, House, Committee on Appropriations, *Independent Appropriations for 1955*, Washington, D.C., 1954.

_____, House, Committee on Armed Services, *Civilian Advisory Panel on Military Procurement*, 90th Cong., 1st Sess., Washington, D.C., 1967.

_____, House, Committee on Armed Services, *Extension of the Universal Military Training and Services Act, Hearings . . .*, 90th Cong., 1st Sess., Washington, D.C., 1967.

_____ , House, Committee on Armed Services, *Hearings and Papers, 53,* Washington, D.C., 1957.

_____ , House, Committee on Armed Services, *Review of the Administration and Operation of the Selective Service System, Hearings,* 89th Cong., 2nd Sess., Washington, D.C., June 1966.

_____ , House, Committee on Armed Services, *Review of the Reserve Program,* 85th Cong., 1st Sess., Washington, D.C., 1957.

_____ , House, Committee on Armed Services, *Selective Service Act, 1917,* 1917 Hearings, 65th Cong., 1st Sess., Washington, D.C., 1917.

_____ , House, Committee on Armed Services, *Universal Military Training and S. Act Extension, 1955 Hearings,* Washington, D.C., 1955.

_____ , Joint Economic Committee, *Economic Report of the President, 1968 and 1969 Hearings . . .,* Washington, D.C., 1969.

_____ , Senate, *How Can the United States Best Maintain Manpower for an Effective Defense System?,* Document 75, Washington, D.C., 1968.

U.S. Congress, Senate Committee on Armed Services, *Career Incentive Act of 1955,* Washington, D.C., 1955.

_____ , Senate, Committee on Armed Services, *Hearings on Military Pay,* 85th Cong., 2nd Sess., Washington, D.C., 1958.

_____ , Senate, Committee on Armed Services, *Hearings on Military Pay Increases,* 88th Cong., 1st Sess., Washington, D.C., 1963.

_____ , Senate, Committee on Government Operations, Subcommittee on National Security and International Operations, *Specialists and Generalists,* Washington, D.C., 1968.

_____ , Senate, Committee on Labor and Public Welfare, *Manpower Implications of Selective Service. Hearings before the Subcommittee on Employment, Manpower and Poverty,* 90th Cong., 1st Sess., March 1967, Washington, D.C., 1967.

U.S. Department of Defense, Chaney, R.L., *Discounting by Military Personnel by Various Ages,* unpublished study, Washington, D.C., 1962.

_____ , *Congressional Briefing Book,* Washington, D.C., April 1965.

_____ , *Estimated Marital Dependency Status of Military Personnel on Active Duty,* as of 31 March 1964, Washington, D.C., November 1964.

_____ , Office of Assistant Secretary of Defense, Manpower, *Project One Hundred Thousand: Characteristics and Performance of "New Standards" Men,* Washington, D.C., March 1969.

_____ , Office of Assistant Secretary of Defense, Manpower, *Average Annual Basic Pay of Military Personnel on Active Duty 30 June 1966, by Years of Active Service,* 14 February 1967, Washington, D.C., 1967.

_____ , Office of Assistant Secretary of Defense, Manpower, *Cost of Military Benefits for Entrants Without Prior Military Service Stated as a Percentage of Basic Pay,* 10 August 1967, Washington, D.C., 1967.

_____ , Office of Assistant Secretary of Defense, Manpower, *Defense Study of Military Compensation,* 5 October 1962, Washington, D.C., 1962.

———, Office of Assistant Secretary of Defense, Manpower, *Fact Sheet, Negro Participation in Armed Forces in Southeast Asia*, 28 March 1968, Washington, D.C., 1968.

———, Office of Assistant Secretary of Defense, Manpower, *Number and Percentage of Entrants Without Prior Military Service that Will Remain on Active Duty Until Retirement for a Total Force Similar to That on 30 June 1965*, 5 May 1966, Washington, D.C., 1966.

———, Office of Assistant Secretary of Defense, Manpower, *Number of Military Personnel on Active Duty, 30 June 1967 by Pay Grade and Length of Service for Pay Purposes*, 5 February 1968, Washington, D.C., 1968.

———, Office of Assistant Secretary of Defense, Manpower, *Number of Retirements from Active Duty of Retired Pay Grade and Service, FY 1963, 1964*, 12 April 1965, Washington, D.C., 1965.

———, Office of Assistant Secretary of Defense, Manpower, *Percentage of Military Personnel on Active Duty, 30 June 1965 Expected to Continue on Active Duty until Retirement by Length of Active Service*, 2 August 1966, Washington, D.C., 1966.

———, Office of Assistant Secretary of Defense, Systems Analysis, Poindexter, John, *Manpower Consideration in Development*, unpublished study, Fall 1967.

———, Secretary of Defense, *Modernizing Military Pay*, Vol. 1, Washington, D.C., 1967.

———, Secretary of Defense, Directorate for Statistical Services, *Selected Manpower Statistics*, Washington, D.C., annual.

———, Secretary of Defense, Statistical Service Center, *Allocation of Military Personnel by Program Category, 1950-1959 and 1960-1962*, Washington, D.C., 7 December 1960 and 5 December 1962.

———, Upton, Emory, *The Military Policy of the United States*, War Document 290, Washington, D.C., 1917.

U.S. Department of Health, Education, and Welfare, Public Health Service, *United States Life Tables: 1959-1961*, Washington, D.C., 1961.

U.S. Department of Labor, *Manpower Report of the President and A Report on Manpower Requirements, Resources, Utilization, and Training*, Transmitted to the Congress March 1966, Washington, D.C., 1966.

U.S. Navy, *Report of the Secretary of the Navy's Task Force on Navy/Marine Corps Personnel Retention*, Vol. 7, Washington, D.C., 1966.

U.S. President's Committee on Universal Training, *A Program for a National Security*, Washington, D.C., 1947.

U.S. Provost-Marshal General, *Second Report to December 20, 1918*, Washington, D.C., 1918.

U.S. Provost-Marshal General's Bureau, *Final Report Made to the Secretary of War by the Provost Marshal General of the U.S. from the Commencement of Business March 17, 1863 to March 17, 1866*, Washington, D.C., 1866.

Articles

Altman, S., "Earnings, Unemployment, and the Supply of Enlisted Volunteers," *Journal of Human Resources*, Vol. 4, No. 1, Winter 1969, pp. 38-60.

Altman, S. and A. Fechter, "The Supply of Military Personnel in the Absence of a Draft," *American Economic Review*, Vol. 57, No. 2, May 1967, pp. 19-32.

Baumol, William J., "On the Social Rate of Discount," *American Economic Review*, Vol. 58, No. 4, September 1968, pp. 788-803.

Cutler, F.M., "The History of Military Conscription with Especial Reference to the United States," *Historical Outlook*, Vol. 14, No. 5, May 1923, pp. 170-175.

Eisenhower, Dwight D., "This Country Needs Universal Military Training," *Reader's Digest*, Vol. 89, September 1966, pp. 49-55.

Fisher, A., "The Cost of the Draft and the Cost of Ending the Draft," *American Economic Review*, Vol. 59, No. 3, June 1969, pp. 239-254.

Friedman, Milton, "An All-Volunteer Army," *New York Times Magazine* (Sec. VI), May 14, 1967, p. 23.

Fuller, J.F.L., "A Military Case Against Conscription," *Human Events*, Vol. 2, May 2, 1945.

Hamilton, H.E., "How Good is our G.I. Student?," *The Educational Forum*, Vol. 11, 1947, pp. 213-222.

Hansen, W.W. and B. Weisbrod, "Economics of the Military Draft," *Quarterly Journal of Economics*, Vol. 8, No. 3, August 1967, pp. 395-421.

Johnson, Keith R., "Who Should Serve," *Atlantic Monthly*, Vol. 217, February 1966, pp. 63-68.

Klotz, B.P., "The Lost of Ending the Draft: Comment," *The American Economic Review*, Vol. LX, No. 5, December 1970, pp. 970-978.

Oi, W., "The Economic Cost of the Draft," *American Economic Review*, Vol. 57, No. 2, May 1967, pp. 39-70.

Phillips, Thomas R., "Traditionalism and Military Defeat," *Infantry Journal*, Vol. 48, March 1941, pp. 18-27.

Richter, Werner, "The War Pattern of Swiss Life," *Foreign Affairs*, Vol. 22, July 1944, pp. 643-644.

Sharpe, Laura M. and A.D. Biderman, "Out of Uniform," *Monthly Labor Review*, Vol. 90, No. 1, January-February 1967, pp. 15-21.

Villard, O.G., "Universal Military Training and Military Preparedness," *The Annals of the American Academy of Political and Social Sciences*, Vol. 241, September 1945, pp. 35-45.

Whittemore, I.E., "Does a Military Interruption Decrease the Chances of Obtaining a Degree?," *School and Society*, Vol. 78, July 25, 1953, pp. 25-27.

A Harvard Study Group, "On the Draft: [Conclusions and Recommendations of a Study Group of Harvard Scholars at the Institute of Politics, John Fitzgerald Kennedy School of Government]," *Public Interest*, No. 9, Fall 1967, pp. 93-99.

"Army Eliminates SRF Mission—an Editorial," *The Army Reserve Magazine*, Vol. 15, No. 8, September 1969, p. 2.

"The Only Innocents," *Economist*, November 29, 1969, pp. 15-16.

Reports and Monographs

American Council on Education, *Conference on Military Manpower*, Washington, D.C., January 1955.

American Friends Service Committee, *Sourcebook on Peacetime Conscription*, Philadelphia, 1944.

Bradford, David Frantz, *The Effects of Uncertainty in Selective Service, Technical Report 144*, Institute for Mathematical Studies in Social Sciences, Stanford, Stanford Univ. Press, 1966.

Canby, Steven and Benjamin Klotz, *The Budget Cost of a Voluntary Military*, The Rand Corporation, RM-6184-PR, August 1970.

Canby, Steven, *Cost Estimates of Fair Pay Based on the 1965 and 1967 Federal Minimum Wage and 30 June 1964 Force Strengths, with Implications for a Volunteer Military*, unpublished manuscript, May 1967.

_____, *Military Manpower Procurement: A Policy Analysis,* unpublished doctoral dissertation, Harvard Univ., 1972.

_____, "Costs of Military Personnel by Duty Billet," Office of the Assistant Secretary of Defense (Systems Analysis), 1967.

Eberly, Donald J. (ed.), *National Service; A Report of a Conference*, New York, Russell Sage Foundation, 1968.

_____, *A Profile of National Service*, New York, Overseas Educational Service, 1966.

Enthoven, Alain, *The Mathematics of Military Pay*, The RAND Corporation, P-1101, June 1957.

Gerhardt, James, "Military Manpower Procurement Policies 1945-1967," Ph.D. thesis, Harvard Univ., 1967.

Hause, J.C. and A.C. Fisher, *The Supply of First-Term Enlisted Manpower in the Absence of a Draft*, Institute for Defense Analyses, Arlington, April 1968.

Huq, A.M., et al., *An Investigation of the Problems Associated with Young Men Who are Mentally Unqualified for Military Service*, prepared for Office of Manpower Policy, Evaluation & Research by the Research Triangle Institute, Final Report SU-225, Durham, No. Carolina, 1967.

Karpinos, Bernard D., *Mental Qualification of American Youths for Military Service and its Relationship to Educational Attainment*, Proceedings of the Social Statistics Section, American Statistical Association, 1966.

Klassen, Albert D., Jr., *Military Service in American Life Since World War II: An Overview*, University of Chicago, National Opinion Research Center, Report 117, 1966.

Lenz, Allen Joseph, "Military Retirement and Income Maximization: An

Examination of Economic Incentives to Extended Military Service," Ph.D. thesis, Stanford Univ., May 1967.

Sharpe, Laura M. and Albert D. Biderman, *The Employment of Retired Military Personnel; A Report Prepared for the Office of Manpower Policy, Evaluation & Research*, Bureau of Social Science Research, Report 371, Washington, D.C., 1966.

Smith, Gorman C., "Differential Pay for Military Technicians," Ph.D. thesis, Columbia Univ., 1964.

Spencer, Samuel R., Jr., "A History of the Selective Training and Service Act of 1940 from Inception to Enactment," M.A. thesis, Harvard Univ., 1951.

Stepan, Alfred C., "Patterns of Civil-Military Relations: The Brazilian Political System," Ph.D. thesis, Columbia Univ., 1970.

Thurow, Lester C., *Impact of Service in the Armed Forces on Non-White Incomes*, unpublished manuscript, April 12, 1967.

Wool, Harold, "The Military Specialist," Ph.D. thesis, The American Univ., 1964-65.

Index

About the Author

Steven L. Canby is a staff member of the Social Science Department, The Rand Corporation, specializing in military strategy and force structuring, defense economics, and military manpower. Dr. Canby received a Bachelor of Science degree from West Point and a Ph.D. in Political Economy and Government from Harvard University. Before joining Rand in 1968 as a systems analyst, Dr. Canby was a regular army officer, taught economics at Harvard, a rapporteur at the John Fitzgerald Kennedy Institute of Politics, and an operations analyst in the office of the Assistant Secretary of Defense for Systems Analysis.

Selected Rand Books

Averch, et al., *The Matrix of Policy in the Philippines*, Princeton University Press, Princeton, New Jersey 1971.

Bagdikian, Ben, *The Information Machines: Their Impact on Men and the Media*, Harper & Row, New York, 1971.

Brodie, Bernard, *Strategy in the Missile Age*, Princeton University Press, Princeton, New Jersey, 1959.

Downs, Anthony, *Inside Bureaucracy*, Little Brown and Company, 1967.

Dresher, Melvin, *Games of Strategy: Theory and Applications*, Prentice-Hall, Inc., Englewood Cliffs, New Jersey, 1961.

Fisher, Gene H., *Cost Considerations in Systems Analysis*, American Elsevier Publishing Company, New York, 1971.

Hitch, Charles J. and Roland McKean, *The Economics of Defense in the Nuclear Age*, Harvard University Press, Cambridge, Massachusetts, 1960.

Johnson, John J. (ed.), *The Role of the Military in Underdeveloped Countries*, Princeton University Press, Princeton, New Jersey, 1962.

Kershaw, Joseph A. and Roland N. McKean, *Teacher Shortages and Salary Schedules*, McGraw-Hill Book Company, Inc., New York, 1962.

Kolkowicz, Roman, *The Soviet Military and the Communist Party*, Princeton University Press, Princeton, New Jersey, 1967.

McKean, Roland N., *Efficiency in Government Through Systems Analysis: With Emphasis on Water Resource Development*, John Wiley & Sons, Inc., New York, 1958.

Nelson, Richard R., Merton J. Peck, Edward D. Kalachek, *Technology Economic Growth and Public Policy*, The Brookings Institution, Washington, D.C., 1967.

Novick, David (ed.), *Program Budgeting: Program Analysis and The Federal Budget*, Harvard University Press, Cambridge, Massachusetts, 1965.

Quade, E.S. (ed.), *Analysis for Military Decisions*, Rand McNally & Company, Chicago, Illinois-North-Holland Publishing Company, Amsterdam, The Netherlands, 1964.

Quade, E.S. and W. I. Boucher, *Systems Analysis and Policy Planning Applications in Defense*, American Elsevier Pub. Co., New York, New York, 1968.

Stepan, A., *The Military in Politics: Changing Patterns in Brazil*, Princeton University Press, Princeton, New Jersey, 1971.

Williams, J.D., *The Compleat Strategyst: Being a Primer on the Theory of Games of Strategy*, McGraw-Hill Book Company, Inc., New York, 1954.

Wolfe, Thomas W., *Soviet Power and Europe 1945-1970*, The Johns Hopkins Press, Baltimore, Maryland, 1970.